KU-537-419

TEAM of TEAMS

NEW RULES OF ENGAGEMENT

FOR A COMPLEX WORLD

GENERAL STANLEY McCHRYSTAL (US Army, retired)

with TANTUM COLLINS, DAVID SILVERMAN

and CHRIS FUSSELL

PORTFOLIO
PENGUIN

PORTFOLIO PENGUIN

UK | USA | Canada | Ireland | Australia
India | New Zealand | South Africa

Portfolio Penguin is part of the Penguin Random House group of companies
whose addresses can be found at global.penguinrandomhouse.com.

Penguin
Random House
UK

Published in the United States of America by Portfolio/Penguin,
a member of Penguin Group (USA) Inc. 2015
Published in Great Britain by Portfolio Penguin 2015
001

Copyright © McChrystal Group, LLC, 2015

The moral right of the authors has been asserted

Charts and graphs by Ali Croft

Printed in Great Britain by Clays Ltd, St Ives plc

A CIP catalogue record for this book is available from the British Library

ISBN: 978–0–241–25083–9

For all the people throughout history who have wrestled with the shape-shifters. Special thanks to those whose experiences have informed this book, from the military to the private sector to the academic world. Without your brave service and wise contributions this book would not exist.

FOREWORD BY WALTER ISAACSON

Whether in business or in war, the ability to react quickly and adapt is critical, and it's becoming even more so as technology and disruptive forces increase the pace of change. That requires new ways to communicate and work together. In today's world, creativity is a collaborative endeavor. Innovation is a team effort.

This book draws timely lessons for any organization seeking to triumph in this new environment. Based on very real and vividly described situations that General McChrystal encountered as a commander in Iraq and Afghanistan, it describes how organizations need to reinvent themselves. This involves breaking down silos, working across divisions, and mastering the flexible response that comes from true teamwork and collaboration.

I have observed this phenomenon in my own study of innovation in the digital age. The greatest innovations have not come from a lone inventor or from solving problems in a top-down, command-and-control style. Instead, the great successes—the creation of the computer, transistor, microchip, Internet—come from a "team of teams" working together in pursuit of a common goal.

I once asked Steve Jobs, often mistakenly considered a lone visionary and authoritarian leader, which of his creations made him most proud. I thought he might say the original Macintosh, or the iPhone. Instead he pointed out that these were all collaborative efforts. The creations he was most proud of, he said, were the teams he had produced, starting with the original Macintosh team working under a pirate flag in the early 1980s and the remarkable team he had assembled by the time he stepped down from Apple in 2011.

Today's rapidly changing world, marked by increased speed and dense interdependencies, means that organizations everywhere are now facing dizzying challenges, from global terrorism to health epidemics to supply chain disruption to game-changing technologies. These issues can be solved only by creating sustained organizational adaptability through the establishment of a team of teams.

High-speed networks and digital communications mean that collaboration can—and must—happen in real time. The distributed, decentralized, and weblike architecture of the Internet empowers each individual to be a collaborator. Likewise the necessity of real-time innovation and problem-solving requires integrative and transparent leadership that empowers individual team members.

This new environment gave Al Qaeda a distinct advantage, allowing the networked organization to strike rapidly, reconfigure in real time, and integrate its globally dispersed actions. At first, this overwhelmed the Task Force led by General McChrystal, a traditional, secretive, siloed military hierarchy that was configured to solve the problems of an earlier era.

The solution was, surprisingly, found in changing management structures. The U.S. military and its allies had to transform the way the special operations community operated, changing the way it waged the War on Terror.

The experience of General McChrystal and his colleagues, and their examination of the experiences of others, taught them that complexity at scale has rendered reductionist management ineffective for solving these issues in our networked world. Efficiency is necessary but no longer sufficient to be a successful organization. It worked in the twentieth century, but it is now quickly overwhelmed by the speed and exaggerated impact of small players, such as terrorists, start-ups, and viral trends.

Management models based on planning and predicting instead of resilient adaptation to changing circumstances are no longer suited to today's challenges. Organizations must be networked, not siloed, in order to succeed. Their goal must shift from efficiency to sustained organizational adaptability. This requires dramatic shifts in mental and organizational models, as well as sustained efforts on the part of leadership to create the environment for such a change.

General McChrystal's experiences leading the Task Force illustrate how this dramatic transformation is possible in all organizations. After identifying the adaptable and networked nature of Al Qaeda, the general and his team explored why traditional organizations aren't adaptable. One conclusion they reached was that agility and adaptability are normally limited to small teams. They explored the traits that make small teams adaptable, such as trust, common purpose, shared awareness, and the empowerment of individual members to act. They also identified the traditional limits of teams, such as "blinks" in the organization between teams where collaboration begins to break down.

The primary lesson that emerged, and is detailed in this book, is the need to scale the adaptability and cohesiveness of small teams up to the enterprise level. This involves creating a team of teams to foster cross-silo collaboration. That way the insights and actions of many teams and individuals can be harnessed across the organization. Innovation and problem solving become the products of teamwork, not a single architect.

Doing this requires increasing transparency to ensure common understanding and awareness. It also often involves changing the physical space and personal behaviors to establish trust and foster collaboration. This can develop the ability to share context so that the teams can decentralize and empower individuals to act. Decisions are pushed downward, allowing the members to act quickly. This new approach also requires changing the traditional conception of the leader. The role of the leader becomes creating the broader environment instead of command-and-control micromanaging.

Harnessing and sharing the power and experiences of many teams allowed the Task Force command to adapt quickly to changing events on the ground and innovate solutions that couldn't have come from a top-down approach.

These lessons, as the authors show, apply to business and other organizations as well. General McChrystal is leading an effort, managed at the Aspen Institute, to make a year of national service, military or domestic, an opportunity and an expectation of all young Americans. Participating in a service corps is one of many ways to learn to work as a team, communicate goals, and empower decentralized decision making.

Whatever field you're in, at whatever stage of leadership, these insights and skills will prove necessary to learn. In addition to being a fascinating and colorful read, this book is an indispensable guide to the organizational change and deep appreciation of teamwork that are essential in today's fast-moving environment.

CONTENTS

· PART V ·
LOOKING AHEAD

INTRODUCTION

"Of course we understand the dangers, we simply have no other choice."

The Afghan minister of the interior was a slightly built, soft-spoken man with a demeanor of unfailing courtesy, so his statement had the tone of patient explanation rather than indignation or defensiveness. As a young man he'd lost a leg in the Soviet War and walked with an awkward limp, but his intellect, energy, and commitment to reshaping post-9/11 Afghanistan were undeniable. When he spoke, I listened carefully.

We were talking about the Afghan Police, for whom Mohammad Hanif Atmar was responsible, discussing the horrendous casualties they were suffering in isolated stations in Taliban-contested areas. Poorly trained, inadequately equipped, and unevenly led, raw police recruits regularly fell prey to drugs, corruption, and insurgent violence. So it was incredibly frustrating to see the ministry continue to recruit new police candidates and deploy them to operational areas *before* they were trained. But, for a variety of reasons, Atmar felt he had no other option.

Most of us would consider it unwise to do something before we are fully prepared; before the equipment is optimally in place and our workers well trained. But as the reader will discover, that's the situation we found ourselves in. And in researching this book, we discovered that that is the situation leaders and organizations far from any battlefield face every day.

The genesis of this story lies in the transformation of an elite military organization, the Joint Special Operations Task Force (described in this volume simply as "the Task Force," or TF) in the midst of a war. We could compare ourselves during that transition to a professional football team changing from one offensive system to another in the second quarter of a critical game, but the reality was far more drastic. The Task Force's shift was actually more akin to that team's moving from playing football to basketball, and finding that habits and preconceptions had to be discarded along with pads and cleats.

But it was anything but a game or a sport. The war against a succession of terrorist groups that had simmered, with periodic outbursts since the 1970s, had gone white hot in the aftermath of 9/11 and the Task Force found itself first in Afghanistan, then, as the fight expanded, in the wider Middle East.

In the spring of 2003 we entered Iraq. What began as a heavily conventional military campaign to unseat the regime of Saddam Hussein had, by the fall of 2003, become a bitter, unconventional struggle against frustrated Sunnis who increasingly coalesced around a charismatic Jordanian extremist who had taken the name Abu Musab al Zarqawi. In the years that followed we (I had rejoined the Task Force in October of 2003) found ourselves in a bitter fight that, in the beginning, was as confounding as it was bloody.

The Task Force hadn't chosen to change; we were driven by necessity. Although lavishly resourced and exquisitely trained, we found ourselves losing to an enemy that, by traditional calculus, we should have dominated. Over time we came to realize that more than our foe, we were actually struggling to cope with an environment that was fundamentally different from anything we'd planned or trained for. The speed and interdependence of events had produced new dynamics that threatened to overwhelm the time-honored processes and culture we'd built.

Little of our transformation was planned. Few of the plans that we did develop unfolded as envisioned. Instead, we evolved in rapid iterations, *changing—assessing—changing* again. Intuition and hard-won experience became the beacons, often dimly visible, that guided us through the fog and friction. Over time we realized that we were not in search of the perfect solution—none existed. The environment in which we found ourselves, a convergence of twenty-first-century factors and more timeless human interactions, demanded a dynamic, constantly adapting approach. For a soldier trained at West Point as an engineer, the idea that a problem has different solutions on different days was fundamentally disturbing. Yet that was the case.

Fortunately, the common denominator of the professionals with whom I served was an almost mystical devotion to mission accomplishment. The Task Force was founded in the wake of the Iran hostage crisis failure, and perhaps those images of wrecked aircraft and the burned bodies of American servicemen at Desert One* still lay behind the force's fierce desire to win. And so in the early 2000s we morphed, and morphed again, in a bitter struggle to first contain, and then reduce, the threat posed by Al Qaeda in Iraq (AQI).

By early 2008 that goal was clearly in sight, and the Task Force's continual adaptation had transformed it into a fundamentally new organization—one that functioned using distinctly different processes and relationships. Because we were so engaged in the fight, we thought and talked constantly about what we were doing. But it was an experience that could only come into true focus when we had the opportunity to deconstruct and study it afterward, enabling us to draw valid conclusions. That's where this book comes in. In 2010 when I left the service, I joined with several former colleagues to explore whether our shared experience was a one-off occurrence that emerged from the unique factors of post-2003 Iraq, or whether it was a microcosm of a broader changed environment that impacts almost every organization in today's world. We suspected the latter, but began a journey to find out.

This book is the work of four very different individuals, three of whom shared wartime experiences, and a fourth who shares our fascination and passion for the subject. Dave Silverman is a 1998 Naval Academy graduate-turned-SEAL who fought in Iraq before deploying on no notice to Afghanistan in 2009 to serve with me in the International Security Assistance Force (ISAF) headquarters. Chris Fussell is another former SEAL who spent many years at the Naval Special Warfare Development Group, including a year as my aide-de-camp in the Task Force, before taking time at the Naval Postgraduate School in Monterey to study

---

*Desert One was the name given to the remote airstrip used by U.S. forces during the failed 1980 attempt to rescue Americans held hostage in Tehran.

multiorganization fusion cells. Tantum Collins, or Teddy as we know him, I met later, as an undergraduate in a graduate leadership seminar that I have been teaching at Yale University since 2010. The incredible impression he made on me led us to ask him to spend his first year after graduation (before heading to Great Britain as a Marshall Scholar to study at the University of Cambridge) leading this effort to capture the conclusions of our experiences and study in this book. I round out the quartet, with a bit more mileage on me than my colleagues, but still more student than teacher in our examination of this critical idea.

The decision to produce yet another book to help shape and lead complex organizations did not come easily. Shelves are crammed with works of varying value, and busy leaders can feel pummeled by contradictory advice from business gurus and management consultants. But the impact of the Task Force experience drove us to test the conclusions we'd reached, because the wider implications for almost all organizations were so serious.

First, although the Task Force struggled in Iraq, we could not claim we were mismatched against a world-class team. Honestly assessed, Al Qaeda was not a collection of supermen forged into a devilishly ingenious organization by brilliant masterminds. They were tough, flexible, and resilient, but more often than not they were poorly trained and underresourced. They were also dogmatic and offensively extreme in their conduct and views. Their strengths and capabilities were multiplied by a convergence of twenty-first-century factors, of which AQI was simply the lucky beneficiary. Much like a Silicon Valley garage start-up that rides an idea or product that is well timed rather than uniquely brilliant to an absurd level of wealth, AQI happened to step onto an elevator that was headed up.

Second, and most critically, these factors were not unique to Iraq, or to warfare. They are affecting almost all of us in our lives and organizations every day. We're not lazier or less intelligent than our parents or grandparents, but what worked for them simply won't do the trick for us now. Understanding and adapting to these factors isn't optional; it will be what differentiates success from failure in the years ahead.

This book won't diminish the challenges or simplify the complexity of succeeding in this new age, but it will serve as a lens through which to understand it, in addition to outlining an approach that can allow an organization to adapt to the new requirements.

To capture the subject effectively, our search moved along two lines. In the first, we founded CrossLead to work with civilian firms facing the challenge of adapting in complex, rapidly changing environments. That effort has grown into an amazing collection of talent—young and mature, civilian and former military or intelligence professionals, academics and practitioners. Through on-site, practical work with client partners, we've seen firsthand the tornado of changing factors—once-comforting constants transformed into variables that defy predictability and challenge traditional models of leadership and management. For many successful organizations, things that once worked superbly now seem ineffective.

In addition to our direct engagement, we also began an effort to study this phenomenon in other domains and theoretical dimensions, to see whether those undertaking serious examination of the subject were drawing similar conclusions. To a great degree, they are. Reviewing published studies and interviewing experts in a wide variety of fields who generously shared their time, we have put our personal experience under the microscope to validate our findings against their wisdom. We don't claim to be academic scholars, but we have been more than willing to let their work help guide us to supportable conclusions.

BUTTERFLIES, GARDENERS, AND TOADS

It is important to state up front what this book is, and what it is not.

This isn't a war story, although our experience in the fight against Al Qaeda weaves through the book. Far beyond soldiers, it is a story about big guys and little guys, butterflies, gardeners, and chess masters. The reader will meet slimy toads, mythical beasts, clanging machines, and sensitive ecosystems.

We hope to help the reader understand what's different in today's world, and what we must do about it. We will argue that the familiar pursuit of efficiency must change course. Efficiency remains important, but the ability to adapt to complexity and continual change has become an imperative. Using our experience in war, combined with a range of examples from business, hospitals, nongovernmental organizations, as well as more unlikely sources, we lay out the symptoms of the problem, its root causes, and the approaches that we and others have found effective. Readers will understand and appreciate the challenges they face, and be able to frame what makes sense for them.

W e do not offer here a series of checklists or a "how to" manual. Instead, in five parts, the reader will journey from problem to solution.

Part I: The Proteus Problem opens in Iraq in 2004 where the world's most elite counterterrorist force is struggling against a seemingly ragtag band of radical fighters. We explore the unexpected revelation that our biggest challenges lay not in the enemy, but in the dizzyingly new environment in which we were operating, and within the carefully crafted attributes of our own organization. To understand the challenge, we'll go to factory floors with Frederick Winslow Taylor and look back at the drive for efficiency that has marked the last 150 years, and how it has shaped our organizations and the men and women who lead and manage them. We then examine how accelerating speed and interdependence in today's world have created levels of complexity that confound even the most superbly efficient industrial age establishments. And we'll find, much to our disappointment, that Big Data will offer no respite from the unrelenting demand for continual adaptability.

Part II: From Many, One examines both the magic and the myths of teams. The reader will find herself in the operating room of Brigham and Women's Hospital as surgeons work to save victims of the 2013 Boston Marathon bombing, and lying on the rolling deck of the MV *Maersk Alabama* next to SEAL snipers whose precise shots save Captain Phillips from Somali pirates. We dissect the processes that create the *trust* and *common purpose* that bond great small teams, and dispel the fallacy that it takes Supermen to forge super teams. Then we'll climb to thirty thousand feet in the cockpit of United Airlines' ill-fated Flight 173 in December 1978 to explore the daunting challenges that even well-trained crews face, and study some of the adaptations, like Mission Critical Teams, that have emerged to deal with increasing complexity. Finally, we'll enter the imaginary land of Krasnovia to investigate why so many small teams and firms falter as they grow in scale. And we'll find that even the elite Task Force suffered from the same malady.

Part III: Sharing looks at how to deal with the continual change and dramatically increasing complexity that whipsaws us at breakneck speed. From the launch pad of NASA's famed Apollo project that put the first human on the moon, to a blacked-out helicopter putting an Army Special Forces operator on a roof in Fallujah, the reader is introduced to *shared consciousness*: the way transparency and communication can be used in an organization to produce extraordinary outcomes across even large groups. And the Prisoner's Dilemma and game theory will illustrate how the simple concept of *trust* is, in large organizations, anything but simple to create.

Part IV: Letting Go probes the history, advantages, and imperatives of truly *empowered execution* in an organization—pushing decision making and ownership to the right level for every action. The reader will follow Commodore Perry's hulking warships to the coast of Japan and awake with me in Iraq to make on-the-spot decisions on who will live, and who will not. Through a fifteen-inch plastic model we'll pursue the model of "Eyes On—Hands Off" leadership. We'll then look at the leaders we've traditionally sought, and why they are perhaps an endangered species in the new environment. Finally, the reader will sit at my side for the daily video teleconference that I used to shape and drive the Task Force's efforts, and travel to the small bases in Iraq and Afghanistan where ultimately the job must be done. In doing so, we'll explore the new, and increasingly important, role of the senior leader.

Part V: Looking Ahead opens with a detailed look at how *trust, common purpose, shared consciousness,* and *empowered execution* drove the successful hunt for Abu Musab al-Zarqawi, travels with Alexis de Tocqueville as he holds a mirror up to America's face, and argues that to succeed, maybe even to survive, in the new environment, organizations and leaders must fundamentally change. Efficiency, once the sole icon on the hill, must make room for adaptability in structures, processes, and mind-sets that is often uncomfortable.

This isn't a scientific study or the result of clinical trials. We don't claim that these concepts are original nor do we offer findings that are the product of years of study by field experts. We recognize there may well be mistakes or conclusions that can be challenged. But we believe that by leveraging the thinking of others to help explain the experience we navigated, readers will find a useful blend of practical and theoretical knowledge to combat the growing challenge we all face.

AN ENDURING CHALLENGE

In the early summer of 2014, as this book neared completion, Sunni fighters operating under the banner of ISIS, the Islamic State of Iraq and

Syria, captured the northern Iraqi city of Mosul and surged southward like an unstoppable wave toward Baghdad. ISIS was led on its surge through Iraq by the charismatic Abu Bakr al-Baghdadi, a figure reminiscent of the villain we had faced off against a decade prior and whom we will discuss at length in this book: Abu Musab al-Zarqawi. Images of abandoned Iraqi Army vehicles being passed by triumphant ISIS fighters reflected the stunning collapse of the Government of Iraq's defenses, and with it, its credibility. Veterans of our war watched from afar in sullen frustration as ground we'd taken foot by foot, and yard by bloody yard, fell to yet another extremist movement that advanced with seeming ease despite being outmanned and outgunned by government forces.

The question "Had our success against Al Qaeda been a cruel illusion?" came immediately to mind. But we knew it hadn't been. What we'd done had been real. Instead, this latest development reinforced some of the very lessons we had drawn. The first was that the constantly changing, entirely unforgiving environment in which we all now operate denies the satisfaction of any permanent fix. The second was that the organization we crafted, the processes we refined, and the relationships we forged and nurtured are no more enduring than the physical conditioning that kept our soldiers fit: an organization must be constantly led or, if necessary, pushed uphill toward what it must be. Stop pushing and it doesn't continue, or even rest in place; it rolls backward.

Before we begin, a thought. There's a temptation for all of us to blame failures on factors outside our control: "the enemy was ten feet tall," "we weren't treated fairly," or "it was an impossible task to begin with." There is also comfort in "doubling down" on proven processes, regardless of their efficacy. Few of us are criticized if we faithfully do what has worked many times before. But feeling comfortable or dodging criticism should not be our measure of success. There's likely a place in paradise for people who tried hard, but what really matters is succeeding. If that requires you to change, that's your mission.

PART I
THE PROTEUS PROBLEM

The soldier held tightly to the twisting figure. The weapon he'd killed with many times before remained hanging at his side; he needed this one alive. His hands, burned dark by the sun, ached as he struggled to maintain a firm grasp. After years of fighting an unpopular war, he would do whatever it took to get home.

Menelaus, king of Sparta, the fiery brother of Agamemnon and husband of the beauty Helen, was on his journey home following the ten-year-long Trojan War. Shipwrecked on the island of Pharos, Menelaus was desperate when the goddess Eidothea told him of her father, the immortal Proteus—the Old Man of the Sea. If Menelaus could defeat him, Proteus would surrender the secrets Menelaus needed to lead his men home to Sparta.

Defeating Proteus would be difficult because the god possessed a special power: he was a shape-shifter, a polymorph. So Menelaus and his men, disguised in sealskins, lay in ambush on the beach. As Proteus emerged salty and frothing from the roiling sea, they sprang into action. . . .

> First he shifted into a great bearded lion
>   and then a serpent—
>   a panther—
>   a ramping wild boar—
>   a torrent of water—
>   a tree with soaring branch tops—

But the Greeks clung firmly. Their normal weapons of little use, with each shift, they shifted, with each new challenge, they changed, clenching their legs tight around the necks of animals that appeared, or digging their fingers into the wooden limbs of trees, or wrapping their arms around swirling balls of mercurial fire.

The Old Man of the Sea was defeated. By adapting, the Greeks found their way home.

A true story, 860 miles to the east of Pharos, three thousand years later . . .

CHAPTER 1

SONS OF PROTEUS

F ive muscled silhouettes, midnight blue against the sand-colored sunrise, moved down an otherwise empty street on the outskirts of the El Amel neighborhood in Baghdad. The morning call to prayer had just ricocheted through the urban sprawl and faded into the thick heat. A few blinds opened, then quickly closed; residents knew when to stay hidden. The door of a small house on the corner swung open and the men shuffled inside. It was September 30, 2004, and one of the biggest operations they would ever conduct was about to begin.

The building appeared unremarkable—another ripple in the pixelated waves of tan cinder block that extended to the horizon. But inside, it housed a temporary organizational nerve center that gathered data and disseminated instructions across the city. Maps, photos of targets, and operational checklists covered the walls. Personal gear—weapons and clothes—lay neatly stacked in the corner. Those pulling security watched the street, weapons in hand. The newly arrived warriors greeted the other members of their team—the analytic and intelligence counterparts to their brawn—with bear hugs. They asked about their families, joked about colleagues. They also met three new additions to the team—fresh out of training and recently arrived in Iraq. The young faces betrayed the tangle of confusion and excitement that the older men knew would soon give way to fear.

The group strode through the halls of their safe house, brushing past photos of the cheerful family that used to live here. Men in combat attire settled into the plush mauve couches in what had once been a living room. If any of them saw humor or pathos in the juxtaposition, they did not mention it. They had learned to compartmentalize the emotions of war, to internalize as "collateral damage" the deaths of bystanders, to accept the savagery of the battlefield as an unavoidable step in pursuit of a brighter future. They had long since exhausted any reflexive appreciation of tenderness or irony.

Turning to a map of the target area, the most grizzled member of the unit reviewed their approach. Grabbing three coasters and a fragment of tile that had dislodged from the floor during earlier fighting, he modeled the paths their vehicles would follow and the dozens of potential booby traps they would have to avoid.

Each sweep of his hand represented the culmination of weeks of work: the decryption and reconciliation of intelligence, the gathering and assembly of special hardware. Such was the art of networked warfare they were starting to master. Although only three men were slated to pull triggers, dozens—across levels of command and in different countries— made vital contributions to the operation.

The war's tactics and the overall strategy differed radically from how they had envisioned fighting. This was not a war of planning and discipline; it was one of agility and innovation. Their unit had developed a rhythm of localized autonomy intercut with frequent communication with their leadership; superiors would watch from a distance, but today's operation was the brainchild of the men in the room and they owned the mission fully.

For security reasons, no journalists—even the most sympathetic— were allowed to embed with units like this; if they had, they would have witnessed a case study in cutting-edge organizational design, a mesh of synchronization and real-time adaptability that suffused the institutional ecosystem of their fighting force. While in previous conflicts even an elite team of this size would have had little strategic heft, in 2004 their firepower meant that their tactical capabilities were tremendous, and information technology meant that news of the operation could reach global audiences almost instantly.

After a final review and some nods, the men pulled themselves off the couches and moved to the kitchen to grab equipment. Four men would stay behind; the other seven locked magazines into place and tightened the straps on their heavy vests. They chatted about the sorry state of Iraq and what it might look like once they finished liberating it. They decried the shameless tactics employed by their enemy. The fresh arrivals didn't speak.

As the operators walked to the door, the commander felt a crunch beneath his boot. On the floor a framed photo lay nestled in a constellation of glass shards: a picture of a girl, heavily made-up and airbrushed, wearing a cap and gown. Nationality aside, the people who had lived here were not unlike the families these men came from, or might one day rear. This family had done nothing to provoke this; they were guilty only of being in the wrong place at the wrong time. The commander had no idea who they were or what had become of them, but he hoped that his work might, in some winding, indirect way, bring them peace. He pulled the front door open.

It was just past nine o'clock, and the temperature had already broken 90 degrees Fahrenheit. They were sweating before they reached their vehicles. For this operation they wore civilian clothes and drove sedans: two Hyundais and a Volkswagen to execute the operation, plus an Opel to monitor from behind—cars chosen to blend with the traffic. After an equipment check, the drivers rolled out.

They eyed every window, rooftop, and pedestrian warily. On a similar operation a week ago, a sniper round had shattered the windshield and blown through the driver's forehead, soaking the upholstered ceiling with a Rorschach test of deep crimson. Eight days later, some of the men in the car could not recall his face. Despite such losses, in the ebb and flow of bombings, raids, and retributions, the operatives saw the tide turning slowly but surely toward victory. The war had been harder than any of them expected but their efforts were not in vain.

Today's operation would be complex, and the more moving parts, the higher the risk. Hostile fire was almost inevitable and, as always, precise intelligence on the enemy was lacking.

The cars drove slowly through crowded streets, through the clamor of vendors seeking customers, parents reprimanding children, and teenage boys harassing hijab-clad girls; through the scents of fresh food, rotting food, and stray dogs. None of the men had been to Iraq prior to this rotation, but the din had started to feel familiar. As they turned the corner of Thirtieth Street, they saw a throng of residents surrounding a newly minted sewage plant, cheering beneath banners celebrating a grand opening ceremony.

The spot where the Volkswagen, their lead vehicle, was supposed to wait had been taken by a dump truck. The drivers adapted wordlessly: the Hyundais circled the block while the Volkswagen found a new spot nearby at 7 Nissan Street. The Opel hung back as its driver feigned interest in a roadside falafel stand, trying hard to mask his accent. The chaos of Iraqi streets disguised activity that might otherwise seem suspicious.

Then one of the Hyundais found its intended route blocked by construction. The driver pulled into an alternate street, glancing at his colleagues to make sure they had registered the change of plan. Their experience together had built a near-telepathic connection. Twelve minutes later than scheduled, all four cars were in position. In the three attack vehicles, the men took a moment for prayer and reflection.

A code word, delivered with the callous finality of a voice that had issued dozens of similar commands before, crackled across their radios. The first Hyundai driver took a breath, and ground the accelerator into the floor.

At the sewage plant ceremony, the outer ring of the crowd consisted mostly of children, more interested in playing with one another than listening to politicians expound on economic revitalization. At the center were fathers and mothers. Smiling faces, framed by black scarves and dark hair, glistened in the heat.

Small bodies thudded against the grille and headlights as the Hyundai punched, full speed, into the group. The driver muttered prayers again before depressing his detonator. Perhaps, in the fraction of a second that it took the radio signal to travel outward from his palm, through the backseat, and toward the trunk, he saw the bloodied jihadist glory into which Iraq had sunk. Perhaps, for a heartbeat, his rage gave way to a pang of regret before the exploding propane tanks and BB pellets in the trunk ripped through the vehicle's steel exoskeleton and tore him apart.

The street, now a mosaic of car shrapnel and bloodied remains, filled with wails. Mothers searched frantically for their sons and daughters. Enemy soldiers—Americans—sprinted to the scene from down the block. They began setting up a perimeter and triaging the wounded.

In the midst of the screaming, nobody heard the Volkswagen approach. Speeding into the pack of soldiers and children who had emerged, stupefied, to collect debris and identify bodies, it detonated its payload.

Thirty-five children now lay dead; 10 Americans and 140 Iraqis wounded. As the final car careered across a median toward the site, coalition forces opened fire, and the vehicle detonated well south of its target.

But the failure of the third vehicle didn't matter to the men in the fourth, who had already disappeared into the traffic. Operations were rarely flawless. As they drove away, the driver stowed the three small garage door openers he had been keeping in his lap. Had his operators experienced any second thoughts, he would have used these to trigger their explosives. The man in the shotgun seat reviewed the footage he had taken of the strike. Within hours, it would be online—its shock value recruiting dozens more bombers to the cause.

For Al Qaeda in Iraq, the operation was a success.

THE BEST OF THE BEST

On the day of the sewage plant bombing, I sat in a Saddam-era double-thick concrete aircraft shelter at Balad Airbase, some sixty miles north of El Amel. Laptop computers and plasma displays connected by an arterial network of wires and cables covered the plywood walls and tables we had hastily built the previous spring. Information flowed nonstop through a "farm" of antennae and satellite dishes into an operations center the size of a basketball court. Specialists scrutinized video surveillance, intercepted communications, captured documents and human intelligence reports, piecing together a mosaic portrait of Al Qaeda in Iraq. The reports they composed were passed on to my subcommanders and me, to be used in planning raids with our special operators. This was the forward headquarters of our Joint Special Operations Task Force.

I had recently turned fifty and had been in charge of the Task Force for almost a year. The post was an honor for any soldier. From 1980 to 2003, nine highly respected major generals (a two-star rank) had embraced this responsibility, five of whom went on to wear four stars. These men, among the best planners, coordinators, and strategic thinkers in the U.S. Army, had set an extraordinary precedent.

Their legacy of accomplishment was why we had been brought in to battle Iraq's growing insurgency, specifically Al Qaeda in Iraq (AQI)—the most prominent and savage of the many terrorist operations that had sprung up in the wake of the U.S. invasion. The United States and coalition forces had entered Iraq to depose Saddam Hussein, which they did in short order. But AQI posed a different type of threat from an army—small, agile, and dispersed. Fighting them required the special skill sets our units possessed.

The Task Force had been built in answer to a previous debacle: the failed rescue of American hostages held by Iranian revolutionaries in 1980. It folded the best special operations units of the world's most powerful military into a single organization. The Task Force had amassed forty years of experience and amazing accomplishments; by any objective standard we were the finest special operations fighting force in the world—"the best of the best." But that didn't seem to be doing us any good now. We had just failed to prevent the deaths of thirty-five children, and were losing a war to a collection of underresourced extremists.

On paper, the confrontation between AQI and our Task Force should have been no contest. We had a large, well-trained, superbly equipped force, while AQI had to recruit locals and smuggle in foreign fighters one by one through dangerous, unreliable ratlines. We enjoyed robust communication technology, while they were often dependent on face-to-face meetings and letters delivered by courier to minimize the risk of detection. Our fighters had persevered through the most demanding training in the history of special operations; theirs had attended a smattering of madrassas scattered across the Arabian Peninsula and North Africa. We could, at will, tap into an unmatched well of firepower, armored vehicles, and cutting-edge surveillance; their technology consisted of IEDs assembled in safe-house basements from propane tanks and expired Soviet mortars.

We were also exemplary in our discipline. Our superior resources had not bred complacency; we were pushing our assets harder than they had ever been pushed. Our operators would wake mid-morning, spend their day reviewing plans and intelligence and briefing the chain of command; then as dusk began to settle, kits would come out, gear would click on, and rotor blades would start to whir. Through the hours of darkness, small teams would go to work, hitting two, three, ten targets in a given night—each operation meticulously planned and executed, every effort oppressively taxing in the way that only the life-threatening can be. By the early morning, weary warriors would sink into bed for a few hours of sleep and then repeat the cycle without interruption for months on end.

The Task Force's unique capabilities made it necessary for us to take a leadership role in the fight in Iraq, but the task was on a scale we had never encountered before. Throughout our twenty-plus-year history, we had successfully executed small, precise, surgical operations; we were now being called on to spearhead a war with no end in sight. The tragedy of the September 30 sewage plant attack was an unwelcome reminder that, despite our pedigree, our gadgets, and our commitment, things were slipping away from us.

As information streamed in about the bombing, the SIGACT (Significant Activity) report's terse account was augmented with valuable details from Task Force liaison officers dispersed across Iraq—details of the casualties, the backgrounds and ages of the men, women, and children who perished, and of how the men in the Opel had slipped through our fingers. We debated what response we should muster.

But we also had to ask a deeper, more troubling question: If we were the best of the best, why were such attacks not disappearing, but in fact increasing? Why were we unable to defeat an underresourced insurgency? Why were we losing?

TEAM OF TEAMS

That question, the answers we found, and their implications for the world beyond our Task Force form the basis of this book. With AQI, we faced a fundamentally new kind of threat, bred by a fundamentally new kind of environment. The war we had to wage was not only different from fighting a nation-state; it was different from any kind of war waged in the twentieth century. Insurgency, terrorism, and radicalization are as old as conflict itself, but by 2004 those phenomena had been coupled with new technological variables to create an entirely new problem set. Most people will, fortunately, never be in the position of fighting a violent insurgency, but the technological and social changes that made AQI's success possible affect us all.

In 2004, we were only beginning to understand the gravity of this shift, but in the months that followed we came to understand that defeating AQI would necessitate learning from them. Just as the cohort of young people born in the 1990s and 2000s are considered "digital natives" in contrast to their "digital immigrant" parents, AQI was an organization native to the information-rich, densely interconnected world of the twenty-first century. It operated in ways that diverged radically from those we thought of as "correct" and "effective." But it worked.

In the course of this fight, we had to unlearn a great deal of what we thought we knew about how war—and the world—worked. We had to tear down familiar organizational structures and rebuild them along completely different lines, swapping our sturdy architecture for organic fluidity, because it was the only way to confront a rising tide of complex threats. Specifically, we restructured our force from the ground up on principles of extremely transparent information sharing (what we call "shared consciousness") and decentralized decision-making authority ("empowered execution"). We dissolved the barriers—the walls of our silos and the floors of our hierarchies—that had once made us efficient. We looked at the behaviors of our smallest units and found ways to extend them to an organization of thousands, spread across three continents. We became what we called "a team of teams": a large command that captured at scale the traits of agility normally limited to small teams. Almost everything we did ran against the grain of military tradition and of general organizational practice. We abandoned many of the precepts that had helped establish our efficacy in the twentieth century, because the twenty-first century is a different game with different rules.

Our struggle in Iraq in 2004 is not an exception—it is the new norm. The models of organizational success that dominated the twentieth century have their roots in the industrial revolution and, simply put, the world has changed. The pursuit of "efficiency"—getting the most with the least investment of energy, time, or money—was once a laudable goal, but being effective in today's world is less a question of optimizing for a known (and relatively stable) set of variables than responsiveness to a constantly shifting environment. Adaptability, not efficiency, must become our central competency.

Today, the challenges faced by our Task Force are shared by contemporary organizations, which, like us, developed tremendous competencies for dealing with a world that no longer exists. Since leaving the military and founding CrossLead in 2011, my colleagues and I have studied the difficulties encountered by a variety of businesses and other groups struggling to survive and prosper in a changed world. In the pages to come, we will explore why most organizations today are ill equipped to meet those challenges, and we will lay out, step-by-step, our experience in Iraq, the solutions we found that worked, and the research we have done subsequently into the broader applications of these solutions.

In 2004 those answers lay in the future. We were struggling to understand an enemy that had no fixed location, no uniforms, and identities as immaterial and immeasurable as the cyberspace within which they recruited and deployed propaganda. The utility of the intelligence we gleaned through arduous and dangerous struggle had a disconcerting way of evaporating like the Opel melting into Baghdad traffic on September 30. But we did have a starting point—a name: Abu Musab al-Zarqawi. It was an alias, but the man was real.

AHMAD AL-KHALAYLEH

Five years earlier, in the Jordanian desert thirty miles east of the Dead Sea, the doors of the high-security Suwaqah prison opened. A few dozen men emerged, including a quiet man whose flowing Afghan robes cut a stark contrast with the prison clothes of those who surrounded him. He was Ahmad al-Khalayleh, or as he came to be known to the outside world, Abu Musab al-Zarqawi.

Raised in the industrial Jordanian city of Zarqa in an average, modest family, Ahmad went off the rails at a young age, dropping out of school and turning to drugs and alcohol. His mother eventually shipped him off to a mosque renowned for its Salafist bent (a deeply conservative strain of Sunni Islam). There, he found his true passion: holy war. He traveled to Afghanistan and Pakistan in search of jihadist glory, hoping to play a glamorous role in fighting the infidel invaders (at the time, Soviets), but he was too late: the Soviets were already withdrawing from the decade-long conflict. Ahmad returned to Amman and made inroads with the radical Islamist community there. His participation in a plot against the state landed him in Suwaqah, where he spent five years deepening his resolve, lifting weights, memorizing the Koran, and using acid to burn off the tattoos acquired in his renegade youth. His time there completed the transformation his mother unwittingly had kicked off a decade earlier from listless thug to charismatic terrorist commander. Fellow inmates came to revere him, prison authorities to fear him. Cowed by his influence, prison authorities allowed him to replace traditional prison garb with the elegant drape of the *shalwar kameez*—the long shirt and baggy trousers bound at the waist and ankles traditional of Afghanistan. This was part of his new identity, as was his adopted name—Abu Musab al-Zarqawi. When the thirty-three-year-old walked out of prison, he was poised to assume what would become a central role in the post-9/11 wars.

He returned to Pakistan, where a new group called Al Qaeda—"the Base"—was taking form. Inspired, he founded a similar organization, Tawhid w'al-Jihad (TWJ)—"the Group of Unity and Jihad." After a few unsuccessful attempts to join brewing conflicts in Pakistan and Chechnya, TWJ established a training camp in Herat, Afghanistan, that taught physical conditioning, bomb making, and chemical warfare. Al Qaeda took an interest, and the two groups grew close.

The U.S. invasion of Iraq was a dream come true for Zarqawi; finally, he would have a chance to prove his mettle. TWJ established itself at the forefront of the resistance, shrewdly playing on the fear and frustration of Iraq's Sunni minority, suddenly dispossessed of political power by Saddam's fall. In 2003, Zarqawi engineered a successful bombing campaign that killed hundreds and made a mockery of the occupying coalition's attempt to secure Baghdad. A massive truck bomb at the United Nations headquarters in the Canal Hotel killed twenty-two, including Sérgio Vieira de Mello, the UN's special representative to Iraq. Two months later, in a barrage of coordinated suicide bombings that killed thirty-five and wounded more than two hundred, an explosives-packed ambulance was used to target the International Red Cross headquarters.

Though the sewage plant strike was horrific, it was not out of the ordinary for Iraq in 2004. By December, there had been more major terrorist attacks in Iraq alone than there had been in the entire world in 2003. In 2005, terrorism in Iraq would claim 8,300 lives, the equivalent of almost three 9/11s in a country with one tenth the population of the United States. Iraq, with less than one half of one percent of the global population, accounted for almost a third of all terrorist attacks worldwide and a majority of terrorism's fatalities in 2005. And it only got worse: the spring of 2006 saw more than a thousand Iraqis dying on Iraqi streets each month. For families like the onetime homeowners in El Amel, local bombings occurred with the frequency of garbage collection in suburban America.

Saddam had been ousted and tried, but where a time lapse of Iraqi streets from 2003 to 2005 should have revealed an increase in order and democracy, it would instead have shown a depressing descent: shops shuttering, roads deteriorating, fewer and fewer people walking around in public, and the incessant orange flicker of suicide bomb attacks. In 2003, oil-rich Iraq's economy contracted more than 20 percent, putting the per capita GDP at $449—less than 2 percent of that of the United States. Television news reported the United Nations Development Program's conclusion that conditions were "dismal."

Iraqis weren't watching it on TV. For them, the experience was visceral. As the fragile edifice of Saddam's government collapsed, electricity shortfalls crippled Baghdad, eliminating lighting, refrigeration, and air-conditioning. In a city where summer days top 125 degrees Fahrenheit, and simply brushing exposed skin against sun-heated metal can produce a painful burn, this is bad news. Water treatment and sewage processing plants sat idle, and human waste backed up into the streets, producing an omnipresent, nauseating stench.

A place with a history as great as any on earth—the onetime "Cradle of Civilization"—had become a living hell.*

The brutality and mayhem were strategic. Zarqawi's goal was a sectarian civil war between Iraq's Sunni and Shia populations. In destroying each other, he thought, they would also destroy any remnant of a real state, thereby creating a window of opportunity for the Islamic caliphate of his dreams. By strategically targeting Shia Iraqis, Zarqawi ignited a cultural tinderbox, and a sectarian bloodbath swept through Iraq. He had cleverly engineered leverage: each carefully chosen strike of AQI's would see its death toll multiplied by the chain of reprisals it would set off. Victims of suicide bombs were joined by those who met dark fates at the hands of the sectarian militias on both sides of Iraq's religious divide: bodies electrocuted and dismembered in underground torture chambers, or discarded in garbage-filled alleys with their heads still covered by suffocating plastic bags.

Even Al Qaeda grew uncomfortable with Zarqawi's extremism. But its leaders could not deny the sheer military power of the organization that

---

*It is worth mentioning that for most Iraqis, things in 2004 were far worse than during the Saddam years. Although he had been a tyrant, driven his nation's economy into the ground, and killed many of his own citizens, the death toll and economic state were not nearly as bad as under AQI's wrath. A useful point of comparison is that through the 1980s and 1990s, the United Nations Human Development Programme ranked Iraq 85th out of 160 countries—solidly in the "medium development" tier, just ahead of Jordan, and alongside China and the Philippines.

the Jordanian had mustered. If they wanted to exert influence in Iraq, they would have to work with him. In October 2004, Zarqawi swore *bay'ah*, allegiance, to Osama bin Laden, and in return the world's most famous terrorist formally lent his brand to the man who had once been Ahmad, the good-for-nothing from Zarqa. AQI was born.

WHITEBOARDS

As members of an entity traditionally focused on targeting terrorist leaders, we in the Task Force were tempted to succumb to the "great man theory" and attribute AQI's success to Zarqawi. He was undeniably bright and able. His strategy of pitting Sunni against Shia had an evil brilliance. But ideas are cheap; plenty of armchair generals have proposals for winning wars, some of them quite clever, but only those who can actually shape and manage a force capable of doing the job ultimately succeed. Zarqawi's AQI certainly profited from Sunni fears, Iraqi resentment of American occupiers, religious fervor, and the general insanity that accompanies violent chaos, but the speed and breadth of their rise was still astounding. The fact that Zarqawi was able to forge a small group of dedicated individuals into a cohesive terrorist organization was not surprising, but his ability to leverage that relatively minuscule group, propagating a distastefully nihilist narrative, into a broadly supported and strategically effective insurgency demanded deeper explanation. We examined a litany of possible variables—the history of the region, the virulence of AQI's ideology, and the no-holds-barred tactics they adopted—but none could adequately account for what we were seeing on the ground.

When we first established our Task Force headquarters at Balad, we hung maps on almost every wall. Maps are sacred to a soldier. In military headquarters, maps are mounted and maintained with almost religious reverence. A well-marked map can, at a glance, reveal the current friendly and enemy situations, as well as the plan of future operations. Orders can be conveyed using a marked map and a few terse words. There are stories of Pentagon office renovations removing a wall only to find behind it another wall covered in maps dating from a previous conflict. For most of history, war was about terrain, territory held, and geographic goals, and a map was the quintessential tool for seeing the problem and creating solutions.

But the maps in Balad could not depict a battlefield in which the enemy could be uploading video to an audience of millions from any house in any neighborhood, or driving a bomb around in any car on any street. In place of maps, whiteboards began to appear in our headquarters. Soon they were everywhere. Standing around them, markers in hand, we thought out loud, diagramming what we knew, what we suspected, and what we did not know. We covered the bright white surfaces with multi-colored words and drawings, erased, and then covered again. We did not draw static geographic features; we drew mutable relationships—the connections between things rather than the things themselves.

Just as my siblings and I had, on long car rides, played a game where we searched for familiar objects hidden in a larger picture, in the Task Force we tried to locate familiar structures and patterns in the chaotic tapestry that was Iraq. Though we couldn't see them, we felt sure they must be there. As we gathered intelligence, we would diagram the relationships between members of the organization. But in place of the straight lines and right angles of a military command, we found ourselves drawing tangled networks that did not resemble any organizational structure we had ever seen. The unfamiliar patterns that blossomed on our whiteboards seemed chaotic and riddled with contradictions—taking them in was like reading a technical document in a foreign language.

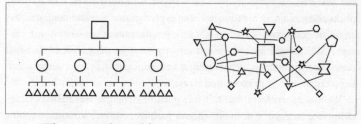

What we were designed for   What we were facing

The actions that we saw on the battlefield indexed more accurately to these unstable linkages than they did to the more familiar, hierarchical structure we were trained to trace. We began to consider the possibility that those familiar patterns we sought might not be there at all—that AQI and this war were fundamentally different from anything we had seen in the past.

AQI's adroit use of information technology had multiplied the effectiveness of tactics employed by guerrilla and terrorist groups for decades. That much was obvious, but there was a bigger change at play. The exponential growth of global interconnectedness meant we weren't just looking at the same roads with faster traffic; we were looking at an entirely different and constantly shifting landscape. In contrast to a standard fighting force structure of subordinate organizations and stubborn personalities, AQI displayed a shape-shifting quality. It wasn't the biggest or the strongest, but, like Proteus, AQI was a daunting foe because it could transform itself at will.

In deeply traditional, tribal Fallujah, the organization dressed itself in the robes of the sheikh and sponsored traditional Islamic poetry festivals. Operatives exerted influence through local proxies on the Mujahedeen Shura Council of Fallujah, respected local religious figures AQI won over or intimidated. But if an AQI operative traveled forty-five miles east to Baghdad, he blended in with the urban landscape, wore city clothes, and drove vehicle-borne IEDs through the city traffic. Not only did they have no standard modus operandi, they had no standard hierarchy. Every time we thought we had landed a debilitating blow to the organization as a whole, removing a ranking leader whose loss should have derailed them, they bounced back. As network theorist and military analyst John Arquilla put it: We killed "about 20 of Al Qaeda's 'number threes' over the past decade, but everyone in a network is number three." To our way of thinking, an organization without a predictable methodology or clear chain of command wasn't really an organization at all—from our vantage, AQI should have devolved into internal anarchy. But it didn't. It continued to function as persistently and implacably as ever, demonstrating a coherence of purpose and strategy.

We saw no evidence that this inexplicable structure was the product of deliberate design; it seemed instead to have evolved through ongoing adaptation. As we would soon learn, it represented something essential about the new world in which we were operating.

ACTOR AND ENVIRONMENT

Years later, in 2010, I took a teaching appointment at Yale University, where I had the opportunity to reflect on these experiences amid a community of wickedly intelligent people. One interaction proved particularly fascinating. Dr. Kristina Talbert-Slagle, a brilliant immunologist who studies AIDS, came to see me, curious about whether the similarities she saw between infections in the human body and insurgencies in a state correlated with my observations. They did; while neither HIV nor AIDS kills anyone outright, the human body is weakened to the point where it is fatally vulnerable to otherwise nonthreatening infections. The environmental factors that weaken the host indirectly strengthen and empower attackers.

In 2004 I lacked this immunologist vocabulary, but I began to realize that an organization's fitness—like that of an organism—cannot be assessed in a vacuum; it is a product of compatibility with the surrounding environment. Understanding that environment would be the key to understanding why we were failing and AQI was winning. We may have had the best equipment and the best special operations units in the world, but we were not—as an organization—the best suited for that time and place.

AQI was successful because the environment allowed it to be. A big piece of this was the failure of the Iraqi state, but an even bigger piece was something that extended beyond national borders—something that was temporal, not geographic.

A great deal has been written about how the world has become "flatter" and faster. People are more connected, more mobile, and move faster than ever before. By lowering what economists call the "barriers to entry"—prohibitive costs associated with entering a market—these changes have ushered in a universe of new possibilities for players operating outside the conventional systems: Mark Zuckerberg, without family connections, starting capital, or an undergraduate degree, changed the world before hitting his mid-twenties; Justin Bieber posted a self-made video online in 2007 and has since sold 15 million albums, accruing close to $200 million in personal wealth; and Abu Musab al-Zarqawi, buoyed by online bomb-making instructions and the power to recruit and disseminate propaganda worldwide, incited a war. Interconnectedness and the ability to transmit information instantly can endow small groups with unprecedented influence: the garage band, the dorm-room start-up, the viral blogger, and the terrorist cell.

The twenty-first century is a fundamentally different operating environment from the twentieth, and Zarqawi had arrived at just the right time. It was more than just chat rooms and YouTube: AQI's very structure—networked and nonhierarchical—embodied this new world. In some ways, we had more in common with the plight of a Fortune 500 company trying to fight off a swarm of start-ups than we did with the Allied command battling Nazi Germany in World War II.

If we couldn't change the environment to suit us better, we would have to change to suit it. The question was how. We were not a handful of renegade fighters operating outside the law and making it up on the fly. The Task Force was a large, institutionalized, disciplined military machine. Though more agile than most forces, we were still a veritable leviathan in comparison with AQI. How do you train a leviathan to improvise?

MANAGING CHAOS

Like many soldiers, I enjoy studying military history. Even the most storied of battles can contain revelations with unexpected applications. In 2004, mired in a fight against the most elusive and intractable of enemies, I was fascinated by Adam Nicolson's *Seize the Fire: Heroism, Duty, and the Battle of Trafalgar*, which chronicles British admiral Horatio Nelson's daring face-off with a superior Franco-Spanish fleet.

On October 21, 1805, the five-and-a-half-foot-tall, forty-seven-year-old Nelson stood on the deck of his consort, the HMS *Victory*, and stared at his enemy. Nelson, who had lost an eye and an arm in earlier battles, knew that Napoleon's Franco-Spanish fleet hoped to decimate his forces, neutralizing the British navy and making way for a flotilla that would launch a land invasion of Britain. If Nelson's force fell, England fell. The British had not been so threatened since they squared off against the Spanish Armada in 1588.

The odds did not look good. Nelson had twenty-seven ships, while the enemy boasted thirty-three. But he had up his sleeve one of the most thoughtfully unorthodox plans in military history.

Traditionally, admirals fought naval battles by arranging their ships in a line parallel to those of the enemy. Both sides would fire volley after volley until one fleet, sufficiently weakened due to loss of life, ships, and ammunition, surrendered. This arrangement maximized use of the cannon arrayed along the length of the warships. It also facilitated centralized control: admirals, positioned toward the middle of their line, could monitor the entire battle and issue orders with relative clarity by way of flag signaling. The face-off becomes a duel of puppet masters. Nelson, however, planned to approach from the side with two columns at a perpendicular angle and punch through the Franco-Spanish line, breaking it into three parts. He hoped to catch the fleet off guard, scatter both sides' ships, and create such chaos that the enemy's commanders would be unable to issue coherent orders.

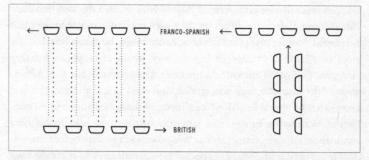

The traditional approach to naval battles contrasted with the Nelson touch, British admiral Horatio Nelson's disruptive approach to facing a superior Franco-Spanish fleet.

Drawn on paper or moved as small models on a tabletop, Nelson's daring move could be executed by even a dilettante. But the difference between the environment of a drawing-room tabletop and the tossing seas off the coast of Spain made managing the maneuver challenging. The 227-foot-long *Victory* was an enormous, heaving machine of wood, iron, canvas, and rope manned by 850 sailors scurrying constantly from the hold below the waterline to the yardarms on the three huge masts. The sailors used a twenty-six-mile maze of hemp-rope rigging to raise and adjust the 6,510 square yards of canvas that made up the thirty-seven sails needed to propel the ship. Managing the sails while loading, aiming, and firing massive guns in careful synchronicity with the ship's roll required the careful orchestration of superbly drilled crews. Micromanaging every sailor's conduct across eight decks during routine sailing would have been difficult, and during battle impossible. It was no drawing-room exercise.

Even getting into position for an attack would be risky. Ships' cannons faced port and starboard and could not be turned to fire toward the bow or stern. Nelson's ships would be exposed to and defenseless against enemy fire during their approach. Once they pierced the line, however, they could fire, point-blank, through the row of French and Spanish ships, causing far more damage than in the conventional face-off.

In the cabin of the *Victory* on September 29 Nelson described the plan to his captains and on October 9 followed up with a secret memo further describing how the fleet should separate into columns to attack the enemy. Maybe more important than laying out a specific strategy, Nelson took care to emphasize the role of the individual captains. At the very core of his plan was what he later termed "the Nelson touch": the idea that individual commanders should act on their own initiative once the mêlée had developed. Noting that plans could be easily foiled, he gave a final, simple piece of advice: "No captain can do very wrong if he places his ship alongside that of the enemy." As historian and archaeologist Roy Adkins wrote, "the plan of attack was settled, and every commander in the fleet knew what he would be doing" as a result of these meetings and memos. Nelson, Adkins explains, "had patiently instilled the idea in his own commanders during many tactical discussions in the days before the battle. He allowed and, indeed, expected his subordinates to use their own initiative, at the same time reducing the fleet's dependence on uncertain methods of communication" such as signaling.

In contrast, the Franco-Spanish fleet, a few miles away, was under more authoritarian rule. As Nicolson observes, Napoleon had forbidden Vice-Admiral Pierre-Charles Villeneuve to tell his captains at any stage what the grand strategy for defeating England might be. Adkins adds that "this reliance on orders from a central command proved a recurring weakness in the French and Spanish navies where, by tradition, commanders of individual ships awaited orders transmitted in flag signals that could be hidden by smoke, cut down by enemy fire, or merely misunderstood."

The sun rose, the hulking ships raised their sails, and Nelson, his craft at the vanguard of the battering-ram formation, led his fleet into battle. Many things could have gone wrong—a slight shift of wind would have meant that the advantage of their "weather gage" or upwind position would have been reversed—but nothing did. They broke through the Franco-Spanish lines and sent ships careening in all directions. Things proceeded largely according to plan—the plan being to disrupt all plans: in the wake of the collision, the French and Spanish command was unable to coordinate an effective response. Despite its technical superiority, Napoleon's side lost— nineteen of its ships were captured by the British, while Nelson's forces did not lose a single vessel. It remains one of the most stunning strategic successes in naval history, but its lesson is often misunderstood.

Nelson was a brilliant man with an ingenious plan who pulled a marvelous trick and won an uphill battle. So goes the story . . . but what enabled Nelson's forces to win was more than just surprise. The seeds of that victory were laid long before Nelson hatched his plan or told each of his men to "place his ship alongside that of the enemy."

In fact, Nelson's maneuver wasn't anything that hadn't been done before: the very same strategy had been used many times to great success, in the British navy no less. While Nelson's tactics echoed those of great admirals before him, his unique innovation lay in his managerial style and the culture he had cultivated among his forces.

At its heart, Nelson crafted an organizational culture that rewarded individual initiative and critical thinking, as opposed to simple execution of commands. As Nicolson explains it, "Nelson created the market, but once it was created he would depend on their enterprise. His captains were to see themselves as the entrepreneurs of battle." The development of these "entrepreneurs" took years of training and experience, but as a result of that investment, Nelson knew his force could emerge victorious from a situation of chaos. Nicolson concludes that "the British had a cultural and not a technical advantage; reliant on the notion of the 'band of brothers.'" The maneuver Nelson pulled that day was clever, but it was just the tip of the iceberg, and the real magic lay beneath the waterline.

At the heart of his success was patient, yet relentless, nurturing of competence and adaptability within his crews. Here, for organizations, lies the critical nexus between theorized strategy and realized victory—the ground where doctrinaire theorists and armchair admirals fall short is the decisive terrain from which true leaders emerge. Nelson's real genius lay not in the clever maneuver for which he is remembered, but in the years of innovative management and leadership that preceded it.

LIMFAC

In 2004, I was reading about Nelson, but I felt more like the hapless French admiral Villeneuve an hour or so into the battle. AQI had created chaos and caught us off guard; moreover, it managed to maneuver coherently in the ensuing mêlée while we—with all our superior firepower—were unable to bring it to bear effectively enough to win the fight.

We had everything in place: men, guns, planes, ammunition, medical supplies. But the system that bound these elements together and channeled them toward our enemy required the equivalent of ships in a row and an admiral who could see everything in order to be effective. In the military, where we love abbreviations, we have a term for the one element in a situation that holds you back—a *limfac* (limiting factor). As we looked at images of charred remains at the El Amel sewage plant, at the networks ensnaring our whiteboards, and at the new environment that surrounded us, we came to realize that our firepower and legacy were failing us not because of a lack of effort or a shortage of clever tactics, but because of something in our Task Force's organizational DNA. We were an outstanding twentieth-century organization, but that was of little use in the twenty-first century. We realized that of all the unexpected and blindingly obvious things, our limfac lay in the mundane art of management.

RECAP

♦ The Al Qaeda in Iraq (AQI) that our Task Force confronted in 2004 looked on the surface like a traditional insurgency. *But under the surface it operated unlike anything we had seen before.* In place of a traditional hierarchy, it took the form of a dispersed network that proved devastatingly effective against our objectively more qualified force.

♦ AQI's unorthodox structure allowed it to thrive in an *operating environment that diverged radically from those we had traditionally faced: the twenty-first century is more connected, faster paced, and less predictable than previous eras. Though we encountered this shift on the battlefield, similar changes are affecting almost every sector of society.*

♦ To win we had to change. Surprisingly, that change was less about tactics or new technology than it was about the internal architecture and culture of our force—in other words, our approach to management.

CHAPTER 2

CLOCKWORK

A combat parachute assault is a difficult, dangerous endeavor. To drop a six-hundred-strong battalion of the Eighty-second Airborne Division onto a pitch-dark landing zone requires intricate planning and coordination. The men must first assemble on an airfield with twelve C-17 transport aircraft standing by (six for men, six for heavy equipment). The paratroopers, fresh from last-minute refresher training, don parachutes and, weighed down by their heavy equipment, file into the planes in careful sequence. Subordinate companies and platoons are "cross-loaded" through the aircraft so that when they reach the airspace above the start of the drop zone, they can jump in synchronized stages, hoping to land in the vicinity of their teammates and equipment. Paratroopers, bundles of ammunition, and vehicles to be "heavy dropped" on pallets under huge parachutes are marked to allow for rapid recognition in the dark.

To the soldiers, it is a familiar process. They spend thousands of hours in drills emphasizing precision and uniformity so that, in combat, they can gather themselves on the ground in the shortest possible time, beat off enemy attacks, and reach their objective. The pursuit of order is relentless. Nonetheless, time and again, paratroopers in combat find themselves scattered across the countryside, minus their vehicles and ammunition, and forced to self-organize into LGOPs (little groups of paratroopers) that accomplish the mission as best they can. Even when they land together, paratrooper battalions are still isolated inside enemy territory, without the luxury of immediate reinforcement, and limited more or less to what they can carry for supplies. To stand any chance of succeeding, they must learn to get the most out of the little that they have; they must be ruthlessly efficient.

Combat parachuting offers a microcosm of the paradox inherent in military operations. The pursuit of predictability—carefully delineated instructions, easily replicable procedures, fastidious standardization, and a tireless focus on efficiency—is foundational to the military's struggle against the chaos always threatening to engulf combat operations. Historically, this quest for order has produced impressive results. However, we were learning in 2004 that efficiency was no longer enough. A look into the origins of this doctrine reveals why it was effective at confronting the threats of the 1900s, but has proved increasingly inadequate at battling the networked mayhem of the twenty-first century.

As long as war has existed, military theorists have strived to reduce its practice to a set of principles. Sun Tzu, Machiavelli, Napoleon, and Clausewitz all contributed to this effort, along with thousands of less familiar names. While there is no single accepted "theory of everything," my teachers at West Point constantly reinforced the importance of a set of commonly accepted principles. One of the most compelling of these states that commanders should mass the effects of overwhelming combat power at the decisive place and time.

Massing combat power usually meant concentrating forces into tightly packed formations that maintained cohesion while battering their similarly configured enemy with club, spear, sword, rifle, or cannon. Normally the side whose line "held" won the day. Ironclad discipline and well-rehearsed drills prepared soldiers to stand or maneuver in the face of arrows, charging cavalry, or withering musket fire. Drill manuals became bibles and the drill field holy ground.

The Roman army was an early and effective employer of the kind of drilled order that we see in a parachute drop. Discipline and incessant drills were hallmarks of life in the legions. The soldier-turned-historian Josephus was said to have described Roman army drills as "bloodless battles," and their successful battles as "bloody drills."

Strict rules governed everything the Roman soldiers did, even the building of their homes. Whether the project was a temporary camp or a permanent fortification in the distant reaches of the empire, the layouts followed the same plan. Every man had a specific construction task and every tent had its place. This standardization enabled the Romans to construct camp defenses quickly and efficiently. Soldiers could move between units and still participate in construction without breaking the orderly flow of work. Messengers could arrive at camps and forts and immediately know where to find the commander. Most important, in the chaos and confusion of an enemy attack, defenders could organize themselves speedily and effectively.

In the winter of 1778, George Washington's ragged army was reborn through a similar focus on discipline and uniformity. Friedrich Wilhelm August Heinrich Ferdinand von Steuben (often referred to as Baron von Steuben), a profane Prussian-born officer who joined the troops at Valley Forge, introduced a training program for drill that was credited with transforming the efficiency and battlefield effectiveness of the fledgling Continental Army.

To achieve efficiency and predictability, armies have long dressed, drilled, and disciplined men into becoming interchangeable parts of a military machine. Beginning at enlistment, conscription, or sometimes impressment, soldiers are groomed and outfitted to look as much alike as possible. Uniforms, besides allowing easy identification on the battlefield, also impact behavior. Frederick the Great affixed otherwise useless buttons to the sleeves of uniform coats to stop his soldiers from wiping their noses with them. Today's uniforms enforce erect posture and bearing. More subtly, they help instill loyalty, pride, and inclusion—all part of "soldierization."

When I joined the Ranger Regiment as a young captain, the Standard Operating Procedures (SOPs) I followed were almost laughably detailed. My rucksack had to be packed with exactly the same equipment as every other Ranger's, and that equipment had to be in exactly the same pocket of the "ruck." A folded entrenching tool (a small shovel) was clipped to the left side and further held with parachute cord tied with prescribed knots. Failure to follow the SOPs brought immediate correction, and sometimes the punishment of a Saturday twelve-mile foot march—carrying the now correctly configured equipment.

Such overweening rigor may seem ridiculous. It has certainly earned the term "military discipline" a reputation as shorthand for any arbitrary exercise in crushing individuality. But most of these regulations developed for a reason. Under fire and often in the dark, Rangers must be able to locate water, gauze, and ammunition in seconds. A correctly packed bag can mean the difference between life and death. When a special operator leaps out of a C-130 transport aircraft twelve thousand feet above the ground, it is very important that his parachute was packed by following the appropriate steps with painstaking attention to detail.

Just as the road to mastering calculus begins with learning basic addition, the mechanized fastidiousness that ensures that all chute straps are in the right place starts with obsessive attention to small things like the knots that secure entrenching tools. Most tasks—how to pack a bag, how to conduct an air drop, how to clear a room of enemy—have been studied and their solutions tested, then practiced by thousands of men and women. Standardization and uniformity have enabled military leaders and planners to bring a semblance of predictability and order to the otherwise crazy environment that is war. Such standards become all the more important as a force grows in size. At the scale of the U.S. armed forces, standardization is a necessity.

The stakes for military organizations are particularly visible and dramatic—wars are won or lost, people live or die—but civilian organizations also wrestle with the basic questions of individuality, standardization, and predictability of outcome. Individual companies and entire economies depend on business leaders' knowing how best to manage for success. While fighting forces have been developing such protocols since Sparta, the notion of top-down, rigidly predetermined, "scientific" management of behavior in the civilian sector is largely the legacy of the nineteenth-century Quaker Frederick Winslow Taylor. His influence on the way we think about doing things—from running corporations to positioning kitchen appliances—is profound and pervasive. For our Task Force and for other twenty-first-century organizational endeavors, the legacy of Taylor's ideas is both part of the solution and part of the problem.

THE PERFECT STEP

What the forty-four-year-old Taylor unveiled at the 1900 Paris Exposition Universelle was so beautiful it inspired people to devote their lives to his vision. In a small tent on the outskirts of that famous world fair, he recreated a fragment of the steel factory he operated 3,600 miles away in Bethlehem, Pennsylvania: a handful of lathes and a few workers, tirelessly churning out metal chips. To the fin de siècle exposition audience, the rate at which his system did this was nothing short of miraculous: the norm was nine feet of steel per minute; Taylor's system could cut fifty.

Industrial manufacturing was the sexy technology of the day, and Taylor's display was akin to Steve Jobs's introducing the first iPhone.

People traveled across Europe and spent hours winding their way through the line outside Taylor's tent before being granted a few minutes to gaze at his system. The French metallurgist Henri-Louis Le Châtelier wrote, "Nobody quite believed at first in the prodigious result . . . but we had to accept the evidence of our eyes." A British engineer compared Taylor's breakthrough to the creation of the electric light. A prominent design engineer determined that the demonstration was nothing less than "a landmark in the history of mankind."

So what had he created? A new steel-cutting machine? A new way of heating or cooling the metal? The brilliance of Taylor's creation was not technological—his machines were very similar to those used by other companies. His genius lay in the regularity of his procedures, regularity much like the intricate execution of a parachute assault. Through a series of experiments, Taylor had determined the optimal temperature at which to cut steel chips, the optimal distance between the machinist and his tools, the optimal way for water to cool the lathe, and the optimal speed for internal conveyor belts. When it all came together, there was not a second of lost time, not an ounce of misplaced material, not a moment of unproductive human effort.

Taylor made *more*, *faster*, with *less*. Though not an engineer by training, he was a habitual optimizer by nature. A childhood friend noted that as a young boy walking around town Taylor would "endeavor to discover the step which would cover the greatest distance with the least expenditure of energy; or the easiest method of vaulting a fence; the right length and proportions of a walking staff." This mind-set, applied to questions of human organization, precipitated the most influential doctrine in the history of management.

At the age of seventeen, Taylor turned down Harvard to work in a factory. An intellectually gifted child of privilege, he had attended boarding school at Phillips Exeter Academy, where he devoted himself rigorously to his studies and consistently ranked as the top student in his class. A lucrative career in law, following in the footsteps of his father, seemed all but inevitable, especially after gaining university admission at the start of his senior year. But around that time, a spate of headaches and deteriorating eyesight convinced his doting parents that he suffered from "overstudying." (He was probably just farsighted.) So in late 1874, he boarded a carriage and returned to his quiet Pennsylvania home. After a few months of dawdling, Taylor yearned for something—anything—to keep him occupied. He signed up for an apprenticeship at Enterprise Hydraulic Works, a small company in downtown Philadelphia that made steam pumps and hydraulic machinery.

At Enterprise, Taylor fell in love with the gritty hustle and bustle of industry. For the first time, he got to know people who worked with their hands for a living. He learned how the contraptions that filled his home were made, learned what life on the factory floor was like, and even made attempts at cursing (by all accounts very awkwardly). This sphere of society was far removed from his upbringing on Cicero and George Fox, but Taylor could tell that industry was reshaping the world. He wrote later that his six months on the factory floor represented "the most valuable part of my education."

Taylor became fascinated by the contrast between the scientific precision of the machines in the shop and the remarkably *un*scientific processes that connected the humans to these beautiful contraptions. Although the industrial revolution had ushered in a new era of technology, the management structures that held everything in place had not changed since the days of artisans, small shops, and guilds: knowledge was largely rule of thumb, acquired through tips and tricks that would trickle down to aspiring craftsmen over the course of long apprenticeships. A veteran machinist wrote that "machinists, as a rule, were not very liberal with information of the right kind. Once in a while someone would give you some good advice, but that was the exception, rather than the rule."

On Taylor's first day at work, a foreman thrust an unmarked ruler under his nose, placed his finger randomly along its length, and demanded that Taylor tell him the exact measurement. A useful trick, Taylor thought, but why not just have numbers on the ruler? When fashioning a tool bit, Taylor was taught to heat the metal and beat it into a diamond-shaped point. But why that shape? There was no explanation. "It was a tradition," he wrote. "It had no scientific basis." Each worker had developed his own system of hammering, melting, and hardening, of work and breaks, etc., which each believed to be superior to that of his colleagues. Because there was no forum for comparing their outputs, everyone could continue to operate under the belief that his own system was best. They could not *all* be right, Taylor thought—there must be *one best way.**

Although Taylor claimed that he "learned appreciation, respect and admiration for the everyday working mechanic," he also developed an intellectual disdain for the casual, intuitive nature of common laborers' work. He came to believe that their protectionism over trade knowledge prevented industry from achieving its potential for scaled efficiency. Technology had leapt forward and now management was the limfac.

At his next position, with Midvale Steel Works, he was put in charge of the factory floor. Everywhere he looked, he saw slack that could be tightened, fat that could be trimmed, seconds that could be shaved off flawed processes.

Confident that the men could do more, he raised minimum output rates. In response, workers, who saw him as an arrogant upstart, sabotaged machines and went on strike. Taylor made them pay for repairs, cut their pay, and fired them.

After two years of struggle, which Taylor later recalled as the most miserable of his life, he had an epiphany: he would not *make* them work harder—he would *show* them that it could be done. He would rigorously study practices that had, for centuries, been left to rules of thumb; he would find "the one best way" to cut steel, prove that method's supremacy, and then have everyone do exactly that. Thus began a set of experiments that would change the working world for generations.

CLOCKWORK

Armed with a pen, a ledger, and a stopwatch, Taylor hovered over workers on the shop floor, timing every procedure, tweaking their actions, and timing again. He hired an assistant to catalogue the duration of every variant of every procedure. Determined to be as "scientific" as possible in his optimizing, he followed the reductionist impulses of classical mechanics, breaking every job down to its most granular elements, analyzing factory labor with similar intellectual tools to those used by Isaac Newton to

---

*Fittingly, *The One Best Way* is the title of Robert Kanigel's excellent and very thorough biography of Taylor (from which we draw much of this vignette).

deconstruct and make sense of the forces of the physical world. In the case of workers at Midvale, this was a series of discrete motions, which he measured, compared, and then reconstructed, calculating the fastest possible way to execute each step. The small gains made by optimizing each tiny element came together to make a substantial difference in efficiency.

Based on his findings, Taylor produced prescriptive instruction cards: instead of being tasked with the general objective of "machining a tire," workers were now told to:

Set tire on machine ready to turn . . .

Rough face front edge . . .

Finish face front edge . . .

Rough bore front . . .

Finish bore front . . .

There was a time expectation for each of these movements.

Though the notion of a "best practice" is now commonplace, at that time a workman's methods were part of his art: variable, personalized, and a matter of pride. For people who perceived themselves as skilled workers, being recast as mindless cogs in a larger machine was degrading: they went on strike and quit. In a petition against Taylor's "humiliating" system, the workers agreed that "any man on whom the stop watch was pulled should refuse to continue to work." Unfortunately for the striking workers, this lacked the impact it would have had a few years earlier: Taylor's system meant that—once researched, evaluated, and formalized—their skilled jobs became simple steps executable by anyone. He could find new, cooperative workers, and with the massive increases in production gained by his efficient system, he could pay them more. Taylor wasn't afraid of workers' quitting; he fired anyone unable to keep pace with what he had calculated to be a hard day's work.

Taylor's methods were cruel, but, for business owners, his results were undeniable. The cost of overhauling boilers dropped from $62 (around $2,000 today) to $11; machining a tire could now be done in one fifth of the previous time; making a cannon projectile now took just ninety minutes instead of ten hours; 1,200 could now do work that would have taken 2,000 people at any other company.

The data vindicated Taylor's belief in the mismatch between the capabilities of technology and the way organizations were run, and confirmed the tremendous potential for improved performance through rigorous, reductionist optimization and standardization. He measured more and more, revealing bottlenecks in the flow of materials and inefficiencies within machines. The physical layout of the room, the nuances of sweeping the floor, the methods of issuing orders, and the protocols for returning materials all fell under the authoritarian choreography of his instruction cards. Right down to screwing the spindle of a popper head, he found an optimal solution to every kink and hiccup of workplace life, shaving off fractions of a second here, cents on the dollar there.

In a small shop, such savings might have been insignificant, which is why rule of thumb worked fine and intrusive management would have been counterproductive. But at the scale of industrial production, where these gains were multiplied across hundreds of identical machines and thousands of workers, small savings added up to significant differences in productivity and profits.

By 1890, Midvale had become an industry leader and Taylor departed to pursue the broader potential of "a workplace ruled by science." Taylor's efforts dovetailed nicely with contemporary scientific thought, heavily influenced by the elegant simplicity of earlier thinkers such as Newton and "the French Newton," Pierre-Simon Laplace. Science at the time was dominated by the notion of determinism—the idea that any initial conditions has only one, inevitable outcome: a ball thrown at a certain speed will have a predictable trajectory, as will a planet in orbit. Throughout the nineteenth century, phenomena that had once been written off as the work of God fell under human mastery. The vision was of a "clockwork universe" in which all laws were coherent and all causes and effects predictable. If you knew the rules and the inputs, you could foresee and sometimes manipulate the outputs. The challenge was taking the clockwork apart to see how it all fit together.

Taylor created a clockwork factory, systematically eliminating variation, studying all labor until he understood it inside and out, honing it to peak efficiency, and ensuring that those precise procedures were followed at scale. Because he could study and predict, he could control. He dubbed his doctrine "scientific management."

Taylor became the world's first management guru. At a paper mill in Wisconsin, he was told that the art of pulping and drying could not be reduced to a science. He instituted his system and material costs dropped from $75 to $35 per ton, while labor costs dropped from $30 a ton to $8. At a ball bearing factory, he experimented with everything from lighting levels to rest break durations, and oversaw an increase in quantity and quality of production while reducing the number of employees from 120 to 35; at a pig iron plant, he raised worker output from 12.5 to 47 tons of steel per day, and decreased the number of workers from 600 to 140.

By the time Taylor's Parisian tent showed the world how Bethlehem Steel could produce fifty feet of metal a minute, the doctrine he had developed to resolve a factory-floor fight at Midvale was the gospel of forward-looking industrialists.

"WE HAVE OTHER MEN PAID FOR THINKING"

Taylor's ideas spread from company to company, from industry to industry, and from blue collars to white (there was one best way to insert paper into a typewriter, to sit at a desk, to clip pages together). They seeped into the halls of government. His philosophy of replacing the intuition of the person doing the job with reductionist efficiencies designed by a separate group of people marked a new means of organizing human endeavors. It was the behavioral soul mate for the technical advances of industrial engineering.

Taylor's success represented the legitimization of "management" as a discipline. Previously, managerial roles were rewards for years of service in the form of higher pay and less strenuous labor. The manager's main function was to keep things in working order and maintain morale. Under Taylor's formulation, managers were both research scientists and architects of efficiency.

This drew a hard-and-fast line between thought and action: managers did the thinking and planning, while workers executed. No longer were laborers expected to understand how or why things worked—in fact, managers saw teaching them that or paying a premium for their expertise as a form of waste. At the paper mill, Taylor encountered a system where workers submitted samples of digester fluid to a chemist at regular inter-vals. Taylor replaced the chemist with a rack of test tubes filled with digester fluid at varying standard conditions. Workers simply had to determine which tube was the best match to their sample and proceed accordingly. As a result, an expensive, skilled worker could be replaced with a cheap, uneducated adolescent. By devising incredibly exact instructions and printing a few charts, Taylor could again afford to lose expensive workers with decades of experience, replacing them with young laborers who were unquestioningly loyal to a centrally designed process.

Taylor told workers, "I have you for your strength and mechanical ability. We have other men paid for thinking." In the book that became the bible of his movement, *The Principles of Scientific Management*, he portrayed laborers as idiots, mocking their syntax and describing them as "mentally sluggish." In one passage he wrote,

> *[A laborer] shall be so stupid and so phlegmatic that he more nearly resembles in his mental make-up the ox than any other type . . . the workman who is best suited to handling pig iron is unable to understand the real science of doing this class of work. He is so stupid that the word "percentage" has no meaning to him, and he must consequently be trained by a man more intelligent than himself into the habit of working in accordance with the laws of this science before he can be successful.*

Taylor's statement is offensive and inaccurate, but he was right in pointing out that many people do things in inefficient ways, and that small inefficiencies multiplied at industrial scale reduce productivity. The world had become vastly more complicated since the time of apprenticeships and small, family-run enterprises. The level of complication had passed a threshold whereby localized improvisation and intuition could not support the magnitude of industrial endeavors. The scope and intricacy of production processes had expanded to the point that they required planners and coordinators to ensure that all the pieces came together efficiently and effectively. The rise of managers as the thinkers who would devise such blueprints—and the reduction of workers to instruments of implementation—seemed to follow as a natural consequence.

Reductionism lay at the heart of this drive for efficiency. Taylor's approach broke work down into its simplest elements—the laying of bricks became a series of five discrete motions; the machining of a tire, a sequence of twelve. Only the managers—the planners and coordinators—had to understand how everything came together. Such a system harnessed the gains of extreme specialization, advocated in the abstract by Adam Smith and David Ricardo centuries earlier. Henry Ford's famous assembly line, which in 1913 compressed the production of a car from days to just ninety-three minutes by dividing the assembly process into a set of specialized roles, was a natural extension of Taylor's train of thought.*

Military planners had relied on many of Taylor's strategies—the segregation of planning and execution, standardization, and an emphasis on efficiency—for centuries before Taylor was born. But Taylor's ideas inspired many military leaders to find fresh ways to create a more efficient fighting force. In the years leading up to World War I, European militaries constructed complicated plans for the mobilization and deployment of their massive armies, built on precisely timed rail movements. Reductionist master planners broke down offensives into the number of feet and inches that each brigade would be expected to advance each hour. Those lower down the chain of command would receive orders similar to Taylor's instruction cards. Historian A. J. P. Taylor famously dubbed this approach "war by timetable."

When America entered World War I, the country turned to reductionist systems to raise production of guns, bombs, and boots to unprecedented levels. Historian Samuel Haber wrote that "efficiency became a patriotic duty. . . . Taylor's advocacy of unrestrained production became common sense." When World War II broke out barely twenty years later, reductionist systems enabled tens of thousands of untrained sharecroppers to become welders and shipbuilders in the span of a few months. One year after Pearl Harbor, America's "arsenal of democracy" was producing war matériel (including the 7,000-ton ship the SS *Frederick W. Taylor*) on a scale that stunned the world. By 1945 U.S. factories had churned out 310,00 aircraft, 124,000 ships, 60,973 tanks (versus 19,326 by Germany), and mind-numbing quantities of trucks, rifles, uniforms, and ammunition. Peter Drucker, the sage of modern management, argued that without Taylor's innovations, America would have been unable to defeat the Nazis.

For Taylor, efficiency was far more than a mere set of business practices—it was a "mental revolution" applicable to the mundane (he experimented persistently with the most efficient way to make scrambled eggs), the trivial (an avid tennis player, he spent years optimizing the

---

*It is worth noting that Ford denied scientific management's influence on him. Nonetheless, it is clear that the two men's approaches derive from the foundational belief in efficiency.

angle of his racket, and eventually won the precursor of the U.S. Open), and the geopolitical. In his words,

> *The same principles [of scientific management] can be applied with equal force to all social activities: to the management of our homes; the management of our farms; the management of the business of our tradesmen, large and small; of our churches, our philanthropic institutions, our universities, and our governmental departments.*

On the domestic front as well as in war, government took an active role in promoting Taylor's doctrine. In 1910, when a group of powerful railroads petitioned the government for a rate hike, the Supreme Court determined that they did not need it: if the railroads just adopted Taylor's scientific management, they could save up to one million dollars a day—more than they would have gained with the rate hike. The lawyer who represented "the consumer" in the case, Louis Brandeis (who would later be appointed to the Supreme Court), wrote, "Of all the social and economic movements with which I have been connected, none seems to me to be equal to [scientific management] in its importance and hopefulness."

Historian Glenn Porter explains, "Scientific management took on some of the trappings of a kind of secular religion; Taylor was the messiah, and his followers, who spread the word, were (and still are) commonly referred to as 'disciples.'" In the 1910s, these disciples descended on factories, mills, and plants across America, ushering in a new era of measured optimization. One, Robert Kent, wrote, "No group of crusaders ever battled for their cause with greater energy, greater faith, than the men in this movement in those early days battled for scientific management."

These acolytes reduced all sorts of domains to neatly defined sets of "scientific principles." Henri Fayol, a mining engineer, wrote a dissertation called *Industrial and General Administration* in which he reduced management to five elements: planning, organizing, command, coordination, and control. Social scientists Luther Gulick and Lyndall Urwick determined that the responsibilities of government leadership were to plan, to organize, to direct staff, to coordinate, to report, and to budget.

Taylor touted his advances as a universal panacea. "In my judgment," Taylor wrote, "the best possible measure of the height in the scale of civilization to which any people has arisen is its productivity." He believed his "mental revolution" would lead to

> *the substitution of peace for war; the substitution of hearty broth-*
> *erly cooperation for contention and strife; of both pulling hard in*
> *the same direction instead of pulling apart; of replacing suspicious*
> *watchfulness with mutual confidence; or becoming friends instead*
> *of enemies.*

Biographer and historian Robert Kanigel writes that "by the late 1920s, it could seem that all of modern society had come under the sway of a single commanding idea: that waste was wrong and efficiency the highest good, and that eliminating one and achieving the other was best left to the experts." Journalist Ida Tarbell went so far as to argue, "No man in the history of American industry has made a larger contribution to genuine cooperation and juster human relations than did Frederick Winslow Taylor. He is one of the few creative geniuses of our time."

In the decades since, Taylor's star has dimmed. His treatment of workers has been widely decried, as has his conception of individuals as mechanistic entities to be manipulated. In the 1960s, MIT professor Douglas McGregor's "Theory X" and "Theory Y" of human resource management offered a famous critique of Taylorist principles: in McGregor's view, Taylor's approach (X) saw humans as fundamentally lazy and in need of financial incentives and close monitoring in order to do work, while McGregor's own Theory Y understood people as capable of self-motivation and self-control, and argued that managers would achieve better results by treating their employees with respect.

Nevertheless, Taylor's *foundational* belief—the notion that an effective enterprise is created by commitment to efficiency, and that the role of the manager is to break things apart and plan "the one best way"—remains relatively unchallenged. The question of the treatment of labor is an argument over the appropriate means to that agreed-upon end. We might recoil today at the brutal consequences of mechanized warfare and the dehumanizing connotations of the assembly line, but the principles that undergird these systems remain firmly embedded in the way organizations of all types approach management and leadership. We still search faithfully for the one best way to do things; we still think of organizational leaders as planners, synchronizers, and coordinators—chess-player strategists responsible for overseeing interlocking troop movements, marketing initiatives, or global supply chains.

The structures of our organizations reflect this ideal. Whether imbued with a "lazy worker" Theory X or a "motivated worker" Theory Y disposition, the "org charts" of most multiperson endeavors look pretty similar: a combination of specialized vertical columns (departments or divisions) and horizontal tiers that denote levels of authority, with the most powerful literally on top—the only tier that can access all columns. At the top, we envision the strategic decision making. At the bottom, we imagine action by those taking direction. The efficiency, strength, and logic that we are inclined to see in such a chart is a natural extension of the separation of planning from execution. From our conception of leadership to the form of our organizations, reductionism laid the foundation of contemporary management.

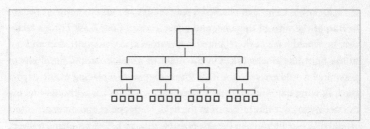

Taylor's system of reductionist planning lent itself naturally to a new generation of neat and tidy hierarchies. At each level, managers would examine objectives, break them apart into separate tasks, and farm these out in discrete packages.

We no longer tell secretaries how to paper-clip pages together, but we do read dozens of online articles that promise "five ways to make your day more efficient" or "seven tips to maximize your productivity." We believe that the reductionist sum of everyone being their "most productive" will lead to the best overall results. We love the idea of a "best practice." Historians attribute to Taylorism the advent of modern time consciousness, the transformation of leisure from unstructured free time to organized recreation, and the approach to managing the federal bureaucracy championed by the Reagan administration. Critic Christopher Lasch argued that Taylorism ushered in "a new interpretation of the American Dream."

A Taylor disciple writing in the 1940s acknowledged that despite all the effort they poured into their crusade, he and his peers never would have "dreamed that in less than a quarter of a century the principles of scientific management would be so woven into the fabric of our industrial life that they would be accepted as a commonplace, that plants would be operating under the principles of scientific management without knowing it, plants perhaps that had never heard of Taylor." Peter Drucker argued that Taylor, more than Karl Marx, deserves a place in the pantheon of modern intellectual thought alongside Darwin and Freud.

Taylor changed not only the way our world is organized, but the way we think about solving problems. Historian Jeremy Rifkin believes, "[Taylor] has probably had a greater effect on the private and public lives of the men and women of the twentieth century than any other single individual."

THE AWESOME MACHINE

If Taylor could have been plucked from the turn of the last century, brought to Iraq at the turn of this one, and given a tour of our Task Force's facilities, he would have been delighted. Operators and units shifted in and out of the fight like clockwork. On the night of a unit rotation, hundreds of personnel would arrive to the fight, those they were replacing would depart the following day, and all these movements would occur without reducing our ability to continue missions in the field. Helicopters and other air assets would fly, quite literally, to the last possible minute before requiring upkeep, and would travel back to the United States on the same transport aircraft that had just a few hours prior brought freshly tuned helicopters into the fight. Pilots would step from one cockpit to another, without missing a beat. Operators' weapons and personal kits sat in precise rows in the pathway between their sleeping quarters and the departure point for missions, enabling them to launch at a moment's notice and creating a common area for updates to be given to the team. From major equipment to the placement of gear on the individual operator, everything about our system screamed efficiency and precision. It was, as we often said, "an awesome machine"—an assembly line for counterterrorism.

This fastidious synchronization across forces had been learned the hard way, through the humiliating failure of Operation Eagle Claw, the 1980 attempt to rescue hostages being held in our embassy in Tehran. In the first stage of a torturously complicated operation to reach, secure, and extract the Americans who had been held captive in the occupied embassy compound for five months—misfortune struck. In a remote part of the Iranian desert, a Navy helicopter, flown by a Marine pilot, collided with an Air Force cargo plane loaded with Army commandos, dooming the mission before the force got within two hundred miles of its target. In the aftermath, the Holloway Commission, appointed by the Joint Chiefs of Staff to review the failure, recommended the creation of a specially focused Joint Task Force to coordinate and plan American special operations. It was a "never again" mentality. We needed a new management tier at the top—a new level of reductionist architects of process to ensure that things clicked together with the precision of Taylor's factory floor at Midvale. Our Task Force, bringing the different military branches' elite teams under one command, was the result.

When I took command in 2003, the Task Force was deeply involved in what was termed the Global War on Terror (GWOT). Operations spanned a wide swath of Africa, the Middle East, and Southwest Asia, but the largest commitment was focused on Iraq. In the aftermath of the initial invasion, we had assumed primary responsibility for targeting senior former leaders of the fallen Saddam Hussein government, made famous by the "deck of cards" unveiled in March 2003—a collection of playing-card-size cards with the names and photographs of fifty-five Ba'athist leaders designated for capture.

At first it had seemed straightforward: we had little trouble gathering up the paunchy, chain-smoking men who had apparently served as stalwart henchmen of an odious dictator. But Zarqawi's insurgency—a different type of threat—was already growing in size and sophistication. In 2003 it was not yet clear that AQI was the primary agent coalescing resistance, but the rumblings could be felt like distant thunder on a summer afternoon—a storm was approaching. Our planned, reductionist precision might have been an outstanding organizational solution for twentieth-century problems, but we were now fighting in a new era.

By early spring of 2004, we understood that Iraq would be different. Special operations forces were designed to employ uniquely skilled operators, in small numbers, for carefully timed raids executed with rapierlike exactitude. Correctly done, such operations were the ultimate symbol of efficiency, and to be used sparingly. But as the scope and complexity of the fight grew it became clear that AQI's surprising breadth and agility demanded increased reliance on the tactical flexibility that only special operations units could provide. Success of the larger mission in Iraq demanded we take on a role at a scale and sustained intensity that were unprecedented—with no discernible end in sight.

Not only the scale of the fight was new; the tools were as well. The development of new information technologies, precision weapons, GPS, night vision, and other advances were also changing how we fought. Descending from blacked-out helicopters that could locate a specific rooftop in a sea of buildings with pinpoint accuracy, operators communicated via headsets with pilots controlling unmanned aerial vehicles that provided constant video surveillance, and, after capturing their target, employed biometric data collection to confirm his identify.

The process that drove our operations in Iraq was a sequence that became known as *F3EA: Find—Fix—Finish—Exploit—Analyze.* It was simple in concept, and much of it was as old as warfare itself. First, the target needed to be *found*; then its position would need to be *fixed* so that we could know where it was in real time; the operators would then *finish* the target, removing the threat from the battlefield; next, the target would be *exploited* for any intelligence (a house might be searched, a person interrogated); and finally, intelligence would be *analyzed*. Then the cycle would begin again. It derived from similar targeting and decision-making processes (like the well-known OODA loop: *Observe—Orient—Decide—Assess* that became associated with fighter pilots) that sought to increase the effectiveness of operations by continually refining understanding of the situation.

At first we had to adjust to the speed and scale of this fight. We had traditionally functioned in a slower rhythm, conducting occasional, exquisitely planned, surgical strikes, but now we were conducting operations nearly every day, often doing multiple raids simultaneously. We quickly came up to speed. This type of work was not fundamentally new—just the same old thing at a larger magnitude. Within a few months, we had built our "awesome machine."

But there were warning signs. We were being asked to take on a new role, with unfamiliar tools, in an environment that we didn't fully comprehend.* While efficient on a scale that the challengers we faced could never have imagined, we were beginning to understand that the new world was not just incrementally different from the old one in a way that could be fixed with a new, yet more intricate set of precise instructions delivered from on high. Our efficient systems provided us with a solid foundation, but they could not bring us victory.

This new world required a fundamental rewriting of the rules of the

---

*Appreciating the magnitude of what one *doesn't* know, as the reader will see, proves to be a major theme in this book. In 2004, we did not yet understand this maxim.

game. In order to win, we would have to set aside many of the lessons that millennia of military procedure and a century of optimized efficiencies had taught us.

LESSONS OF THE LAST WAR

In 1930, France began construction of its famed Maginot Line, named for the minister of war and World War I veteran André Maginot. Like millions of his countrymen, Maginot had seen firsthand the death, disease, and suffering of static trench warfare. As the Holloway Commission would do decades later, he applied "never again" thinking to avoid repeating the horrors of the past.

Built over ten years, the Maginot Line was a modern-day version of the Great Wall of China: an impenetrable system of tunnels, resupply routes, and interlocking fields of fire for both individual soldiers and large artillery. Its various subterranean floors included not only soldiers' quarters, but hospitals, telephone bureaus, and even a subway. Running the length of the Franco-German border, and extending ten to twelve miles below ground, it was a marvel of military planning and an intimidating deterrent to any invaders coming from the east.

In 1940 the Germans approached the line and stopped—their maneuver a feint. Simultaneously Panzer divisions knifed through Belgium, the Netherlands, and Luxembourg—neutral countries that could offer no substantial defense. Aided by improvements in tank technology, German forces could now move far faster than the columns of troops in World War I. They blazed through the Lowlands and struck France from the north in a flanking maneuver around the impenetrable (but immovable) Maginot Line. The Luftwaffe simply flew over it. Outflanked and stunned, France surrendered in less than two months.

Today, the Maginot Line is often used as a metaphor for stupidity, but the reality is complicated. The line largely worked as designed—the muddy trenches and carnage of World War I did not reappear, and Germany was unable to mount a land invasion via the Franco-German border. Arguably, had the line not been built, the Germans might have taken a more direct route into France and achieved victory even more swiftly. But despite its formidability, André Maginot's creation was insufficient for a new environment of tanks, airplanes, and an enemy command that chose not to play by the rules. Instead of deterring a German attack, it helped stimulate a new type of war.

In 2004, as we planned clockwork raids designed to make the most of every drop of fuel, we were manning a managerial Maginot Line: our extraordinarily efficient procedures and plans were well crafted and necessary, but not sufficient.

Like the proverbial general always fighting the last war, the French had crafted a solution to avoid the pain of World War I, and we had designed an organization that could avoid repeating the embarrassment of Eagle Claw. And just as the development of the tank changed the realities of military defense, the proliferation of new information-age technologies rendered Taylorist efficiency an outdated managerial paradigm.

Over the past century, the kind of organizational measures that ensure the success of combat parachute assaults have proliferated throughout the military, industry, and business. In today's environment, however, these solutions are the equivalent of the provincial apprenticeship models that Taylor stumbled upon in 1874. In Iraq, the inexplicable, networked success of our underresourced enemy indicated that they had cracked this nut before we had. Managerially, AQI was flanking us.

RECAP

♦ Our Task Force's structure and culture of *disciplined, stratified reductionism* had its roots deep in military organizational history.

♦ This organizational culture is not unique to the military; since the Industrial Revolution, most industries have subscribed to management doctrines informed by or similar to Frederick Taylor's "Scientific Management," a system that is excellent for achieving *highly efficient execution of known, repeatable processes* at scale.

♦ We were realizing in 2004 that despite the success of this approach throughout the twentieth century, it had its limits. Like the Maginot Line, it was insufficient for tackling a new generation of threats. *Efficiency is no longer enough.*

CHAPTER 3

FROM COMPLICATED
TO COMPLEX

The year is 1882. Halfway around the world from Taylor and his factories, the Ottoman governor of Damascus has decided to implement major educational reforms. Tarek, a poor, pious Muslim who resents the reforms, goes down to the town square, gets on a soapbox, and begins to agitate against the government. Do the authorities need to worry about him? Perhaps. In all likelihood, the Ottoman regime knows almost nothing about him personally because he is not well connected or aligned with any of their institutional enemies. But even without knowledge about Tarek as an individual, the regime can anticipate that the number of people who might turn out to see him preach is small—only people who are within daily communication and traveling radius of his soapbox will be aware of his protest. Moreover, the town square lies within government control. If things get out of hand, they can shut down the operation almost instantly. Maybe they will arrest him, or maybe they will let him say his piece and leave. Either way, they can predict with some accuracy that he does not represent a threat to the state.

Fast-forward to 2010 and Tarek is standing on the street in Sidi Bouzid, Tunisia. He is shouting at the top of his lungs about local police corruption. With access to his data trail, twenty-first-century Tunisian authorities may know a lot about Tarek: where he shops, what he likes to buy, what Web sites he visits at the Internet café, who his Facebook friends are, what kind of religious and political beliefs he holds. With simple study and a basic computer, they can come to far more refined conclusions about him than the Ottoman governor in 1882 could have. But in 2010 the range of outcomes

that this Tarek can generate is far greater than his government can anticipate, because he lives in a vastly more complex world.

The first Tarek is fictional. The second is Tunisian fruit vendor Tarek
al-Tayeb Mohamed Bouazizi, and when he douses himself with gasoline
and self-immolates, events spiral out of control at breakneck speed: A
crowd protests his death, and his cousin records the scene on his iPhone.
Videos appear on YouTube within two days, along with a picture of Tarek,
aflame and dying. More protests erupt. Videos of those protests wind up
on Facebook. Arabs everywhere see their Tunisian brethren in the streets.
Not only Al Jazeera, but *The New York Times* and *The Guardian* make
trips to the small town of Sidi Bouzid. Within three months, the thirty-year
reign of Hosni Mubarak is brought to an end some 1,400 miles away in
Cairo, Muammar Gaddafi starts losing control of Libya after four decades
in power, and Syria begins its descent into intractable civil war.

Despite having more data about Arab societies—and about individuals
like Tarek—than at any time in history, no government, search engine, or
social media platform foresaw Tarek's self-immolation or the impact it
would have.

The two Tareks illustrate the contradiction between the tremendous
technological progress witnessed during the past century, and our
seemingly diminished ability to know what will happen next. Though we
know far more about everything in it, the world has in many respects
become less predictable.

Such unpredictability has happened not *in spite* of technological progress,
but *because* of it. The technological developments of recent decades are of a
fundamentally different variety from those of Taylor's era. While we might
think that our increased ability to track, measure, and communicate with
people like Tarek would improve our precise "clockwork universe" management, the reality is the opposite: these changes produce a radically different
climate—one of unpredictable complexity—that stymies organizations based
on Taylorist efficiency. It is because of these changes that the Task Force's
"awesome machine," excellent by all twentieth-century metrics, was failing.

Understanding specifically what had changed, why it reduced predictability, and how that impacted management would prove critical to solving our problem. And we weren't alone. In our later analyses, we found
that phenomena we witnessed on the ground in Iraq had been observed
in a wide variety of domains, from agronomy to economics.

COMETS AND COLD FRONTS

Getting a handle on the problem of the two Tareks begins with the story of an eclectic mathematician and meteorologist working at MIT in 1961. Edward Lorenz had been using then-cutting-edge computers to try to crack weather for about a year. Weather was a tricky problem. While events such as the return of Halley's Comet could be precisely calculated decades in advance, and tides and eclipses had surrendered long ago to scientific prediction, weather remained elusive. Lorenz hoped that the new technology would enable him to find a similar level of clockwork determinism in the Earth's climate. He ran computer simulations, created rudimentary graphics to better visualize the trends in his data, and hoped to discern some sort of pattern.

One day, Lorenz took a shortcut in order to reexamine one particular simulation. Instead of running the whole sequence from the beginning (computers were much slower), he began halfway through. He keyed in the numbers from an earlier printout himself to make sure the initial conditions were exactly the same, then went off to grab a cup of coffee, giving the machine time to spit out its new predictions. The new run should have duplicated the earlier one exactly, as Lorenz had made no changes and had double-checked all of the inputs himself. But when he saw the new printout, he was astonished: it diverged so wildly from its predecessor that the pair seemed to be "two random weathers out of a hat."

Lorenz pored over his results, searching for a bug somewhere in the code or in his computer. After weeks of analysis, he found the culprit. It wasn't in the code or the machine; it was in the data. The two "identical" simulations he had run were actually *very* slightly different. The original sequence that caught Lorenz's attention had been produced by the algorithm. The computer's memory stored six decimal places for any value, but Lorenz had entered the reproduced sequence from the printout, which displayed only three. He did not foresee a problem in entering the printout's rounded-off numbers, assuming that the difference between .506127 and .506 would be inconsequential.

In a clockwork universe it *would* have been inconsequential. The calculations that had successfully predicted eclipses, tides, and comets behave in straightforward ways; a small error in input data would lead to a small error in prediction—forecasting an eclipse a few minutes early or late.

But weather is different. Lorenz's tiny "rounding error" existed in a more interdependent and volatile environment than the void through which Halley's Comet orbits. Tiny eddies of air can be influenced by an almost immeasurably small event—something like the fluttering of a butterfly's wings—and these eddies can affect larger currents, which in turn alter the way cold and warm fronts build—a chain of events that can magnify the initial disturbance exponentially, thereby completely undermining attempts to make reliable predictions. Lorenz's program had been correct.

When, several years later, Lorenz presented a paper about his findings, he titled it "Does the Flap of a Butterfly's Wings in Brazil Set Off a Tornado in Texas?" The phrase "the butterfly effect" entered the world.*

Lorenz's butterfly effect is a physical manifestation of the phenomenon of *complexity*—not "complexity" in the sense that we use the term in daily life, a catchall for things that are not simple or intuitive, but complexity in a more restrictive, technical, and baffling sense. This kind of complexity is difficult to define; those who study it often fall back on Supreme Court justice Potter Stewart's comment on obscenity: "I know it when I see it." Things that are complex—living organisms, ecosystems, national economies—have a diverse array of connected elements that interact frequently. Because of this density of linkages, complex systems fluctuate extremely and exhibit unpredictability. In the case of weather, a small disturbance in one place could trigger a series of responses that build into unexpected and severe outcomes in another place, because of the billions of tiny interactions that link the origin and the outcome. In an ecosystem, one slightly mutated virus may spread like wildfire, causing a huge population depletion that, in turn, propagates through the

---

*Contrary to popular belief, the concept's origins do not lie in Ray Bradbury's 1952 short story "A Sound of Thunder." However, the story does capture a version of the same phenomenon. In it, mankind of the near future uses a time machine to leap back thousands of years and hunt dinosaurs. Hunters cannot bring their prey back to the twentieth century, or even step foot on the prehistoric ground while on the hunt (they have built levitating pathways) because of the danger that tampering with the past could negatively influence the present. One hunt goes wrong and the hunter slips, stepping briefly off the pathway, and crushing a butterfly, before hopping back on. When he and his guides return to the present day, "there was a thing to the air, a chemical taint so subtle, so slight that only a faint cry of his subliminal senses warned him it was there." Language is used differently; a different man has been elected president. The death of a butterfly, relayed and magnified by eons of ecosystem twists and turns, resulted in a different society.

food chain, transforming the local biological order. In the case of economies, the capsizing of a single bank can have no effect at all, or cause cascading failure throughout the system.

Being *complex* is different from being *complicated*. Things that are complicated may have many parts, but those parts are joined, one to the next, in relatively simple ways: one cog turns, causing the next one to turn as well, and so on. The workings of a complicated device like an internal combustion engine might be confusing, but they ultimately *can* be broken down into a series of neat and tidy deterministic relationships; by the end, you will be able to predict with relative certainty what will happen when one part of the device is activated or altered.

Complexity, on the other hand, occurs when the number of *interactions* between components increases dramatically—the interdependencies that allow viruses and bank runs to spread; this is where things quickly become unpredictable. Think of the "break" in a pool game—the first forceful strike of the colored balls with the white cue ball. Although there are only sixteen balls on the table and the physics is that of simple mechanics, it is almost impossible to predict where everything will end up. In a perfect world, with an impossibly level table, balls that were identical down to the micron, and a player who could strike with the precision of one millionth of a degree, a computer could foresee where the balls would slow to a halt. However, introduce even the slightest deviation in the trajectory of a single ball, and quickly *all* the balls that it touches, and all the balls that they touch, will diverge. The density of interactions means that even a relatively small number of elements can quickly defy prediction.

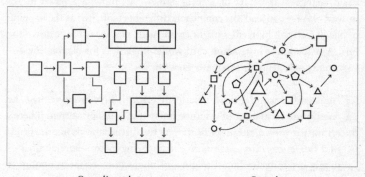

Complicated   Complex

Because of these dense interactions, complex systems exhibit *nonlinear* change. Linear phenomena are those whose output is proportional to input: you can put $100 or $200 into a set of bonds that will give you a 5 percent return in five years; doubling your input will double your eventual profit from $5 to $10. The change in outcome is proportional to the change in income. Such a function could be represented mathematically as: $Y = 1.05x$. Human minds feel at home with linear functions. *Non*linear functions, on the other hand, make us uncomfortable. They come in many forms, including exponential functions like $Y = 5^x$, and they quickly defy our intuitive understandings of growth and scale. Initial differences in the base or slight increases or decreases in x have massive consequences. When we invest money in a risky stock, we are resigning ourselves to the nonlinear capriciousness of a complex system (the stock market), where a single news story or a rogue trader across the world can cause a stock to plummet, skyrocket, or flatline.

To grasp how quickly nonlinear situations can spiral beyond our capacity to comprehend or predict, consider a game of chess: Chess is rule bound and the number of possible moves is limited, but it is *interdependent*—what happens to one piece changes the relationships between, and the behavior of, the others. Jonathan Schaeffer has calculated that there are 197,742 different ways for the players' first two turns to transpire. By the third move, the number of possibilities has risen to 121 million. Within twenty moves, it is more than likely that you are playing a game that has never been played before. Nobody knows exactly how many games of chess potentially exist because, according to Schaeffer, the figure "is so huge that no one will invest the effort to calculate the exact number." A small change at the start of a chess game—say, moving a pawn to A3 instead of A4—can lead to a completely different result, just as the flapping of one of Lorenz's butterflies might create huge, nonlinear havoc down the line. A reductionist instruction card would be useless for playing chess—the interactions generate too many possibilities.

The significance of Lorenz's butterfly effect is not, however, just the nonlinear escalation of a minor input into a major output. There's uncertainty involved; the amplification of the disturbance is not the product of a *single, constant, identifiable* magnifying factor—any number of seemingly insignificant inputs might—or might not—result in nonlinear escalation. If every butterfly's fluttering *always* led to a hurricane halfway across the world two days later, weather would be predictable (if insane). The butterfly's fluttering leads to a storm only if thousands of other minor conditions are just right. And those conditions are so precise as to be practically immeasurable, rendering the outcome unpredictable.

According to Taylor's idea of efficiency, an understanding of the initial conditions of a system and the forces at play within it enables managers to compute the end result. But in a complex system with dense interconnections (even one as seemingly "clockwork" as a chess game), one would need an impossible resolution of data in order to make reliable medium- to long-run predictions. There *are* causes for the events in a complex system, but there are so many causes and so many events linked to one another through so many direct and indirect paths that the outcome is *practically* unpredictable, even if it is theoretically deterministic.

As Lorenz explained, "if a little flap could lead to a tornado that would not otherwise have happened, it could equally well prevent a tornado that would otherwise have formed." The weather in his example depends on the myriad other interdependent variables with which that flapping wing would—directly and indirectly—interact. As a result, compared with something like the trajectory of a comet, the development of weather has a far, far wider range of potential outcomes.

In popular culture, the term "butterfly effect" is almost always misused. It has become synonymous with "leverage"—the idea of a small thing that has a big impact, with the implication that, like a lever, it *can be manipulated to a desired end*. This misses the point of Lorenz's insight. The reality is that small things in a complex system may have no effect or a massive one, and it is virtually *impossible to know which will turn out to be the case*.

This broad spectrum of possible outcomes throws a wrench into the conceptual clockwork. In the Task Force, as in most large organizations, our actions were the product of our planning, and our planning was predicated on our ability to predict. (Or more precisely, our perception of our ability to predict—our belief that we understood the workings of the clock.) But by 2004 our battlefield behaved a lot more like the capricious movements of a cold front than like the steady trajectory of Halley's Comet. New communications technologies had joined individuals like Tarek to millions of others in a dense tangle of interconnectedness. These events and actors were not only more interdependent than in previous wars, they were also faster. The environment was not just complicated, it was *complex*.

EMMYLOU'S WAYWARD SWIRL

My granddaughter, Emmylou, was born on June 4, 2014. She will grow up in a world defined by the near-instant transmission of information and rapid transportation of people, goods, and services. She is a "digital native," while I will always remain, at best, the holder of a green card. I do not know how she will perceive the differences between real and virtual presence, but I know she will navigate these converging spheres differently and far more deftly than previous generations. The very social fabric of her world is being woven with the fiber optic cables of social media—a shift whose consequences we cannot begin to predict. The world of Emmylou is one that many could have scarcely imagined twenty years ago.

Products, events, nations, phenomena, and individuals have become more connected to, dependent on, and influenced by one another than ever before. Boeing's primary assembly of its 787 Dreamliner, for instance, requires about one thousand workers at its Everett, Washington, plant. But it depends on wings from Nagoya, Japan; horizontal stabilizers from Foggia, Italy; cargo and access doors from Sweden; wingtips from Korea; and landing gear from Gloucester, United Kingdom. Like most of what we buy or use, any given Dreamliner is the product of a vast network of sources.

The increased interdependence that goes into creating our physical products is nothing compared with the leaps in digital connectivity witnessed in recent years. The rise of crowdsourced fund-raising campaigns, viral online trends, and mobile payment systems testifies that the spread of technology has brought almost all of us into a much broader web of connectivity than we were in a decade or two ago.

In Iraq, we saw this rise in interdependence manifested almost daily. An operation in one city would lead almost instantly to a chain reaction of AQI actions and civilian responses across the country. The tiniest rumors—sometimes true, sometimes not—would spread like wildfire through online forums.

At the same time, almost all processes have become much, much faster. Tiny increments of time now spell the difference between success and failure. Keeping up with the increased pace of news was a problem not just for our Task Force; it presents a challenge for almost all organizations, especially those actually in the news business. A century ago, at newspaper offices, beat reporters would write about assigned topics, editors would review the stories, and the editor in chief would look over the final product before sending it to press. Breaking a story meant getting it out a full day before the competition. Fast-forward to March 17, 2014, when the *Los Angeles Times* was the first news company to break a story about a nearby earthquake. Their edge? The article was written entirely by a robot—a computer program that scans streams of data, like that from the U.S. Geological Survey, and puts together short pieces faster than any newsroom chain of command could. This program earned the paper a few minutes of lead time at most, but today, those minutes are critical.

In New York, commercial realtors charge a premium for "co-located" financial real estate that places traders nearer to servers, allowing them to shave microseconds off near-light-speed transactions. For similar reasons, a group of American and European trading firms recently spent $300 million on a new transatlantic cable that will decrease trade time by 5.2 milliseconds. One young banker summed up the rationale behind going to such lengths to procure seemingly minuscule advantages: "Speed is money."

Speed has always been important to armies, but for most of history it was limited to what a horse or a human could do. The Romans built excellent roads to facilitate military movement, but even a crack legion could only go about 20 miles a day. During the Civil War, Confederate general Thomas Jonathan "Stonewall" Jackson's troops earned the moniker "foot cavalry" after they covered 646 miles over a forty-eight-day period, but the fastest speed they achieved was 6 miles per hour, and that was for a limited duration forced march.* In the twentieth century automobiles, tanks, and eventually airplanes, jets, and rocketry changed the speed of war dramatically, but the ones and zeros of the digital world fly still faster.

When we read about new technologies or hear about the promise of a globalized, interconnected world we tend to assume that technological advances will enable us to do what we have always done, only better. But there is a second side to this coin. The same technologies that provided organizations like the Task Force with enhanced transportation, communication, and data abilities simultaneously imbue our operating

---

*Most people (not carrying a weapon and pack) walk comfortably at about 3 mph. For soldiers to march 6 mph (10 minutes per mile) requires an uncomfortable (and unsustainable for most people) jog/walk.

environment with escalating nonlinearity, complexity, and unpredictability. Speed and interdependence together mean that any given action in any given time frame is now linked to vastly more potential outcomes than the same action a century or even a few decades ago: endeavors that were once akin to a two- or three-ball pool problem now involve hundreds of collisions.

Boeing might gain in efficiency by outsourcing its production processes, but that outsourcing also means that events in a dozen countries across three continents have the power to disrupt its operations. The successful assembly of a plane now depends not just on a few factories' remaining intact, but on safe passage across oceans, acceptable labor conditions in Japan, a lack of natural disasters in Sweden, stable exchange rates, and flexible supply chain management.

In Iraq, we encountered unprecedented levels of disruption. An operation on one side of the country would spontaneously incite reactions from a cell on the other that we did not even know existed; one misstep of ours or one piece of effective AQI propaganda could make the social media rounds and spark riots within hours; one video of a militant attack would have an immediate effect on insurgent recruitment numbers and sectarian reprisals, and all of these events happened almost every day.

In fact, the developments of recent years have led to a completely different—and less predictable—world. Because of speed and interdependence, street vendor Tarek al-Tayeb Mohamed Bouazizi could set off a chain of events that toppled multiple governments faster than the rest of the world could even process the news. Of course, there were successful revolutionaries and butterfly-effect phenomena before the information age, but new technologies have created an unprecedented proliferation of opportunities for small, historically disenfranchised actors to have a butterfly effect. Some of this has positive consequences, like entrepreneurial success. Other manifestations are devastating: terrorists, insurgents, and cybercriminals have taken advantage of speed and interdependence to cause death and wreak havoc. But it *all* exhibits the unpredictability that is a hallmark of complexity; today, we all find ourselves surrounded by hurricanes. In the Task Force, we saw this in the effects of snowballing insurgencies, but these changes have left their mark not only on the battlefield, but almost everywhere.

When hackers infiltrated the Associated Press's Twitter account in

2013 and sent out a message claiming the White House had been hit by two explosions and President Obama was injured, the Dow Jones fell 143 points in a brief but widespread market panic. The tweet was deleted as soon as it appeared, but its momentary presence was enough to trigger both impulsive human behavior and the high-frequency trading algorithms now used throughout the markets, which "read" the news and perform trades in response in mere nanoseconds. One trader saw the Associated Press–induced flash crash as "a comment on how vulnerable the markets are to random pieces of information."

A more lighthearted example: When musician Dave Carroll's guitar was broken by United Airlines baggage handlers, he spent nine months navigating the company's telephone-directory maze of customer service representatives to no avail, so he wrote a song called "United Breaks Guitars" and posted the video on YouTube. Within one day the video had racked up 150,000 hits and Carroll received a phone call from an abashed director of customer solutions at United. Within three days the video had more than a million hits and United's stock price fell 10 percent, costing shareholders $180 million in value—600,000 times the value of the guitar. Within a week, the song peaked as the number one download on iTunes, and the company made a public show of donating $3,000 (the cost of a new guitar) to the Thelonious Monk Institute of Jazz at Carroll's request (the makers of his broken instrument, Taylor Guitars, sent him two for free after watching his video).

All of this creates challenges for systems built for a simpler era. The global aid system, for instance, which once depended on connecting individual donor governments to individual recipient governments, has in recent decades transitioned from "few to few" to a "many to many" market, in which thousands of NGOs try to link up with millions of recipients.

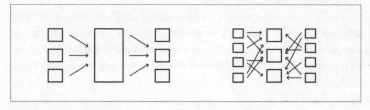

Few to few   Many to many

The system now includes some fifteen thousand donor missions in fifty-four recipient countries every year. The result is that health workers in some sub-Saharan African states spend so much time meeting Western delegates that they can only do their real jobs in the evening. The world of "many to many" has produced tremendous gains in some sectors, but these gains have come at a high cost in others—specifically those that require coordination at scale.

Challenges like those faced by aid agencies and the myriad other organizations caught in what author and development consultant Ben Ramalingam dubs "the emergent, wayward swirl generated by social media" create questions about how we confront domains that were once predictable but are no longer. Practitioners wrestling with these questions use slightly different terminology from the optimistic "interconnected." They use phrases like "discontinuity," "disruption," or the recently minted military acronym VUCA (volatility, uncertainty, complexity, and ambiguity). They know that the world in which Emmylou will grow up is not just marginally different from that of previous generations; it is vastly faster and more interdependent, and thus essentially complex in entirely new ways. She lives in the wayward swirl—a totally different place from the clockwork universe. We get in trouble when we try to use tools designed for the latter to tinker with the former.

SQUARE PEG, ROUND HOLE

Many great thinkers—most notably the nineteenth-century polymath Henri Poincaré—have observed aspects of the phenomenon that we now call "complexity," but the concept's coming-out party was thrown in a 1948 paper in *American Science*. "Science and Complexity" by Warren Weaver clocked in at a mere eight pages and involved no original research—it was an essay on the nature and aims of scientific thought— but it has left an enduring mark.

Weaver argued that science up through the 1800s had concerned itself with questions of "organized simplicity": problems involving one or two variables, like the attraction between two magnets or the rotation of the Earth around the sun.* But, Weaver observed, this was not the way much

---

*Weaver also noted that the first half of the twentieth century had concerned itself predominantly with questions of *disorganized* complexity—problems like the behavior

of the real world worked. Living organisms, for instance, "are more likely to present situations in which a half-dozen, or even several dozen quantities are all varying simultaneously, and in subtly interconnected ways." Such traits, he noted, are found in ecosystems, economies, and political systems. In other words, the real world is full of the knotted interdependencies of complexity, and science was not equipped to deal with this—indeed, science actively avoided these unpleasant truths, preferring to simplify things to fit the clockwork universe. Such efforts, Weaver maintained, are futile. You cannot force a square peg into a round hole, and you cannot force the complex to conform to rules meant for the merely complicated.

A pool table of sixteen balls, he argued, presents a fundamentally different type of problem from a pool table with only two or three balls (just as cold fronts are fundamentally different from comets). The table with sixteen balls confounds prediction. "On what does the price of wheat depend?" is far more complex still. Problems of organized complexity involve "a sizable number of factors which are interrelated into an organic whole." These problems are just too complex,* he wrote, "to yield to the old nineteenth-century techniques which were so dramatically successful on two-, three-, or four-variable problems of simplicity."

Once scientists, historians, and journalists began looking, evidence in support of Weaver's observation was everywhere, perhaps most visibly in the history of human tinkering with nature's complex ecosystems. The attempt to fix the greyback beetle problem in Queensland, Australia, is a famous case in point. When an infestation of beetle grubs decimated sugarcane fields in the 1930s, agronomists were delighted to learn of the *Rhinella marina*, or cane toad, whose appetite for greyback beetles had successfully kept the pest in check in Hawaii. The Australian government imported 102 of these miracle critters in June 1935, and released them into the Little Mulgrave River.

---

of a gas, where the sample size of molecules is so high that one can approximate it with averages. This too is a much simpler challenge than that of organized complexity, but it is less relevant to our argument.

*Weaver actually used the word "complicated," which he employed interchangeably with "complex" throughout his work (distinguishing them from things that are "simple"). At the time of his writing, the terminology in the field was far less crisp than it has become since his paper kicked off the discipline. But the ideas he was trying to get across are better captured by what we today refer to with the word "complex."

Today, if you scoop a net through the waters of the Little Mulgrave River—or those of any nearby river, lake, pond, or estuary—it will come up full of what looks like mud but is actually a mass of glossy black cane toad tadpoles. Given an abundance of quiet ponds, and the absence of Hawaiian predators, an unexpectedly large proportion of the forty thousand eggs that a female toad can lay in one summer survive to adulthood in Australia. The agronomists' projections for toad survival were based on a smaller figure. This was the equivalent of incorrectly estimating the "base" number in the exponential function of population growth—the kind of incremental difference that would not have been a problem for predicting the return of Halley's Comet, but would turn out to be a big, big problem for Australian wildlife.

The toads multiplied and multiplied. They spread to parks, gardens, freeways, and ponds. They ate fish, frogs, small birds, and crabs, as well as rare species like the pygmy marsupial mouse. One researcher found that cane toads would attack and eat Ping-Pong balls. The only things they do not eat, apparently, are Australian greyback beetles: differences in the life cycles of the Australian and Hawaiian species mean that the beetles and toads were never in the fields at the same time. Furthermore, the toads can kill not only by eating other animals, but also by being eaten: their poisonous skins meant that dogs, ducks, and snakes died in droves after biting into them. Fences, traps and other barriers have fallen like miniature Maginot Lines to the toads' amphibious assault. The species now covers 40 percent of Queensland and has moved into other states. An American ecologist summed it up as "classic human disaster . . . an ecosystem is at threat by being chopped away at the base, and that will have repercussions all the way up through the food chain in which the toad has insinuated itself."

The list of catastrophic attempts at ecological intervention stretches from the cane toad to the kudzu vine that has spread over some seven million acres of American land, to the million-strong flocks of starlings that blacken American skies (a Shakespeare enthusiast who wanted to bring every species mentioned by the playwright to the New World introduced sixty starlings into New York's Central Park in 1890; they have since spread geographically and now roost in flocks that can devour twenty tons of potatoes per day).

As with butterflies and weather, the lesson here is not that *all* introduced species will spread like crazy. Any of these fauna might just as easily have died out within a few weeks, if only some slight properties of the environment had interacted differently or if the base number had been marginally different. Complex systems are fickle and volatile, presenting a broad range of possible outcomes; *the type and sheer number of interactions prevent us from making accurate predictions.* As a result, treating an ecosystem as though it were a machine with predictable trajectories from input to output is a dangerous folly.

L ikewise, economic systems—the products of complex knots of human factors—confound linear attempts at prediction and control. It is because of this complexity that economist and philosopher Friedrich Hayek argued against state-run economic planning. In his landmark essay "The Theory of Complex Phenomena," he drew a distinction between "the degree of complexity characteristic of a peculiar *kind* of phenomenon" and "the degree of complexity to which, by a combination of elements, any kind of phenomena can be built up." In other words, some systems are *essentially complex* (like the human brain, or society), whereas other systems (like a big machine, or a factory) might appear complex because they have a lot of moving parts, but are essentially complicated.

He argued that national economies, unlike industrial production, could never be transformed into mechanical systems with reductionist solutions: their behavior results from the decision making of millions of people, and all these decisions influence one another, making it impossible to forecast how markets will move—as in a game of chess, there are just too many possibilities for a prescriptive instruction card. Butterfly effects in the economy, triggered by tiny initial disturbances, are common.

This complexity has only grown denser as economies have globalized. The hacker attack on AP demonstrates that these nonlinear disturbances are becoming more likely. In the words of British sociologist John Urry, "when China gets a cold . . . the US sneezes."* To extend the Lorenz butterfly metaphor, we seem, increasingly, to live in a world of hurricanes.

A predictive hubris, perhaps bred by centuries of success at applying

---

*This quote has a complicated history: the original statement, of which there are now many popular variations, is thought to have originated with Austria's Prince Klemens von Metternich: "When France sneezes, Europe catches a cold." Metternich was referencing the spread of popular revolutions across Europe in the nineteenth century, and surely never imagined that his quote would be modified to apply to the economies of China and the United States.

Newtonian models to complicated problems, has fooled us into believing that with enough data and hard work, the complex riddles of economies can be decoded. But as Weaver pointed out, you cannot force the square peg of complexity into the round hole of the complicated. The average forecasting *error* in the U.S. analyst community between 2001 and 2006 was 47 percent over twelve months and 93 percent over twenty-four months. As writer and investor James Montier puts it, "The evidence on the folly of forecasting is overwhelming . . . frankly the three blind mice have more credibility than any macro-forecaster at seeing what is coming." In November 2007, economists in the Survey of Professional Forecasters—examining some forty-five thousand economic-data series—foresaw less than a one-in-five-hundred chance of an economic meltdown as severe as the one that would begin one month later.

Debates still rage about whether we understand economics well enough to exert even slight interventions like adjusting discount rates, but the graveyard of centrally planned economies such as the Soviet Union's—much like the necropolis of planned interventions in ecosystems—would seem to validate the idea that some things cannot be fitted into a reductionist straitjacket. Attempts to control complex systems by using the kind of mechanical, reductionist thinking championed by thinkers from Newton to Taylor—breaking everything down into component parts, or optimizing individual elements—tend to be pointless at best or destructive at worst.

BACK TO MANAGEMENT

Frederick Taylor's managerial solutions were unequivocally designed for complicated problems rather than complex ones. The Midvale Steel Works factory floor may have been a cacophonous circus of whirling gears and white-hot iron, but the machines worked in straightforward ways and the management structures Taylor created functioned like organizational analogs of those mechanical devices: Tasks moved from one worker to another, from one corner of the factory to another. Change was linear. Problems with one machine could not organically spread to others. Inversely, a single innovation could not "go viral" and turn factory owners into billionaires overnight. Companies would steadily ratchet their way toward success or failure over the course of years.

The predictability of this environment enabled Taylor to break complicated processes down into independent, repeatable actions and, at a larger scale, to divide whole organizations into independent departments. Because he could anticipate that tomorrow would bring the same eight varieties of pulp as today, he could reduce the chemistry of papermaking to a simple chart; because he knew that the same machines would be in place with the same flow of water, he could give workers precise instruction cards for their actions. The industrial world, where almost everything could be measured and mechanized—where individual variables could be isolated, tested, and optimized—lent itself to this model. As complicated as it was, it almost all lay under the manager's capacity for calculation, prediction, and control. Planned efficiency became the lifeblood of "good management." Everything else, from physical design to organizational structure to leadership behavior, was a natural extension of this goal.

As we have crept toward the "many to many" environment of complexity, we have engineered increasingly *complicated* solutions: gifted managers have developed intricate protocols and organizational hierarchies to cover all likelihoods. The baseline belief that any problem can be known in its entirety has never faded. Anyone who has worked in business or government for a few decades can testify to the seemingly endless increases in rules and paperwork. Nowhere was this more visible than at the Pentagon, where the growth of the Department of Defense manifested itself in an ever-expanding set of codes and procedures.

In Iraq, we were using complicated solutions to attack a complex problem. For decades we had been able to execute our linear approach faster than the external environment could change, and as a result we believed we were doing something different from other organizations. In fact, we were as bureaucratic as anyone else; we were just more efficient in our execution. Efficiency was the defining excellence of our "awesome machine," and it had enabled our assembly line of counterterrorism to keep humming along. But by 2004, the world had outpaced us. In the time it took us to move a plan from creation to approval, the battlefield for which the plan had been devised would have changed. By the time it could be implemented, the plan—however ingenious in its initial design—was often irrelevant. We could not predict where the enemy would strike, and we could not respond fast enough when they did.

It is hard, if not impossible, to draw a firm line separating the complicated from the complex. The different domains that deal with complexity use various taxonomies for differentiation.* For our purposes, the ability to *predict* is the most relevant criterion, and determining exactly when things become unpredictable is tricky. All the phenomena we have discussed are at some levels predictable: We can predict the rainfall in a particular city tomorrow with relative accuracy, just not in six months. We can reliably anticipate that inflation will cause shopkeepers to raise their prices this month, but not whether it might trigger a recession in a year.

It is helpful to frame things in terms of timescale: for our purposes, we can think of a phenomenon as exhibiting complexity *over a given time frame* if there are so many interactions that one cannot reasonably forecast the outputs based on the inputs. By this definition, weather would be complex over the time span of a day but not a month. This is why it is relevant not only that things have become more interconnected, but also that processes have become *faster*. These two variables combined mean that the amount of interactive complexity previously contained in many months of, say, local conversation and letter exchange might now be squeezed into a few hours of explosive social media escalation.

Knowing the outcome of a war at its start has always been impossible (otherwise we would not have to fight them), and no one working at Ford in 1915 could foresee what automobiles and production processes would look like in 1950. But on more immediate time horizons, for much of the past century, things remained manageable: an enemy's troops could move only so far overnight; a competing automobile could be brought to market only so fast. Military thinking has always had to accommodate unpredictability—or "friction": the divergence of reality from plan—but strategists could reliably predict events further out than we can now. In Iraq, *every day* brought with it the unpredictability of an entire war. Suicide bombings seemed tactically capricious, and any person with access to the Internet, cleaning products, and ball bearings could become a threat overnight. Monitoring and developing contingency plans to deal with fifteen enemy submarines is one thing; doing the same for a population of thirty million people is practically impossible (not to mention

---

*Some taxonomies of "complex" include systems that automatically adjust in response to disruption—"resilient" systems—which we will address later.

potentially unethical). As with Lorenz's butterflies, it was impossible to tell which events would lead to what kinds of results.

This is the new world we all share. There are too many events occurring simultaneously for any entity—even one equipped with the surveillance capabilities of our Task Force—to monitor; and with the ability of individuals and small groups to communicate with millions of people, there is no way to be sure which of those events will transform into a threat.

Events like the YouTube spread of Tarek al-Tayeb Mohamed Bouazizi's protest, the hacker attack on AP, and Dave Carroll's explosively popular ballad—along with the whole family of "viral" disruptions that characterize contemporary life—were unthinkable thirty years ago. Even the word "viral" hints at the fact that today's environment resembles an organism or an ecosystem—the kind of interconnected system whose crisscrossing pathways allow phenomena to spread. This is a very different environment from the linear, one-to-the-next connectedness of items on Taylor's merely complicated factory floor. The amount of nonlinear change that once took months to play out can now happen in the time that it takes to type 140 characters.

BIG DATA WILL NOT SAVE US

In Iraq, cutting-edge technology had provided us with the holy grail of military operations: near-perfect "situational awareness" or COP ("common operational picture"). This was the first war in which we could see all of our operations unfolding in real time. Video feeds from unmanned aerial vehicles (UAVs or drones) gave us live footage of missions, while microphones carried by our operators provided audio. We enjoyed access to data on population, economic activity, oil exports, generation of electricity, and attitudes (through polling); we were connected to our partner organizations in real time. A technology called Blue Force Tracker tagged all of our vehicles with GPS monitoring, so our maps always showed the exact positioning of our forces. While this profusion of information proved of great value, it was never very useful for prediction. In a simpler world, our leaps in data would have been of great predictive value, but the reality of increased complexity meant that when it came to foresight, we were essentially chasing our own tail—and it was getting away from us.

Meteorologists looking to predict the weather might think that forecasts might be perfected if they could just get enough information about butterfly wings. Science historian James Gleick explains the folly in pursuing this. Even if we covered the Earth in a lattice of sensors spaced one foot apart, and even if every one of these sensors provided flawless readings, we would *still* not know whether it would rain in a month, because the small spaces between those sensors hide tiny deviations that can be of massive consequence. Our herculean effort would produce at best a marginally improved predictive capacity, just as the Task Force's real-time information was a powerful tool, but did not enable us to predict terrorist attacks.

We hear a great deal about the wonders of "Big Data," which certainly has advanced our understanding of the world in dramatic ways. Retailers can track who bought what, and where they bought it. Sociologists can sift through vast amounts of political, economic, and societal information searching for patterns. There is tremendous potential for this technology, but, as with Blue Force Tracker and the other tools at our disposal in Iraq, it is unlikely that it will enable effective long-term prediction of the type that we crave. Data-rich records can be wonderful for explaining *how* complex phenomena *happened* and how they *might* happen, but they can't tell us when and where they *will* happen. For instance, data on the spread of a virus can provide an insight into how contagion patterns look in our networked world, but that is very different from knowing exactly where the next outbreak will occur, who precisely will end up getting sick, and where they will go next. Gaining understanding is not always the same as predicting.

Data can determine "average" outcomes with great accuracy: how much time a person in a given age demographic is likely to spend on Facebook every day, or even, based on an individual's habits, what she is most likely to do on a given day. A friend who works at a company that uses Big Data to generate these sorts of insights once joked that he could tell me what I was going to eat for lunch. But of course he couldn't; he could only tell me what I was *likely* to eat for lunch, and a hallmark of complexity is that small, occasional deviations can have massive impact.

Data might have enabled the Tunisian authorities to determine what

Bouazizi was *most likely* to do on the day he self-immolated, but that would have done nothing to foresee what he actually did or the calamity that ensued. If you're trying to track one hundred, one thousand, or ten thousand Bouazizis, it's inevitable that at least a few of those will depart from expectation, rendering plans based on "expected outcomes" useless. And thanks to the wayward swirl of an interconnected, complex, nonlinear environment, when Bouazizi diverged from expectation the impact was exponential.

Big Data will not save us because the same technological advances that brought us these mountains of information and the digital resources for analyzing them have at the same time created volatile communication webs and media platforms, taking aspects of society that once resembled comets and turning them into cold fronts. We have moved from data-poor but fairly predictable settings to data-rich, uncertain ones.

Like most organizations, our Task Force understood very little of this in 2004. So we kept trying to predict and plan better because that is what we had learned "good management" to be.

Civilian organizations are encountering the same problem. Management practices are unable to help companies cope with volatility. This is evidenced by the increasingly shorter lifespan of firms—fifty years ago, a Fortune 500 firm was expected to last around seventy-five years. Today this life expectancy is less than fifteen years and is constantly declining. The Fortune 500 list of 2011 featured only sixty-seven companies that appeared on the list of 1955, meaning that just 13.4 percent of the Fortune 500 firms in 1955 were still on the list fifty-six years later. Eighty-seven percent of the companies simply couldn't keep up; they had either gone bankrupt, merged with other companies, been forced to go private, or fallen off the list completely. The churn has been so incredible that the companies on the list in 1955 would be unrecognizable to readers today.

As corporate strategist and professor Robert Grant puts it:

> *In the last quarter of the twentieth century, macroeconomic dis-*
> *equilibrium, exchange rate volatility, the microelectronics revolu-*
> *tion, and the emergence of newly industrializing countries marked*
> *the end of postwar economic stability. Since economic and market*
> *forecasts provided the foundation for strategic planning, inability*

*to predict demand, prices, exchange rates and interest rates repre-
sented a fundamental challenge to companies' ability to plan.*

Similarly, management thinker Gary Hamel writes that companies
now find themselves in "ecosystems" and "value webs" over which they
exert almost no control, giving them little ability to predict or plan their
own destinies. In such settings, the ritual of strategic planning, which
assumes "the future will be more or less like the present," is more hin-
drance than help. This was exactly what we were finding with the institutional strictures—planning routines and an organizational structure
and culture firmly embedded in the notion of predictive mastery—that
governed the Task Force. Our complicated solutions were flailing in a
newly complex environment. The inevitable outcome of this approach is
perhaps best summarized by Henry Mintzberg, author of *The Rise and
Fall of Strategic Planning*: "Setting oneself on a predetermined course in
unknown waters is the perfect way to sail straight into an iceberg."

RECAP

♦ The technological changes of recent decades have led to a more *interdependent* and *fast-paced* world. This creates a state of *complexity*.

♦ *Complexity* produces a fundamentally different situation from the *complicated* challenges of the past; complicated problems required great effort,
but ultimately yielded to prediction. Complexity means that, in spite of
our increased abilities to track and measure, the world has become, in
many ways, vastly *less predictable*.

♦ This *unpredictability is fundamentally incompatible with reductionist
managerial models based around planning and prediction*. The new environment demands a new approach.

CHAPTER 4

DOING THE RIGHT THING

That AQI was successful was obvious. They steered clear of most icebergs and—more remarkably—even when they hit one, they did not sink; they patched the hole and built a better boat. It was this capability that most frustrated and intrigued us.

How they were so successful was less clear. AQI's network was organic and associative, held together by a property we could not identify. The messy networks drawn on our whiteboards showed no "proper" structure, and without a structure, logic held that the organization should have collapsed on its own. But it did not. They were decentralized, but they were also coherent. The scope of attacks like the September 30 sewage plant bombing demanded well-coordinated directives, tight accounting, and widespread information exchange of a kind we were used to seeing only in the most disciplined military units. Their deadly missions far exceeded what could be achieved by distributing a handbook and some Internet propaganda to an informal smattering of acolytes.

Even as AQI metastasized across Iraq, growing in scale and reach, they somehow preserved their agility. In the first phase of our fight, our Task Force had focused on hunting down former associates of Saddam Hussein. Most of this activity was concentrated on the area between Baghdad and Tikrit, where Saddam's officials and high-ranking officers had estates along the fertile banks of the Tigris. (It was at one of these farms, on the outskirts of Tikrit, that we captured Saddam in December 2003.) Using our best night raid procedures—our carefully honed "one best way" for bagging bad guys—we made relatively short work of

Saddam's apparatchiks: we used our fast-roping skills; we "offset" our assaults from the actual targets and foot-marched in to maximize surprise; we deployed "close quarters battle" tactics when we entered houses, clearing them room by room and floor by floor.

When the war shifted from defeating Saddam to countering the AQI-led insurgency, we applied these same tactics—but it was much harder. Although AQI's center of gravity lay far from the posh precincts where we found Saddam's people, they had been watching. They knew that we preferred to operate at night because of our night-vision advantage, so they departed their safe houses at dusk, dispersing and sleeping in the surrounding fields. They saw how we assaulted and cleared houses, so they began placing machine guns in "pill boxes" at the tops of staircases lying in wait. They knew we sought to capture their leaders to gain intelligence, so many of them took to sleeping in suicide vests.

It did not matter if they lost firefights, botched procedures, and fielded less capable fighters. It did not matter that there was no single process that they could execute anywhere near as well as we could. AQI could adjust and survive.

We were stronger, more efficient, more robust. But AQI was agile and resilient. In complex environments, resilience often spells success, while even the most brilliantly engineered fixed solutions are often insufficient or counterproductive.

Scientist Brian Walker and writer David Salt, in their book on the subject, describe resilience as "the capacity of a system to absorb disturbance and still retain its basic function and structure." In a complex world, disturbances are inevitable, making such a capacity to absorb shocks increasingly important. As a result, resilience is increasingly being studied across a wide variety of disciplines, from psychology to hydrology. Few examples of the concept are more dramatic than the shifting Dutch approach to water.

THE THREAT FROM BEHIND

On the last day of January 1953, a windstorm on the North Sea and a full moon joined forces to create a massive storm tide that swamped low-lying areas in the east of England and Scotland. On the other side of the North Sea, in the southwest corner of the Netherlands where the Rhine River fractures into a tangle of estuaries and low-lying islands, the tide swept over the dikes and poured into the aptly named province of Zeeland (Sealand). It swallowed up homes, schools, and hospitals, claiming more than 1,800 lives. For this small, developed, prosperous, and water-savvy country, it was a shocking calamity.

Water has shaped everything about the Netherlands, from the postcard-pretty canals of Amsterdam to the country's famously consensus-driven politics, a legacy of the cooperation required to drain large tracts of land. Legislating where water goes is an almost instinctive Dutch impulse, and it had stood them well in the past. In the wake of the tragedy, the government responded with a "never again" urgency. The Dutch had been building walls against the sea for a millennium, but now they would build a wall mightier, stronger, and longer than any the world had ever seen.

The Delta Works, completed in 1997, was a massive forty-year-long construction project that links dams, storm surge barriers, and sluices, and effectively shortens the coastline in need of protection by dikes. The American Society of Civil Engineers considered the Delta Works one of the "Seven Wonders of the Modern World." Had the system been in place in 1953, it would have protected Zeeland from the North Sea flood. However, as with the Maginot Line, a robust protection against a known threat is not always sufficient; in complex systems, threats can flow from many places.

In 1993 and 1995, snowmelt in the Swiss Alps met with heavy rainfall downstream and the Rhine swelled, surging from Switzerland through Germany to the Netherlands. Like the German tanks that had traversed some of the same territory a half century earlier, the waters ignored the ingeniously built defense now facing the wrong way. This time the flood "came from behind." Though it was not nearly as catastrophic as the 1953 event, Zeeland flooded, 250,000 people were evacuated, and hundreds of millions of dollars in damage occurred.

As with the cane toad's toxic spread across Australia, the problem was partly of human creation: people have been "improving" the workings of rivers for thousands of years—straightening their wayward courses and fencing them in with dikes to protect the surrounding land against foreseeable calamities. Such predictive design is fine in complicated environments, but often dangerous in complex ones. While a "command and control" approach of high levees and floodwalls decreased the risk of small floods, it actually increased the risks of larger, more devastating floods, because it narrowed the channels of rivers, forcing the water to rise higher and flow faster. At the same time, due to subsidence, the land behind the dikes sank lower, and increasing numbers of people moved into areas that had been floodplains, losing their sense of the natural dynamics of rivers. The Dutch department of water management estimates a river flood in Zeeland today could now put four million people at risk. The drive to optimize created a new type of threat.

This time, however, the Dutch are taking a different approach. "Room for the River," the new water management plan for the region, reverses centuries of "command and control" responses to nature. It includes measures such as creating new bypasses and lowering dikes so that farmland along the rivers can serve as floodplains for the inevitable overflow of the rivers. These measures will reduce high water levels in the Rhine, Meuse, and Waal rivers and increase their resilience to flooding.

It is, in the words of one journalist, "a radical, even heretical notion in a land where dikes have been piled ever higher for more than a millennium." But as an expert at a major storm surge facility explained: "If you fight nature, nature is going to strike back. Water needs space." Room for the River accepts the reality that floods are inevitable, representing a shift in mentality from making the Netherlands floodproof to making it flood *resilient*.

In the Netherlands, people are coming to understand that "the early command and control approach was not working." Other countries and organizations are now following suit, stepping away from predictability and focusing on increasing resilience instead.

"Resilience thinking" is a burgeoning field that attempts to deal in new ways with the new challenges of complexity. In a resilience paradigm, managers accept the reality that they will inevitably confront unpredicted threats; rather than erecting strong, specialized defenses, they create systems that aim to roll with the punches, or even benefit from them. Resilient systems are those that can encounter *unforeseen* threats and, when necessary, put themselves back together again. Investor and writer Nassim Taleb captures a similar concept with the term "antifragile systems." Fragile systems, he argues, are those that are damaged by shocks; robust systems weather shocks; and antifragile systems, like immune systems, can *benefit* from shocks.

Though the concept's popularity has increased in recent years, many resilience techniques are not new. In environmental infrastructure they often mark a return to the kind of cautious coexistence with nature that defined much of human history. Resilience thinkers argue that we have inadvertently "fragilized" many of the systems that surround us. Our urge to specialize, reap efficiencies, and impose our demands for unnatural predictability has, like the rerouting of the Rhine, created new threats and damaged our ability to bounce back.

As environmentalists David Salt and Brian Walker explain in their book *Resilience Thinking*,

> *Humans are great optimizers. We look at everything around us, whether a cow, a house, or a share portfolio, and ask ourselves how we can manage it to get the best return. Our modus operandi is to break the things we're managing down into its component parts and understand how each part functions and what inputs will yield the greatest outputs . . . [but] the more you optimize elements of a complex system of humans and nature for some specific goal, the more you diminish that system's resilience. A drive for efficient optimal state outcome has the effect of making the total system more vulnerable to shocks and disturbances.*

Resilience thinking is the inverse of predictive hubris. It is based in a humble willingness to "know that we don't know" and "expect the unexpected"—old tropes that often receive lip service but are usually disregarded in favor of optimization.

M ost of the time, our instinct is to protect ourselves through prediction and by massing strength against the predicted threat. John Doyle, a professor of engineering at Caltech, describes these types of systems as "robust-yet-fragile": man-made engineering feats like the Delta Works that are brilliantly designed, ambitious in scale, but ultimately simpler, more mechanistic, and more rigid than the environment they attempt to regulate. Their robust responses to a single threat make them brittle and unresilient.

Andrew Zolli, a resilience thinker and writer, uses the Egyptian pyramids as an example of robustness. The fact that they are still standing proves the pyramids are extremely robust—they have successfully resisted all the stressors the architects had in mind when building them: wind, rain, and the other anticipated degradations of time. But if an unexpected stressor—say, a bomb—blew a pyramid apart, the structure would not be able to reassemble itself. A coral reef, on the other hand, survives hurricanes not by being robust, but through resilience. Storms will destroy a certain proportion of coral, but if the reef is at a healthy size, it will regenerate in short order. (One reason coral reefs are now failing is that the damage inflicted by humans—unlike periodic storms—is too fast and unrelenting to allow the critical mass of regrowth needed for resilience. Even a resilient system can be broken when too much comes at it too fast.)

Robustness is achieved by *strengthening parts* of the system (the pyramid); resilience is the result of *linking* elements that allow them to reconfigure or adapt in response to change or damage (the coral reef). Our approach to many environments—from the factory floor to the battlefield—has concentrated on building and hardening robust structures to withstand specific anticipated dangers. But all those environments are, as we discussed in the previous chapter, increasingly susceptible to unforeseen and unforeseeable disruptions. To survive them, we need to become both robust *and* resilient.

The insights of resilience thinking are applicable to many domains in which people are searching for a way forward in the face of uncertainty. The key lies in shifting our focus from *predicting* to *reconfiguring*. By embracing humility—recognizing the inevitability of surprises and unknowns—and concentrating on systems that can survive and indeed benefit from such surprises, we can triumph over volatility. As Zolli puts it, "if we cannot control the volatile tides of change, we can learn to build better boats."

EFFICIENCY AND ADAPTABILITY

The focus of management for a century has been on *efficiency*: getting the most of a desired output (we can call this variable y) with the least of the available input (x). In Taylor's steel mill, y was yards of steel cut and x was hours of machine use; for our Task Force—at least initially—y was operations and x was men and matériel.

The problem, as we discussed, is that you can only optimize for efficiency if you can identify x and y sufficiently far in advance to build a dependable system for converting one into the other; the pursuit of efficiency is grounded in prediction. If you know that your company will be producing cars and only cars for the foreseeable future, then building an assembly line that is optimized for the axles and airbags, and can convert a little human labor and steel into a lot of cars, makes sense. But such a system becomes useless when you suddenly have no need for cars and instead need helicopters by week's end; all the efficiency in the world has no value if it remains static in a volatile environment.

We had built an "awesome machine"—an efficient military assembly line—but it was too slow, too static, and too specialized—too efficient—to deal with that volatility. It was the equivalent of the Delta Works or the Maginot Line: robust at doing specific, long-planned-for things, but incapable of swift, effective responses to the unexpected. We were robust, but not resilient.

When we realized that AQI was outrunning us, we did what most large organizations do when they find themselves falling behind the competition: we worked harder. We deployed more resources, we put more people to work, and we strove to create ever-greater efficiency within the existing operating model. Like obnoxious tourists trying to make themselves understood in a foreign country by continuing to speak their native tongue louder and louder, we were raising the volume to no good end.

If AQI's presence in Baghdad had been static, and *if* their movements had been constrained by the speed of tanks or marching, we could have built a nifty master plan for removing their fighters while defending our sites and efficiently rotating personnel and equipment in and out of the fight. It would have been a math problem, albeit a complicated one rife with danger. As with the world wars, the more efficiency we could add to the solution, the faster the conflict would come to an end.

Those certainties, however, did not exist. That long-range master plan is of little use when a Koran-burning scandal in one city sets off a global furor in Internet chat rooms and, overnight, a ruthless cell in another place is activated and deploys tactics we have never seen before. Or when intelligence collected in Mosul indicates that a major attack on civilians will take place in Basra unless a SEAL team launches a raid that night—a raid for which there is no time to plan, let alone send data back and forth from Washington. Connecting all these dots on the fly would require a flexibility that our Task Force just did not have.

Peter Drucker had a catchy statement: "Efficiency is doing things right; *effectiveness* is doing the right thing." If you have enough foresight to know with certainty what the "right thing" is in advance, then efficiency is an apt proxy for effectiveness. In the wayward swirl, however, the correlation between efficiency and effectiveness breaks down. The Task Force had built systems that were very good at doing things right, but too inflexible to do the right thing.

Following Taylor's advice, we worked to get a lot of y with a little x, y being operations and x being men and matériel, but an efficient conversion of x to y wasn't what we needed. We needed to get the right things in the right place with speed and accuracy, so we could seize opportunities that might evaporate in just a few minutes. In effect, we needed a system that, *without knowing* in advance what would be required, could adapt to the challenges at hand; a system that, instead of converting a known x to a known y, would be able to create an unknown output from an unpredictable input.

Just as flood protection systems can be robust but not resilient (and the former often comes at the cost of the latter), management systems can be efficient but not adaptable. In 2004, we did not have an efficiency problem; we had an *adaptability* problem.

Like the Dutch hydroengineers, our Task Force needed to recover some of the old wisdom that had been cast aside in the quest for efficiency: the able mechanics who found themselves superseded by reductionism were undoubtedly more adaptable than the untrained workers following instruction cards who replaced them. They had a contextual understanding of the larger picture, not just a single bolt. But we could not simply revert to the past. We needed flexibility but we also needed the advantages of scale that accompany efficiency. We had to find a way to create that adaptability while preserving many of our traditional strengths. This would prove difficult— many of the practices that are most efficient directly limited adaptability.

NETWORKED

Tiers of rank are an essential component of every large fighting force. Rank is used to assign authority and responsibility commensurate with demonstrated ability and experience. Leaders of higher ranks are expected to possess the skills and judgment required to deploy their forces and care for their soldiers. In large armies, clarity of power has always been essential to impose the order necessary to maneuver thousands of recently recruited or conscripted famers and shopkeepers on the confusing ground of a lethal battlefield. Even when in bivouac or on routine marches, leaders like Frederick the Great of Prussia imposed harsh punishments for transgressions, hanging any soldier caught looting. Frederick knew that strong officers were needed to keep the army from degenerating into an unruly, dangerous mob that murdered, robbed, and raped its way across the countryside.

Respect for leaders is necessary, and rigorously demanded. Soldiers are taught to come to the position of attention when addressed by a senior sergeant or commissioned officer; "Yes, First Sergeant" or "Yes, sir" reflects the expected deference to rank. In battle, refusal or hesitation to follow orders can spell disaster. But at the same time, the rigid hierarchy and absolute power of officers slows down execution and stifles rapid adaptation by the soldiers closest to the fight. When a subordinate must spend time seeking detailed guidance from a distant officer in order to respond to a rapidly evolving opportunity, the price for traditional order and discipline becomes too high.

Speed and interdependence had rendered our environment in Iraq incompatible with the vertical and horizontal stratification that had maintained military order for centuries. The distance that carefully regulated information had to travel, and the wickets through which decisions had to pass, made even the most efficient manifestation of our system unacceptably slow. The chains of command that once guaranteed reliability now constrained our pace; the departmental dividers and security clearances that had kept our data safe now inhibited the exchanges we needed to fight an agile enemy; the competitive internal culture that used to keep us vigilant now made us dysfunctional; the rules and limitations that once prevented accidents now prevented creativity.

Our Task Force's rigid top-to-bottom structure was a product of military history and military culture, and finding ways to reverse the information flow—to ensure that when the bottom spoke the top listened—was one of the challenges we would eventually have to overcome. More difficult, however, was breaching the *vertical* walls separating the divisions of our enterprise. Interdependence meant that silos were no longer an accurate reflection of the environment: events happening all over were now relevant to everyone. Cordoning off separate institutional entities works only if their operating theaters are not inextricably linked; keeping Navy SEALs and Army Special Forces operators apart was fine as long as the problems they were sent to address were decoupled. Flying a small team around the world on short notice to rescue a hostage can be done without cross-functional collaboration—what interaction does take place between teams, like the transfer of rescued civilians or the exchange of aircraft, can be foreseen and planned by commanders like me. That was the mentality that drove the thinking of the Task Force for two decades, but it no longer worked.

To beat AQI, we would have to change into a type of force that the

United States had never fielded. There was no manual for this transformation, and we had to conduct it in the middle of a war. We often said we were "redesigning the plane in midflight."

There was no manual, but there was a blueprint. We had watched it take shape on our whiteboards. The alternative to our line-and-block charts had already been developed and tested by Abu Musab al-Zarqawi.

AQI was not concerned with efficiency. Through trial and error, they had evolved a military structure that was not efficient but was adaptable—a network that, unlike the structure of our command, could squeeze itself down, spread itself out, and ooze into any necessary shape. There was space between our forces—both geographically and in our communications sharing—that created safe pockets in which the enemy was able to nest, and seams into which they could expand. AQI learned to live and operate in the gaps of our system.

Just as AQI had watched and learned from us at the start of the war, we would have to swallow our pride and learn from them. The messy diagrams on our whiteboards were not glitches—they were glimpses into the future organization of adaptable teams. Soon our whiteboard bore the observation "It Takes a Network to Defeat a Network." With that, we took the first step toward an entirely new conversation.

RECAP

♦ Prediction is not the only way to confront threats; developing resilience, learning how to reconfigure to confront the unknown, is a much more effective way to respond to a complex environment.

♦ Since the pursuit of efficiency can limit flexibility and resilience, the Task Force *would have to pivot away from seeing efficiency as the managerial holy grail*. To confront a constantly shifting threat in a complex setting, we would have to pursue adaptability.

♦ Our foe, AQI, appeared to achieve this adaptability by way of their networked structure, which could *organically reconfigure* with surprising agility and resilience. We realized that in order to prevail, *our Task Force would need to become a true network*.

PART II

FROM MANY, ONE

In 1989, the International Basketball Federation (FIBA) revoked a rule that had barred professional NBA players from participating in the Olympics. The American men's basketball team, which already boasted one of the strongest winning records in Olympic history, leapt from great to legendary. The first squad to take advantage of this legislation steamrolled their way across Barcelona's courts in 1992. Their narrowest margin of victory, in the gold medal game, was 32 points. Head coach Chuck Daly did not have to call a single time-out in the entire tournament. Ten of the team's twelve players would later be named to a list of the fifty greatest players in NBA history. As Patrick Ewing put it, "It was like, the [non-NBA U.S. team] lost back in '88, and so then they sent in the Navy SEALs . . . We were the elite forces." It was known as "the Dream Team."

This set the tone for years to come. The 1994 World Championship team was "Dream Team II," followed by the "Dream Team III" in 1996, both of which claimed the gold, undefeated. Players on opposing teams would often ask to take photos with and get autographs from their heroes on the American bench before games—relationships of master and apprentice, not peers.

In 2004, the team, a combination of veterans and rising talent, featured the likes of LeBron James, Dwyane Wade, Carmelo Anthony, Tim Duncan, and Allen Iverson. Massimo Bulleri, an Italian playing against them in a friendly, recalled, "I stepped onto the floor and said to myself, 'I am only dreaming. I am playing against my idols.'"

But in their opening game—now one of the most famous upsets in athletic history—they lost to Puerto Rico. As CNN put it, they were "humiliated by . . . minnows." The 92–73 loss to the island of four million was the biggest in U.S. international basketball history (including *the competitions when NBA players were barred). The United States then edged their way past Australia and Greece by razor-thin margins and lost to Lithuania, barely qualifying for the semifinals. There, they fell to Argentina before squeezing past Spain to win the third-place match. Prior to 2004, the United States had lost only two games total in all Olympic tournaments; in this one alone, they lost three. At the awards ceremony, Bulleri (the Italian team guard) looked down on them from the silver medal platform. Argentina won gold.*

What was an embarrassment for America was vindication for coaches worldwide who have spent years saying "There is no I in team"; it proved that teams can be either far less or far more than the sum of their rosters.

CHAPTER 5

FROM COMMAND TO TEAM

O n December 28, 1978, United Flight 173 took off from John F. Kennedy International Airport in New York, bound for Portland, Oregon. It would stop en route in Denver. The DC-8, a four-engine, long-range, narrow-body jet airliner, is more slender than most large passenger jets. It resembles a steel pen with wings. Just ten years old and recently overhauled, this one was in the prime of its flying life.

Before takeoff, the eight crew members performed the standard barrage of safety checks—they visually inspected the wheel wells, verified the pressure in the hydraulic systems, and tested the emergency lights. Captain Malburn A. McBroom had worked for United for more than fifteen years, and logged more than twenty-seven thousand flight hours without incident, five thousand of those hours at the helm of a DC-8.

The plane landed in Denver with 181 passengers on board, as scheduled and without complication. Sitting on the runway, it weighed 248,627 pounds. When it took off at 2:47 p.m., it started to shed about a fifth of that weight as its engines began burning through the 46,700 pounds of fuel in its three tanks: enough for the flight, plus reserve fuel for an additional FAA-regulated forty-five minutes and a further company-regulated twenty minutes. Together, the four Pratt & Whitney JT3D engines hanging from its wings consumed roughly 13,209 pounds of fuel—the weight of a small school bus—every hour.

At 5:00 p.m., the flight neared Portland under ideal landing conditions: thirty miles of visibility, almost no wind, scattered clouds, and cool air. McBroom radioed Portland Approach: "Heading for runway 28. We have the field in sight."

Then the tiniest of problems popped up: an indicator light failed to illuminate. A piston on the right main landing gear had given out as it was lowered into landing position and had damaged the indicator system. As a result, the light did not illuminate even though the landing gear was down and locked in place.

As the piston slipped, the landing gear fell more quickly than usual, and crew members interviewed later recalled "a thump . . . and a yaw to the right." The plane radioed the tower to report its problem and state that it would enter a holding pattern to diagnose. On the spectrum of things that can go wrong with an airplane, this was fairly minor. Visual checks could be performed to verify that the gear had lowered, and even if it had not, the worst-case scenario involved grinding to a halt on the runway, damaging a wing but almost certainly leaving passengers alive and intact. An off-duty captain traveling aboard and consulting in the cockpit joked, "Less than three weeks to retirement, you better get me outta here." McBroom replied, "The thing to remember is don't worry."

The plane banked and entered a holding pattern. The crew discussed the issue at length, and consulted the thick manual that contained instructions for such situations. The atmosphere was hectic, with questions being fired back and forth, many of them ignored. McBroom maintained consistent focus on the issue at hand: contingency plans for a rough landing.

The crew debated the significance of various gauges and readings. They determined that the gear was down, but expressed concern that some antiskid functionality and pneumatic suspension might be impaired. Flight attendants informed passengers that the landing might be bumpy, prepared them to assume the brace position, and made sure everyone knew how to use the emergency exits in case they couldn't pull up to the jetway. The captain juggled communication with his crew, the control tower, and the company that made the plane.

After covering the main items on their checklist, the crew turned to smaller potential kinks. The flight engineer reminded them that, after landing, the "last guy to leave has gotta turn the battery external power switch off." The off-duty captain disappeared for a few minutes to grab a spare flashlight, in case they lost power on the ground.

The plane approached the airport a second time at 5:48 p.m., but there was another incoming flight, so Flight 173 yielded. In the cockpit, the captain and flight engineer discussed the placement and relative competencies of individual flight attendants. A few minutes later they checked in with the tower; there was another plane circling and McBroom again gave the other plane right-of-way.

As they circled again, the crew delved into a detailed discussion of what things would be like on the runway. After landing, the captain said, he would call maintenance in San Francisco to provide a report of what happened. They would make sure the tower knew their plans so they could exit the plane quickly and avoid "a million rubberneckers." Captain McBroom asked his first officer, "Why don't you put all your books in your bag over there, Roc," to avoid making a mess of the cockpit.

McBroom had the flight engineer walk through the cabin to check on the passengers. Flight attendants had, by that point, done this several times, but the thinking was that an extra reassuring voice couldn't hurt. He said, "I don't want to hurry 'em . . . [I'll land] in another oh, ten minutes or so." "They're pretty calm and cool," the flight engineer reported.

At 6:02 p.m., Captain McBroom told the tower, "it'll be our intention in about five minutes to land . . . we would like the equipment standing by, our indications are the gear is down and locked, we've got our people prepared for an evacuation in the event that should become necessary."

McBroom then realized that they had forgotten to check the gear warning horn, so they tested the circuit breaker, and McBroom sent the off-duty captain back into the cabin to perform one final check of passengers. At 6:06 the first flight attendant entered the cockpit. "Well," she said, "I think we're ready." McBroom radioed the tower again: "Okay, we're going to go in now, we should be landing in about five minutes." He felt confident the crew had prepared as thoroughly as possible.

In fact, they had now spent a full seventy minutes preparing—five minutes beyond their spare-fuel capacity. McBroom had been so focused on softening a rough landing that he lost track of one of the most basic and important instruments in front of him: the fuel gauge.

As McBroom made visual contact with the runway and pitched the control wheel downward, the first officer informed him, "I think you just lost [engine] number four buddy."

McBroom radioed the tower requesting instant approach. Then they lost another engine, leaving only two operating. At 6:11 p.m., they made contingency plans.

> CAPTAIN: There's ah, kind of an interstate highway type thing along that bank on the river in case we're short.
>
> FIRST OFFICER: Okay.

Two minutes later, they lost the remaining two engines, rendering the highway out of reach.

> CAPTAIN: Okay, declare a mayday.
>
> CAPTAIN TO TOWER: Portland tower, United one seventy three heavy Mayday we're—the engines are flaming out—we're going down—we're not going to be able to make the airport.
>
> TOWER: United one. United one?

At 6:15 p.m. PST, 201,927 pounds of metal ripped through two houses and dozens of trees just outside Portland, skidding 1,500 feet before coming to a rest. The lack of fuel meant there was no fire and the houses the plane struck happened to be empty, but eight passengers, a flight attendant, and the flight engineer were killed; twenty-four people suffered serious injuries.

Compare the tragedy of United Flight 173 to the story of US Airways Flight 1549—the plane that Captain Chesley Sullenberger ditched in the Hudson River in 2009. Shortly after the flight took off from LaGuardia Airport, a flock of Canada geese in the midst of their annual migration flew into both engines, causing immediate engine failure. Barely two thousand feet above the ground, the crew had only moments to respond. All emergency checklists and technical training designed to confront engine failures were premised on the assumption that such failure would transpire at cruising altitude above twenty thousand feet—an incapacitating event so low was unprecedented.

In less than four minutes, the crew turned the plane around, prepared passengers for a crash landing, and splashed the Airbus A320 into the Hudson River. Everyone survived.

United 173 had crashed despite having an hour of spare fuel, no incapacitating technical issues, and clear protocols for dealing with a landing gear failure. US Airways 1549 saved all of its passengers and crew minutes after encountering an unprecedented and critical issue for which they had no technical preparation at all.

There were innumerable differences between the circumstances and individuals on these two flights that might have contributed to the different outcomes, and some were beyond human control. One clear difference, however, was man-made and, as it turned out, highly relevant to the problems our Task Force was encountering. In 1978 airline crews were structured as a *command*: Malburn McBroom oversaw and divided responsibilities, assigned tasks, and issued orders in a system designed for efficiency; in a crisis each and every crew member turned to him and awaited guidance. By 2009, effective airline crews were meant to function as *teams*—Sullenberger was a talented pilot who performed well under pressure, but if he had had to devise and issue individual sequential instructions to every member of the crew in the few minutes they had to act, Flight 1549 might not have made it. The structural and functional distinctions between commands and teams have serious ramifications for adaptability.

Anyone who has ever played or watched sports knows that instinctive, cooperative adaptability is essential to high-performing teams. Our Task Force certainly knew it: though at a macro level we were stiff and clunky, our constituent units—our SEAL teams, Rangers, and Army Special Forces—were famously among the finest adaptive teams in the world.

As we would discover, the mysterious fluidity of AQI's network derived from many of the same traits that our units—and teams in many other fields—possess. Understanding what made our own constituent teams adaptable, and how this differed from the structure and culture of our Task Force at large, would be key to our transformation.

CAPTAIN PHILLIPS

"Navy SEAL" has become shorthand for a superhuman combination of strength, bravery, and skill, but the remarkable quality of SEAL teams has less to do with individual talent than most people think.

Four months after the passengers of Flight 1549 were retrieved from the Hudson, another spectacular water rescue riveted news viewers around the world: On April 8, 2009, four pirates armed with AK-47 assault rifles had boarded the container ship the MV *Maersk Alabama* and taken control of the bridge. In the ensuing scuffle, the pirates had seized the *Maersk Alabama*'s American captain, Richard Phillips.

With Phillips being held by force on a small lifeboat, hostage negotiations ensued in the midst of a standoff between the pirates in the lifeboat and the two U.S. Navy ships dispatched to the scene: the USS *Bainbridge*, a destroyer, and the USS *Halyburton*, a frigate. When Phillips attempted to escape, his captors grew violent, binding his hands and beating him with their rifles. Hostility escalated within the lifeboat as the pirates became desperate; they took to keeping a gun pressed to Phillips's back.

On April 12, three Navy SEAL snipers, watching the lifeboat through their night vision scopes, observed the situation from the fantail of the *Bainbridge*. They had been dropped from a C-17 transport plane, landed in the cold water, cut their parachutes, and linked up with the warships. From the back of the destroyer, they waited, watching their crosshairs rise and fall with their breath and the waves.

The snipers' primary rule was that lethal force could be applied only to save an American life. When they saw the AK-47 pressed to Phillips's back, the team decided action was warranted. But they knew that merely injuring a pirate would almost certainly result in the killing or maiming of Phillips. They also knew that if a fatal but imperfect shot hit the pirate nearest Phillips, it might cause an involuntary muscle spasm that would pull the trigger of the gun held to his back. The lifeboat had only two small windows, which limited already-poor nighttime visibility. At any time, the SEALs could get clear shots at two of the pirates at most. They needed three perfectly placed shots delivered in unison. So they waited.

At a little past 7:00 p.m. local time, two of the pirates, tired of languishing in the three-day-old air that filled the cabin, opened a small hatch at the front of the boat's hull. The third pirate, in the lifeboat, remained under a sniper's sights.

The pirates may have had time to take one deep breath of the saline breeze. With shots taken from the back of the *Bainbridge*, aiming at targets on a bobbing lifeboat seventy-five feet away, the three snipers struck each of the three pirates in the head simultaneously, killing them instantly. Phillips was freed and reunited with his crew and family.

As details of the rescue mission emerged—especially the swift, accurate sniping—the already excited news coverage reached fever pitch. "The operation was nothing short of perfect," remarked a Fox News commentator. "Our Navy SEALs saving the life of an American captain held hostage, taking out three Somali pirates in three shots, all direct hits to the head." An MSNBC pundit quipped that the hijacking "has got the whole country brushing up on our East African geography and our Indian Oceanography and our 'How freakin' impressive are our US Navy SEALs-ology.'" Television programs produced a flurry of special features about the supersoldiers whose marksmanship had saved the day. Americans enjoy the exciting, cinematic vision of a squad of muscle-bound goliaths boasting Olympian speed, strength, and precision; a group whose collective success is the inevitable consequence of the individual strengths of its members and the masterful planning of a visionary commander. But, like many cinematic conceits, this one misses the deeper and more important truth. SEAL teams *are* extraordinary, but for different reasons.

A hit on a moving target from seventy-five feet is, without question, difficult. But in the subculture of military snipers, it is not particularly dazzling. In 1969, a legendary Marine sniper in Vietnam shot an enemy sniper from several hundred yards away. The shot, fired with less precise rounds and from a less powerful rifle than those used today, struck the hidden Vietcong fighter in the eye after traveling through his own scope. Adept marksmen can harness the wind to curve bullets around buildings and strike targets from a mile out. In recent years, coalition sharpshooters have struck targets in Iraq and Afghanistan from distances in excess of eight thousand feet. In the Olympics of sniping, what the SEALs lying on the back of the *Bainbridge* did on April 12 would not even qualify for competition. But in terms of complexity, effective teamwork, and calm under pressure, it set a high mark: three operators stilled their breath, adjusted for the motion of the sea, waited for the precise moment, then executed as one, with full confidence in themselves and their mission. In the Olympics of sniping, that's a whole new event.

Before crackling across the snipers' neurons, down their forearms, and to the tips of their trigger fingers, the decision to fire had formed in a collective team consciousness that had developed through years of practice, cooperation, bonding, and service. The sniper trio, in constant contact with their troop commander, had lain in place for hours before taking advantage of a split-second opportunity: two pirates sticking their heads out to get air. This time frame did not allow for additional checklists, protocols, or second thoughts. The snipers had to think as a unit and feel sure of the trust of their superiors. Only then could they evaluate their tactical options in the proper strategic context and, when the opportunity arose, act instantly, in unison, in the dark of night, on a rocking boat, with a hostage's life on the line and the world watching.

SEAL teams accomplish remarkable feats not simply because of the individual qualifications of their members, but because those members coalesce into a single organism. Such oneness is not inevitable, nor is it a fortunate coincidence. The SEALs forge it methodically and deliberately.

BUD/S

In Coronado, California, just outside of San Diego, a few dozen men are probably, as you read this, soaking wet, freezing cold, and gasping for air. They are taking part in the Naval Special Warfare Center course called Basic Underwater Demolition/SEAL training (BUD/S), a six-month program required of all aspiring SEALs. Three "phases" take these would-be warriors through intensive physical conditioning, diving, and land warfare, aiming to assess their combat readiness. In every phase, the tasks are grueling, both physically and mentally.

The physical training in the first phase involves endless miles of running in wet sand while wearing boots; timed obstacle courses; open-water swims in the frigid Pacific; and regular tests of navigating big waves in small, easily flipped, inflatable boats. A failure to meet standards (twenty-eight minutes for four-mile beach runs, seventy-five minutes for two-mile ocean swims) or follow instructions (such as the exacting rules for room cleanliness) is usually punished with the order to "get wet and sandy," by running down to the 60-degree water and covering one's body with rough sand. Alternatively, trainees might be put through "log PT" (physical training)—holding wooden beams above their heads; or "surf torture"—lying faceup in the chilly surf for around an hour and a half, with breaks of a few minutes to prevent hypothermia. Halfway through the first phase, they enter "Hell Week": a five-day crescendo of intense activities during which trainees are allowed four hours of sleep, total.

The second phase adds open- and closed-circuit combat diving. Recruits must weather underwater attacks and take off, repair, and reassemble their scuba gear while remaining submerged with no oxygen supply. They have to tread water for five minutes wearing seventy pounds of equipment, and swim fifty meters underwater in one breath. Instructors swim alongside, watching, ready to resuscitate them because so many candidates simply pass out on their return lap, determined not to surface for air. Candidates must endure "drown proofing," which involves being dropped into a deep pool with both hands and legs bound, and retrieving objects from the bottom of the pool with their teeth.

The final phase focuses on land warfare. Held on San Clemente Island where, in the only-somewhat-joking words of an instructor, "no one can hear you scream," SEAL candidates go through training in weapons, close-quarters battle, rappelling and fast rope operations, and simulations with live ammunition and explosives. Candidates must demonstrate a mastery of land navigation, patrolling, basic raid techniques, ambush tactics, and Claymore mine placement. The course concludes with full-scale simulated assaults. By the time these students finish, don their Navy dress uniforms, and pose for their BUD/S graduation photos, they are on their way to becoming some of the world's most capable and dangerous fighting men. They are still months away from receiving the coveted Navy SEAL trident insignia, but they have made it past a legendary obstacle to their goal.

BUD/S has earned a reputation as one of the toughest trials in the military. Of the 160-some students in each entering class, around 90 will drop before the course ends, most in the first few weeks. One year, so many people dropped or were injured that the instructors canceled BUD/S and not a single person graduated. The attrition helps perpetuate the same supersoldier image that the media latched on to in the wake of the Phillips rescue, but the primary purpose of BUD/S is not weeding out the physically weak.

Coleman Ruiz looks like a Navy SEAL. Six foot two and 195 pounds, he was captain of the Naval Academy wrestling team before being selected as one of sixteen graduates in his year eligible to put themselves to the test at BUD/S. Later, midway through his thirteen-year career in the SEALs, he found himself on the other side of the wet-and-sandy drills, serving as Officer in Charge (OIC) of First Phase. He maintains that physical prowess has little correlation to success in BUD/S. "Almost universally," he says, "I would hear 'I'm quitting because I can't keep up and I'm letting my team down.' I heard that the most. . . . But rarely, rarely, *rarely* do we ever drop a guy who's running slow. Most of the quitters—physically, they were doing fine." The people who leave *could* meet the challenges; they just realize they don't *want to*. As Ruiz puts it, "They just had different priorities . . . we had a saying that they would leave because of 'my girlfriend, my dog, my cat, and my checkbook.' They can take it, they just realize it isn't for them." Of those who quit, only about 10 percent could not keep up physically.

The physical challenges of BUD/S are, in fact, fairly achievable. Running four miles in twenty-eight minutes—a seven-minute mile pace—requires training, but not Olympian genes; 1.47 million people completed the 3,200 10K (6.2-mile) races held in America in 2012. A serious runner in your neighborhood could likely maintain roughly a seven-minute pace, matching the BUD/S required pace over a greater distance. The BUD/S bar for swimming is equally attainable. Ironman competitions, completed by thousands every year, involve a 2.4-mile swim—just over the BUD/S requirement—in addition to 111.8 miles of biking and 26.2 miles of running. The average swim time clocks in at seventy-six minutes—almost exactly the Third Phase cutoff for BUD/S (and the SEALs get to use flippers). In September 2013, Diana Nyad swam 110 miles from Cuba to the United States in fifty-six hours—faster than the BUD/S required pace, over a distance fifty-four times longer. She was sixty-four years old at the time.

Of course, SEALs' physical challenges are amplified by the relentless conditions of BUD/S—running four miles in twenty-eight minutes on sand after three days of no sleep is more challenging than maintaining that pace on a treadmill. Nonetheless, as Ruiz points out, the notion that physical prowess is the primary determinant of success or failure is false. In the absence of debilitating medical conditions, "If a person wants to do it, they can," says Ruiz.

"GET A SWIM BUDDY"

The purpose of BUD/S is not to produce supersoldiers. It is to build superteams. The first step of this is constructing a strong lattice of trusting relationships. This will seem intuitive to anyone who has been on a team, but it runs against the grain of reductionist management; in a command, the leader breaks endeavors down into separate tasks and hands them out. The recipients of instructions do not need to know their counterparts, they only need to listen to their boss. In a command, the connections that matter are vertical ties; team building, on the other hand, is all about horizontal connectivity.

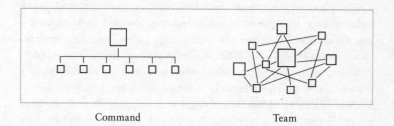

Command   Team

At BUD/S, few tasks are tackled alone. On the first day, instructors divide trainees into boat crews of five to eight people that remain constant for six months. Diving activities include underwater gear exchange, completing buddy missions while sharing one air tank, and nighttime navigation—an exercise simulating explosive demolitions in the pitch-black of deep sea, where pairs of divers with no GPS or visibility swim for miles, following memorized directions, one holding a watch and the other a compass. They communicate using taps and squeezes.

While most military discipline is used to integrate the individual soldier into the military's rigid hierarchy and perfect his ability to execute orders passed down from above, BUD/S takes a different approach. The formation of SEAL teams is less about preparing people to follow precise orders than it is about developing trust and the ability to adapt within a small group. To that end, BUD/S instructors have constructed a training course that is impossible to survive by executing orders individually. Ruiz sees his main job as "taking the idea of individual performance out of the lexicon on day one."

"If someone isn't pulling their weight during log PT, you'll drop the log. If the whole team isn't working together during boat passage, you'll get flipped. And failure is always punished," says Ruiz. Even surf torture is more survivable with linked arms and collective body heat.

From the program's start, trainees must travel with a "swim buddy," even if they are just going to the dining hall. Those who travel alone usually receive orders to "get sandy," and someone in the class will be punished, at random, for allowing this one individual to be moving with-out a swim buddy. "Get a swim buddy" is a jeer leveled at those who see themselves as mavericks. Swim buddies often become lifelong friends.

This is about more than the feel-good effects of "bonding." It is done because teams whose members know one another deeply perform *better*. Any coach knows that these sorts of relationships are vital for success. A fighting force with good individual training, a solid handbook, and a sound strategy can execute a plan efficiently, and as long as the environment remains fairly static, odds of success are high. But a team fused by trust and purpose is much more potent. Such a group can improvise a coordinated response to dynamic, real-time developments.

Groups like SEAL teams and flight crews operate in truly complex environments, where adaptive precision is key. Such situations outpace a single leader's ability to predict, monitor, and control. As a result, team members cannot simply depend on orders; teamwork is a process of reevaluation, negotiation, and adjustment; players are constantly sending messages to, and taking cues from, their teammates, and those players *must* be able to read one another's every move and intent. When a SEAL in a target house decides to enter a storeroom that was not on the floor plan they had studied, he has to know exactly how his teammates will respond if his action triggers a firefight, just as a soccer forward must be able to move to where his teammate will pass the ball. Harvard Business School teams expert Amy Edmondson explains, "Great teams consist of individuals who have learned to trust each other. Over time, they have discovered each other's strengths and weaknesses, enabling them to play as a coordinated whole." Without this trust, SEAL teams would just be a collection of fit soldiers.

BUD/S builds trust between members, beginning with the seemingly arbitrary demands to walk to meals together and ending (for those who complete training) with SEALs willing to place their lives in one another's hands.

"THE BELIEVER WILL PUT HIS LIFE ON THE LINE"

While building trust gives teams the ability to reconfigure and "do the right thing," it is also necessary to make sure that team members know *what* the right thing is. Team members must all work toward the same goal, and in volatile, complex environments that goal is changeable.

Taylor despised workers' free association—their attempts to establish horizontal bonds—because it created too many potential divergences from the plan. He had reason to worry about his workers messing around when not told exactly what to do: they usually had little awareness of what the company needed and no incentive to provide it. His system resolved the problem by parsing the needs of the company into smaller interim goals, overseen by leadership who understood how subcomponents assembled into a whole. As you travel down a traditional org chart, motivation and contextual awareness become more limited and specific, and more remote from the organization's overall strategic aims. When managers talk about "alignment," they usually mean people knowing what the interim goal is at their level (the production of three axles by 5:00 p.m.). A good manager will nestle these interim goals efficiently, linking them in a tight chain that leads to the desired outcome.

If the chain is well designed, there may be no urgent need to spend time and money providing the assembly line workers with a broad structural overview of the process. As long as they can do their part and get paid their wages, it is not important that they care deeply about the factory as a whole or understand its position within the broader corporate strategy. This does not hold in team settings.

Team members tackling complex environments must all grasp the team's situation and overarching purpose. Only if each of them understands the goal of a mission and the strategic context in which it fits can the team members evaluate risks on the fly and know how to behave in relation to their teammates. Individual SEALs have to monitor the entirety of their operation just as soccer players have to keep track of the entire field, not just their own patch of grass. They must be collectively responsible for the team's success and understand everything that responsibility entails.

The Navy needs to know that operators can make the right call in dangerous, high-risk settings where plans are changing constantly. As a result, BUD/S invests deeply in ensuring that every SEAL is holistically aligned in purpose with the strategic function of his unit and with the objective of any given mission and his specific role.

Testing for a sense of purpose at its broadest and most visceral is simple: make the experience unpleasant enough and only the truly committed will persevere. The physical hardship of BUD/S is a test, not of strength, but of commitment. "We could tell from interviews who would drop," Ruiz says. "It was the ones who were in it for themselves: 'I want to *try* BUD/S,' 'I think I'll enjoy the challenge.' Nobody enjoys BUD/S—it's hell." The successful ones, he explained, "were the guys who said, 'I wanna be on the SEAL teams. I wanna fight overseas.' It seems like a small difference, but it means everything."

The trainees who make it through BUD/S believe in the cause. And that matters—team members placing their lives at risk want to serve alongside committed patriots, not bodybuilders who signed up because they saw an opportunity for personal growth. As Ruiz puts it, "The believer will put his life on the line for you, and for the mission. The other guy won't." Purpose affirms trust, trust affirms purpose, and together they forge individuals into a working team.

By the time trainees reach Third Phase, they are intimately familiar with their teammates' combat styles and trust one another with their lives. They have learned to assess, quickly and holistically, any operating environment—determining what tactical x they have and what y the group needs—and they have developed a fluency with their teammates that allows them to reconfigure, adapt, and deliver. Through this combination of dense connectivity—trust—and their understanding of the situation and commitment to an outcome—purpose—teams like the SEALs can tackle threats more complex than any leader can foresee.

SEAL teams offer a particularly dramatic example of how adaptability can be built through trust and a shared sense of purpose, but the same phenomenon can be seen facilitating performance in domains far from the surf torture of BUD/S.

"THAT PERSON WILL BE ABLE TO RUN A MARATHON AGAIN"

Dr. E. J. Caterson is shockingly nonchalant about blood and guts. As he flips through photos of his team's work, it feels like you're looking at evidence of a miracle, a total scam, or Hollywood's newest visual effects breakthrough: gore fades into smooth skin, protruding bone fragments into functional limbs, facial lacerations into cheeks that could spearhead a Proactiv ad.

Dr. Caterson is a member of one of the world's finest reconstructive plastic surgery teams. They have reattached faces, salvaged legs, and saved lives. Seven years ago, they worked on a patient whose face had been torn off when she was mauled by a pitbull. The team opened up the dog's stomach, removed the face, and reattached it. Today, if you saw this patient on the street, you wouldn't bat an eye.

In person, Caterson is unassuming—well dressed and a little scruffy, with an indefatigable passion for his work. Determined to finish explaining the ins and outs of his work before he has to appear for a surgery, he changes into his scrubs in the office while describing the nuances of a skin graft. Later, on the way to the operating theater—at this point jogging—he insists on taking a detour to set us up with guest passes for the Harvard Medical School Library. "The stuff in there is just so incredible. They have Phineas Gage's skull! You really have to see it."

His colleague Dr. Matthew Carty works out of the same office in Boston's Brigham and Women's Hospital. Dr. Carty has shaved more recently and is a few years older, but is equally vivacious.

On April 15, 2013, Carty and Caterson were working on an extreme facial fracture: "A sixteen-year-old kid was riding a skateboard, got hit at fifty miles an hour by a car on the highway," Carty recalls. The operation had taken ten hours, and at 3:00 p.m. the surgeons were about to head home to their families when their resident came in and said, "Hey, a bomb just went off."

A few minutes earlier, two pressure-cooker bombs had ripped through the finish line of the Boston Marathon, killing three people and seriously injuring more than two hundred.

"[The team] just walked right from the OR to the emergency room," Caterson says, where other teams converged. "Because we had just done our big operation for the day, we were warmed up. We were ready to go." Casualties started rolling into the ER but, as Carty remembers, "No one had any sense of what the scope of the event was. As far as we knew, this could be three thousand people."

Working with trauma surgeons, orthopedic surgeons, and vascular surgeons, they helped devise treatment plans for injured patients as they streamed in, before triaging them to the operating room. These surgeons had all collaborated in the past and now made decisions as a collective, Caterson explains as he clicks through surgical photos on his computer. Before and after images of patients look Photoshopped.

Caterson stops on one "before" image—an almost unrecognizable mutilation of bone, muscle, and skin that, after a moment of squinting, comes into focus as the remnant of a knee: Most people, Caterson says, would conclude "that limb is nonviable; he needs an above-knee amputation." But an above-knee amputation means up to a 70 percent increase in energy expenditure to walk for the rest of one's life, leading to cardiovascular and pulmonary issues. It also places increased strain on the hip, often triggering early joint failure.

The team went to work. They took skin grafts from the victim's leg and back to salvage his knee during an interim period, and let that heal. Then they took a 40 cm strip from his back in one direction, a 22 cm strip in another direction, threaded together by a single, 2 mm-thick blood vessel, and used it to make a pattern of skin that was based on the blood vessel with stitching finer than a human hair. They took away the bone, and placed it back in the man's leg. Eight surgeries later, he had recovered with a functioning knee—the result of a meticulously reconstructed mechanism in the absence of the anatomic stump that is normally necessary for a below-knee amputation. "That was a complete deviation from normal practices," Caterson says, before thinking for a moment. "But as a result, that person will be able to run a marathon again."

Everything the surgical teams did that day was "a complete deviation from normal practices." Brigham and Women's had never simulated a mass casualty situation across multiple trauma services. There was no real plan, and certainly no rehearsal. Their response was simply an extension of what they do every day—*adapt*. A unit functioning as a command, with members waiting for instruction from authority, would have been too hidebound to respond effectively. There is no med school course on removing a human face from a dog's stomach, and in time-critical situations, no time to conduct a study or draw up a blueprint. The human body is a complex and interdependent system, and surgeries can diverge from a plan. "Every patient is different. Nobody has an identical fracture," Carty observes. "Operations are unpredictable. You always have to adapt."

For our operators in Iraq, a million incidents could derail a carefully assembled plan. Two men sleeping on a street could change the "infil route." A sudden need for air support halfway across the country could reduce the assets available for backup, which in turn would alter the level of risk that our operators could take on. An unexpected civilian presence on target could change the parameters of acceptable action—even the best technology and the finest intelligence cannot tell you exactly what to expect. And once the first shot is fired, reality diverges from expectation very quickly.

When details emerged about the raid that killed Osama bin Laden, news reports played up the drama of the Black Hawk helicopter that crashed as the force was landing, portraying it as a catastrophic anomaly that nearly derailed the mission. While it was certainly not part of the plan, such a divergence was also not unexpected: the sheer tactical complexity of special operations almost guarantees that at least one critical variable will come loose between planning and execution. Almost none of the hundreds of raids the team had conducted together had proceeded exactly as expected, and mechanical failure was par for the course. The men in Abbottabad regrouped within minutes, set up a different infiltration route, and accomplished the mission.

One can make contingency plans, but these can account for only a modest number of possibilities. A contingency plan is like a tree that branches at every variable outcome (if they fire when we arrive, choose path A, if not, choose path B). But when dozens of saplings shoot out from those branches every second, the possibilities become so overwhelmingly complex as to render complete contingency planning futile.

Our operators' most useful preparation lay in the trust they had built, shared hardship by shared hardship, over years of service. It is often said that trust is learned on the battlefield. But for groups like the SEALs, the oneness imbued by trust and purpose is a *prerequisite* to deployment. Entering the battlefield as a group of individuals without those characteristics would be like walking into a firefight without wearing body armor.

The SEAL team in Abbottabad had not planned for the helicopter crash, just as Captain Sullenberger's crew had not planned for the bird strike, and the Carty-Caterson team had not planned for the marathon bombing, but all were capable of adjusting to the unexpected with creative solutions on the spot, coherently and as a group.

Their structure—not their plan—was their strategy.

EMERGENT INTELLIGENCE

In his book *Emergence*, Steven Johnson debunks "the myth of the ant queen." The myth is that the sophisticated structure of ant colonies is the result of the architectural and managerial brilliance of the colony's queen.

When we look at the ants' remarkable engineering innovations—the dense networks of tunnels resembling subways, the "town dump" where workers deposit inedible hulls of food, the "cemetery" for fallen comrades, and the emergency escape hatch for the queen—it's tempting to think that a very clever ant foresaw how all these elements would converge. This is, after all, how human buildings come into being. We envision an insect hierarchy, at the head of which sits the queen, organizing the labor of her minions and directing battles with rival populations.

The truth is that the queen is a larva factory. Her sole job is to produce new ants—a critical role, but not a managerial one. The myth survives because of our assumption that order is always directed from the top down.

In reality, no individual ant has the brain power to design a colony; ants have 250,000 brain cells, humans have around 100 billion. The colony's structure emerges from the aggregation of individual instinctive behaviors—digging, foraging for food, collecting trash—triggered by primitive communications—ants recognize patterns in the pheromone trails left by other ants.

The field of "emergence" examines how complex patterns and forms can arise from a multiplicity of simple, low-level interactions. Emergence has been used as a paradigm for exploring everything from the crystalline beauty of a snowflake, to the explosive development of cities,* to the capricious behavior of economic markets.

Adam Smith's "invisible hand" of the market—the notion that order best arises not from centralized design but through the decentralized interactivity of buyers and sellers—is an example of "emergence" *avant la lettre*. It stands in direct contrast to what Alfred Chandler dubbed the "visible hand" of management—the reductive planning that has dominated most organizations for the past century. Smith's invisible hand, like the leaderless ant colony, illustrates the core insight of emergence as it relates to our study of teams: in situations defined by high levels of interaction, ingenious solutions can emerge in the absence of any single designer; prices can settle without a central planner; complex operations can be executed without a detailed plan. Johnson describes emergence

---

*One of the most frequently cited "founding texts" of emergence is Jane Jacobs's book *The Life and Death of Great American Cities*, which explores how cities evolve without a central planner.

as producing "unpredictable creativity," and identifies the ingredients necessary to unleash such creativity as "connectedness and organization." In other words, *order can emerge from the bottom up*, as opposed to being directed, with a plan, from the top down.

The competitive advantage of teams is their ability to think and act as a seamless unit (this is sometimes called "joint cognition").* Any computer scientist can tell you that a room full of individual computers can solve vastly more complex problems if you connect the machines to compute in parallel. In fact, with a few dozen desktops—the resources of a basic middle-school computer lab—you can create a supercomputer by doing just this. It requires a big initial time investment to integrate them—the equivalent of putting aspiring SEALs through BUD/S—but the gains in capacity are enormous.

This is not to say that simply throwing *more* computers or Navy SEALs at a problem is the answer; the key lies not in the number of elements but in the nature of their *integration*—the wiring of trust and purpose. Parallel computing, joint cognition, and the oneness of a team all work toward the same goal: building a network that allows you to solve larger, more complex problems. The creation and maintenance of a team requires both the visible hand of management and the invisible hand of emergence, the former weaving the elements together and the latter guiding their work. Programs like BUD/S are designed to foster emergent intelligence that can thrive in the absence of a plan.

This was exactly what the aviation industry had in mind when it set out to solve problems like the crash of United 173.

UTTER PREVENTABILITY

A few months after the crash of United 173, a National Transportation Safety Board report concluded that there was no disabling problem with the plane; Flight 173 "could have landed safely within 30 or 40 minutes after the landing gear malfunction." The captain had been so concerned

---

*Technically the field of "joint cognitive systems" refers to interaction between people or groups of people and computer technology (thus it is relevant to flight crews but not always to surgeons and SEALs). The general point stands that a thorough integration of minds—even if only human—can unlock far more complex solutions than a set of individual thinkers.

with the landing gear that he stayed airborne too long. "The probable cause of the accident was the failure of the captain to monitor properly the aircraft's fuel state and to properly respond to the low fuel state and the crewmembers' advisories regarding fuel state."

McBroom was an experienced and capable pilot with thousands of flight hours on the aircraft he was piloting that day. So how was he undone by such a minor hitch? Even the most qualified people have bad days. Perhaps this was just a regrettable outlier. Statistically, however, it was not.

At the time of the Flight 173 crash, the airline industry had a big and confusing problem on its hands: onboard airline fatalities had been increasing for a decade. This baffled analysts, because it occurred during the golden age of aeronautics. Throughout the 1960s and '70s, the space race between the United States and the Soviet Union saw jet engines and plane designs repurposed and refined to escape Earth's atmosphere. In 1969, aeronautical engineering leapt forward with the invention of Harrier jets that could take off and land vertically. Commercial aviation was also booming, as the Concorde supersonic jet and Boeing's signature commercial craft—the 727, 737, and 747—all had their maiden flights. Planes acquired more sophisticated safety features every year, and yet they kept crashing.* Because of its utter preventability, the Flight 173 crash came to represent the crest of this wave. The ensuing investigation would transform the industry.

If planes were now safer, investigators reasoned, the rash of accidents must be a reflection of increasing rates of "human error." Were pilots receiving less training? Were airlines not giving employees enough rest between shifts? Was the pressurized air at thirty-two thousand feet depriving captains' brains of oxygen and causing irrational decision making? The conclusions of the Safety Board pointed elsewhere: "This accident exemplifies a recurring problem—*a breakdown in cockpit management and teamwork* during a situation involving malfunctions of aircraft systems in flight" (emphasis added).

---

*Although plane crash *rates* did drop, the volume of air travel rose steeply, and overall fatalities increased. More critically, there seemed to be a pattern of planes' safety features underwhelming—the vehicles would crash even in situations that they were supposedly capable of surviving (like a faulty gear light).

The report found that fatalities were increasing not *in spite of* recent technological advances, but *because of* them. As planes incorporated more features, more dials, and more power, they became more sophisticated in aggregate, and the number of possibilities for minor malfunctions—like a faulty indicator light—rose. The number of branches on the contingency tree had become too great for the pilot and his crew to memorize. Something that was once merely complicated had passed the threshold of complexity. For crews trained in checklist-based efficiency, minor deviations from the plan led to unnecessary deaths. As Taylor found in his first factory nearly a century before, and as we would find in Iraq twenty-five years later, technology had changed in such a way that management had become a limfac.

The FAA brought in NASA—an organization whose explorations into the vast and unpredictable beyond had brought it into contact with tremendous complexity. NASA determined that a shocking 70 percent of air crashes stemmed exclusively from human error. In the case of Flight 173, the time spent retrieving flashlights, putting on jackets, zipping books into bags, and reassuring passengers was a deadly waste. Of course, no crew member would have knowingly risked lives just to keep books from spilling across the cockpit, but they were so determined to follow procedure that they lost track of what mattered. They were doing things right, just not doing the right thing. They were following the plan, and as a result, spiraling outward from one faulty piston, an escalating, butterfly-effect set of responses led to ten deaths, twenty-four injuries, and millions of dollars in damage. The crew's attachment to *procedure* instead of *purpose* offers a clear example of the dangers of prizing efficiency over adaptability. The procedures were not the cause of the crash—indeed, the checklists existed to promote safety. But to reach the ultimate goal of those procedures—a safe landing—effectively, a better human interface was needed.

An aggravating factor was the breakdown in communication: McBroom had attempted to keep track of everything himself, and did not take full advantage of the support offered by his crew. He ran a command, in which crew members were instruments for executing the pilot's designs. In the final half hour of the flight, the flight engineer asked multiple times for a fuel check. At 5:48, twenty minutes before the crash, he noted to McBroom that the fuel pump lights had started to blink. At 5:50 he said, "Fifteen minutes [to landing] is gonna—really run us low on fuel here," and at 6:02, *after* McBroom had announced plans to land in five minutes, he said, "We got about three on fuel and that's it." McBroom—intent on other questions—simply was not listening.*

The aviation industry was faced with two possible ways forward. They could continue to try to mitigate risk, attempting to control for ever more specific contingencies: the FAA could add United 173 as a case study in flight school; they could alter emergency checklists to include explicit reminders instructing a particular crew member to check the fuel gauge every five minutes. Such instructions would reduce the likelihood of fuel exhaustion the next time an indicator light failed. But they would do nothing to prevent overreaction and teamwork failure in the face of any of the other thousands of minor glitches that might occur. Worse, an overemphasis on fuel procedures might well create a new blind spot, just as the overemphasis on landing gear procedure had eclipsed fuel monitoring.

Alternatively, they could focus on risk *adaptation* instead of mitigation, accept the inevitability of unexpected mechanical failures, and build flexible systems to combat these unknowns; they could build a better managerial boat to navigate the volatile seas of complexity.

NASA believed that the dwindling ability of flight crews to adapt to unforeseen events stemmed from the captains' attempts to control and plan for everything in a vehicle that had become too sophisticated for that to be possible. Champions of the iconic Mission Control room where hundreds of experts crowded into one space to facilitate real-time communication and adaptation (which we will investigate further in later chapters), they concluded that building trust and communication between crew members was more important than further honing specific technical skills.

In June 1979, NASA hosted a workshop where, attendees remember, the opening speaker began his remarks by saying, "Ladies and gentlemen, the plane is no longer the problem."†

---

*Tragically, the flight engineer issuing these warnings perished on account of their not being heeded.

†Although this phrase is usually attributed to the NASA conference opening speaker, there is no transcript of the remarks. It is possible that it came about in a less formal

"CHARM SCHOOL"

The solution, which came to be known as Crew Resource Management (CRM),* was developed in consultation with social psychologists, sociologists, and other experts, and focused on group dynamics, leadership, interpersonal communications, and decision making.

In 1981, United Airlines implemented the first comprehensive CRM program. Its intensive seminars demanded that participants diagnose their own and others' managerial styles. It trained juniors to speak more assertively and captains to be less forceful, turning vertical command-and-control relationships into flexible, multidirectional, communicative bonds. Instructors exhausted students with team-building exercises. They complemented flight simulators and technical training with a BUD/S-like emphasis on trust and purpose. Predictably, pilots resisted. Raised on the empirical rigors of technical training, they dismissed CRM as "charm school" and "psycho-babble."

But CRM increased aviation safety.

In 1989, another United plane was en route to Chicago when an engine disintegrated and the debris destroyed the hydraulic systems used to raise and lower the wing flaps—the plane's steering mechanism. It was like being on a freeway at rush hour and having the steering column collapse, except at thirty thousand feet. The chances of such an event were considered so remote that no safety procedure had been designed for it. But the CRM-trained crew on Flight 232, working together with an instructor pilot who had been onboard as a passenger, devised and implemented a plan to keep the airplane under some degree of control by manipulating the differential and continual thrust of the two remaining engines. With no functional steering mechanism and no plan for how to deal with such an event, the crew managed to crash-land the plane in Sioux City, Iowa, saving the lives of 185 of the 296 people onboard. When replicated in a

---

way. Nonetheless, it became the catchphrase for the conference and the changes that followed.

*NASA had been conducting studies of resource management in aircraft throughout the late 1970s and arriving at CRM-type conclusions. The phrase "Crew Resource Management" appears about 1986, and wasn't formally adopted until 1993. However, the birth of the program as we know it is generally attributed to Flight 173.

simulator, it was found to be impossible to successfully maintain control and guide the airplane safely onto a runway using engine thrust alone. That the crew had come so close to succeeding was remarkable.

Cockpit recordings revealed crew members discussing procedures, possible solutions, and courses of action, as well as how to attempt the emergency landing and prepare the passengers. Through intense interactions—thirty-one communications per minute—they improvised an extraordinary solution. The pilot in command, Captain Al Haynes, later said, "If we had not let everybody put their input in, it's a cinch we wouldn't have made it." The accident report credited CRM and noted that the crew members' performance "greatly exceeded reasonable expectations." The FAA subsequently made CRM training mandatory for all airline crew members in the United States.

By 1991, more than 90 percent of crew members surveyed found "charm school" useful. Since then, air travel has continually grown safer: 2012 and 2013 had the fewest deaths and fatalities since 1945 (a year with just 1 percent of today's air travel), and the time between serious airline accidents had been steadily increasing for three decades. Annual fatal accident rates in North America have hovered well below one per million aircraft departures since the turn of the twenty-first century—a level they had always previously exceeded.* Arnold Barnett, an MIT professor of statistics and expert in aviation safety, determined that passengers had a one in one million chance of dying from 1960 to 1969. From 2000 to 2007 that chance dropped to one in twenty million, leading Barnett to conclude that today "an American child about to board a U.S. aircraft is more likely to grow up to be President than to fail to reach her destination."

This is not because flights today encounter fewer risks. If anything, rising complexity means they encounter more. The Line Operations Safety

---

*The data set of plane crashes is difficult to analyze because there are not enough to constitute a statistically significant sample size. As a result, even CRM's creators are very careful not to draw a direct causal link between contemporary fatality and crash rates and CRM. As a pioneer of CRM wrote in a recent essay, to determine the impact of the training "the most obvious validation criterion, the accident rate per million flights, cannot be used. Because the overall accident rate is so low and training programs so variable, it will never be possible to draw strong conclusions." However, crew feedback and causal relationships found in anecdotal evidence strongly suggest that CRM has played a key role in the reduction of fatalities.

Audit (LOSA), a system for monitoring flight safety, concludes that 98 percent of all flights today face one or more threats that, if mishandled, could prove fatal—threats on par with the landing gear failure on Flight 173—and that human error occurs on 82 percent of flights. But for crews trained in risk adaptation, rather than only risk mitigation, this is not catastrophic. Just as paradoxical as the simultaneous rise in "plane safety" and fatalities that puzzled analysts through the 1970s, we now live in a world where risk exists everywhere, but we have never been safer.

The accident report deconstructing the success of Flight 1549 noted that Sullenberger's crew's technical training had been completely irrelevant to the solution they achieved. No procedure for low-altitude dual-engine failure existed *anywhere* in the industry. It was their interactive adaptability, the report found, that proved crucial:

> Because of time constraints, they could not discuss every part of
> the decision process; therefore, they had to listen to and observe
> each other . . . [the captain] and the first officer had to work almost
> intuitively in a close-knit fashion.

The report concluded, "The captain credited US Airways CRM training for providing him and the first officer with the skills and tools that they needed to build a team quickly and open lines of communication, share common goals, and work together." Sullenberger's modesty is also honesty: US Airways 1549 was saved not by one mind, but by the ability of the captain, the first officer, and the flight crew to come together and pull toward a common goal.

CRM proved so successful that spin-off programs have been developed for dozens of other settings, from operating rooms to offshore oil rigs to nuclear power plants, all united by the common desire to become better at confronting complexity and risk.

In emergency medical care, rising complexity also resulted in a drive to replace command structures with teams. A 1966 report called "Accidental Death and Disability: The Neglected Disease of Modern Society" observed that Americans were less likely to survive a car crash on U.S. highways than to survive a Vietcong gunshot wound. The reason? Military trauma surgical teams. Domestic medical units used the same technologies as their military counterparts, but not the same team structure. Domestic teams were a command, not dissimilar to McBroom's flight crew: a lead surgeon worked directly on the patient with support from assistants who followed his instructions. As Boston surgeon Dr. Carty explains: "It was usually one guy—usually a man—who came in and kind of ruled everything and everybody bowed to that person's will."

Medicine—and especially surgery—has a reputation for fostering large egos. "There are a lot of aggressive assholes," admits Dr. Carty. "That's the industry norm." Medical school is fiercely competitive, compensation structures in private practices can incentivize fighting for every patient, and turf battles are common and usually come at the expense of the patient. As doctor and writer Atul Gawande put it, "We have trained, hired, and rewarded physicians to be cowboys, when what we want are pit crews for patients." Emergency care, however, is different.

During the Vietnam War military surgeons discovered that moving the lead surgeon *away* from the patient and having him stand at the foot of the bed during resuscitation and evaluation allowed for more actions to occur simultaneously. This practice made the lead surgeon, in effect, a team player—enabling the problem-solving efforts of others, rather than telling them what to do.

In medicine as in aviation, technology had outpaced the capacity of any individual practitioner to be on top of it all; once this was recognized, there was a movement toward "cross-functional trauma teams," with more even distribution of authority and leadership. Research showed that these changes cut average times for complete resuscitation in half, from 122 to 56 minutes.

These changes eventually made their way back to civilian trauma teams, and in 1973, the federal government passed the EMS Systems Act, giving rise to modern trauma care, and the high-performance team response, epitomized by Carty and Caterson's group, that, forty years later, would help save so many lives on that April afternoon in Boston.*

---

*The strength of such teams when confronting the unexpected was visible not only at Brigham and Women's. Patients were seen at twenty-seven hospitals across the greater Boston area, including five level-one trauma centers within two miles of the blast site, and of the more than 260 people injured but not killed in the initial blast, every single one survived.

It is no coincidence that CRM and EMS systems emerged at roughly the same time. Preston Cline, the associate director of leadership ventures at the University of Pennsylvania's Wharton School, has spent years researching "Mission Critical Teams" (MCTs)—small teams whose failure will likely lead to loss of life, and whose time frames for action often involve critical periods of ten minutes or less. Cline notes that not *one* of the dozens of teams he has observed was founded before 1950, and most have sprung up in the past thirty years. The British Army dates back to 1707 but the Special Air Service (SAS)—its first special operations unit—emerged in 1950;* the U.S. Secret Service was founded in 1865, but only developed its Counter Assault Team in 1979; the U.S. Navy celebrated its 187th birthday before it established Naval Special Warfare in 1962.

The proliferation of such groups reflects the increasing complexity of the world—or rather, the tactical understanding that *responding* to such a world requires greater adaptability, and adaptability is more characteristic of small interactive teams than large top-down hierarchies. We can now do the things we used to do—get from New York to Portland, raid a building, provide trauma care—more quickly and effectively than we could fifty years ago, but doing them has become more complex and confusing, to the point that they are beyond the effective control of a single person.

"A combination of increased mobility, increased information, and increased impact means that we have reached a tipping point," notes Cline. "Previously, we had a historical pattern of disruption followed by stabilization—'punctuated equilibrium'—but now that pattern itself has been disrupted. Today, we find ourselves in a new equilibrium defined by constant disruption. This creates the kinds of problems that only MCTs can solve."

For United 173 and US Airways 1549, the difference between command and control on the one hand, and adapt and collaborate on the other, was the difference between success and failure. The proliferation of teams across a diversity of complex environments—from special

---

*The Special Air Service (SAS) was first fielded during World War II under the command of the legendary leader David Stirling, but was then disbanded and not formally organized as a regiment until 1950.

operations to trauma care—evidences their ability to thrive in the midst of the sort of challenge that our Task Force faced.

We had honed the traits of trust and purpose at the team level, but our organization at large was the complete opposite—it was a classic command. Because our Task Force was used to clean lines and right angles thinking, AQI's networked structure had puzzled us. It took us too long to recognize what we were seeing: the connectivity of small teams, scaled to the size of a full enterprise. None of AQI's individual elements was better than ours, but that did not matter; a team, unlike a conventional command, is not the sum of its parts. Even if their nodes were weak, their network was strong.

Our challenge, now that we understood it, was to find a way to reshape our structure to create teamlike oneness across an organization of thousands.

RECAP

♦ Fundamental structural differences separate commands from teams. The former is rooted in reductionist prediction, and very good at executing planned procedures efficiently. The latter is less efficient, but much more adaptable.

♦ The connectivity of trust and purpose imbues teams with an ability to solve problems that could never be foreseen by a single manager—their solutions often emerge as the bottom-up result of interactions, rather than from top-down orders.

♦ In recent decades, teams have proliferated across domains previously dominated by commands in response to rising tactical complexity.

♦ The adaptability of the Task Force's teams represented a valuable start, but we would have to build that same adaptability at a much greater scale.

CHAPTER 6

TEAM OF TEAMS

On an airfield in the small East Asian republic of Krasnovia,
three dozen American diplomats sit on a plane. They have been
in the same seats for twenty-four hours, their hands bound.
The terrorists onboard are demanding that the United States release
twelve members of their sect who were captured and imprisoned four
years earlier for a bombing in Pakistan. Otherwise, the group's leader
pledges in a public statement, the first hostage will be killed before noon.
Negotiations are falling apart. The Krasnovian government, never close
with the United States, has said that it can do nothing to intervene.

Several thousand feet above the western Pacific, Navy SEALs exit a
blacked-out C-17, their parachutes catching the night air. It is 0020
hours: twenty minutes past midnight. The SEALs land in the water, ren-
dezvous with specially designed delivery boats, climb aboard, and begin
their high-speed transit across turbulent seas to reach their target.

Meanwhile, on the plane, one of the hostages—a diabetic Foreign Service officer—starts going into shock. Another two—an elderly couple on
what they had decided would be their final rotation prior to retirement—
are feverish and vomiting. Even if the militants on the plane don't kill
them, it looks like a few Americans won't make it through another
twenty-four hours.

Several hours after the SEAL insertion, thirty Rangers and four Air
Force special operators, wearing knee and elbow pads, thud onto the
tarmac of a near-silent airfield. The padding does little. Several of the
soldiers, though blessed with the limber resilience of youth and peak

fitness, jog in obvious pain to remove obstacles blocking the essential runways and taxiways, and set up a series of infrared lights. Seen through night goggles, the field is now fully illuminated; to the naked eye, it remains pitch black. Within minutes, other members of the Jump Clearing Team, riding motorcycles dropped by the same plane as they were, finish surveying the airfield and confirm that it is ready. They radio to command.

On cue, the first dark-gray MC-130—a special operations variant of the hulking "Hercules" transport plane*—descends from the clouds, landing in the darkness and taxiing quickly to a preplanned off-load site. The roar of the Hercules engine is soon joined by several more. Once the tires touch the tarmac, even before the planes roll to a full stop, they begin to lower their ramps. Modified Land Rover trucks, bristling with machine guns, roll out, and drive off to points around the airfield. By 0322 hours their target is secure.

The dance of the Russian dolls continues, as smaller aircraft now roll out the back of the MC-130s. Rotors stowed for the flight are raised into position, and the high-pitched whirl of helicopter engines harmonizes with the thumping of blades pummeling the air. The diminutive MD-500 "Little Bird" choppers are ready for takeoff. Four gunship variants, armed with a combination of 5.56 miniguns and 2.75-inch rocket pods, lead the formation. Six more, each carrying four goggled operators perched on benchlike seats on the outside of the birds, follow. By 0351 hours, their weapons at the ready and their feet dangling in the wind, Army Special Forces commandos wing at treetop level toward their objective.

In the plane, the terrorists begin to feel frustrated. They are running out of food and did not expect their work to take this long. Two of them pull a senior diplomat from his chair and start beating him with the butts of their guns. One of his ribs breaks. As he falls to the floor there are several explosions, then gunshots. The hostages assume the killing has finally begun.

It has, but not as expected. Amid shouting and the pop of several more shots, Army Special Forces operators move up the aisles of the aircraft methodically engaging the hostage takers. The terrorists, torn between

---

*The Lockheed C-130 Hercules is a large four-engine transport plane that has been used by the U.S. armed forces for half a century.

the impulse to kill their captives and to defend themselves against the sudden assault, accomplish neither, and die.

By 0435 hours the operation is largely complete. The seemingly unrelated actions of the forces had indeed all been component parts of a larger, intricate operation. SEALs had seized a critical oil rig onto which the Krasnovians had positioned air defense radar. Shutting down the radar, the SEAL operation opened a corridor through which American aircraft were able to infiltrate undetected. Minutes later, the MC-130s exploited the radar breach, allowing Rangers to seize the airfield and provide a location from which the Army Special Forces operators could launch the rescue operation.

It was splendid choreography—parade ground precision. The timing of every part of the operation was exquisitely synchronized. Throughout the execution a Task Force battle staff on a U.S. Navy vessel a few miles offshore monitored the operation of this well-oiled machine. In a few hours, they would call "end of exercise" and begin packing for the trip back to the United States.

It had been a tiring week, but none of it was real. It was all part of a program of drills designed to hone the Task Force's ability to execute the most complicated counterterrorism missions anywhere in the world. It was impressive, and beautifully orchestrated, but at the dawn of the twenty-first century, it bore little resemblance to the actual operations we would conduct in Iraq, Afghanistan, and elsewhere against Al Qaeda.

Since its inception, the Task Force has conducted a regular cycle of training exercises, battling fictional Krasnovians and other simulated foes, to refine the force's ability to execute missions like Eagle Claw. Relentlessly, quarter after quarter, year after year, intricate solutions to seemingly impossible situations have been developed, planned, rehearsed, and practiced around the world.

Operations like those against the Krasnovians brought together all elements of our Task Force, in a reductionist clockwork planned from above. The SEALs seized one target, the Rangers secured another, and Army Special Forces rescued the hostages. Though their efforts came together in the final product, there was almost no interaction between them during the course of the operation. Each of the subordinated forces perceived themselves as supremely adaptable, but the overall Task Force developed a preference for complicated, "mechanical" operations.

Contingency plans were developed and rehearsed, but real flexibility was limited.

If the threats we faced in the real world had been like Eagle Claw—slow-building crises that culminated in a single, foreseeable flash point—these exercises would have prepared us well. After years of training, we were ready for another Iranian—or Krasnovian—hostage crisis. But by 2004, the type of threat that Krasnovia posed was as fictional as the state itself. We were pitted against an enemy and a broader environment defined by interdependence, speed, and unpredictability. And we had lured ourselves into a sense of false efficacy. Every time we ran exercises, we confirmed that the SEALs were outstanding at seaborne operations, that Army Special Forces were unparalleled at hostage rescue, and that the Rangers excelled at airfield seizure. We assumed that it followed that we, as a force, were unbeatable. We should have known better.

On its own, each team exhibited horizontal bonds of trust and a common sense of purpose, but the only external ties that mattered to each team ran vertically, connecting it to the command superstructure, just like workers on an assembly line. Meaningful relationships *between* teams were nonexistent. And our teams had very provincial definitions of purpose: completing a mission or finishing intel analysis, rather than defeating AQI. To each unit, the piece of the war that really mattered was the piece inside their box on the org chart; they were fighting their own fights in their own silos. The specialization that allowed for breathtaking efficiency became a liability in the face of the unpredictability of the real world.

MECE

There is a catchy acronym in the consulting world, "MECE," which stands for "mutually exclusive and collectively exhaustive." A MECE breakdown takes something—say, customers—and segments it into a series of categories that do not overlap, but together cover everything. Customers might be divided into "paying customers" and "nonpaying customers." Every customer will fall into one of these categories, and no customer will be in more than one place. There is something very satisfying about the way a MECE framework clicks together. It is a tidy, effective way to organize categories. But it is not always an effective way to organize people.

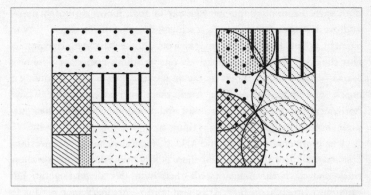

MECE   Non-MECE

The classic org chart is a neatly MECE structure. The connections that matter are the sparse vertical ones between workers and their managers. A car company's VP of North American marketing strategy worries about his relationship with the CEO to whom he reports, but probably does not worry much about his relationship with the VP of Southeast Asian operations, just as a worker affixing tires on that company's assembly line is concerned with following the directions given to her by her boss, but not about the worker tightening screws on the steering column. The tasks for which those two VPs or two automotive workers are responsible are designed to exist independently—they do not need to know each other, they do not even need to speak the same language; they have no need for interactive fluency. A classic military command, a corporate hierarchy, or a flight crew like Captain McBroom's would be fairly MECE: a leader plans and assigns tasks from above, and everyone else stays in his box.

Picture a MECE sports team, and you'd have a ridiculous spectacle: players ignoring one another and the ball, their eyes fixed on the coach, awaiting precise orders. A coach might be able to devise a more *efficient* way to execute any given play than whatever it is the players would improvise in the heat of the game. But the coach has no way of predicting exactly how the game will develop, and no way of effectively communicating instructions in real time fast enough to be useful to all players simultaneously (even if she could conceptualize it on the instant). The team is better off with the cohesive ability to improvise as a unit, relying on both specialization (goalies *mostly* stay in goal; forwards *mostly* don't) and overlapping responsibilities (each can do some of the others' jobs in a pinch), as well as such familiarity with one another's habits and responses that they can anticipate instinctively one another's responses. The best teams—like the three snipers on the deck of the *Bainbridge*—know their coach (or commander or boss) trusts them to trust each other. Those horizontal anti-MECE bonds of trust and overlapping definitions of purpose enable them to "do the right thing."

Where org charts are tidy and MECE, teams are messy. Connections crisscross all over the place, and there is lots of overlap: team members track and travel through not only their own specialized territory but often the entire playing field. Trust and purpose are inefficient: getting to know your colleagues intimately and acquiring a whole-system overview are big time sinks; the sharing of responsibilities generates redundancy. But this overlap and redundancy—these inefficiencies—are precisely what imbues teams with high-level adaptability and efficacy. Great teams are less like "awesome machines" than awesome organisms.

Our small operational teams understood all this instinctively—they trusted one another and within their units they had a clear and shared sense of purpose. They were adept at responding instantaneously and creatively to unexpected events. But all that behavior stopped where the edge of the team met the wall of the silo.

I n October 2003, just after I took command of the Task Force, I inspected the intelligence facilities at our small base at Baghdad International Airport (BIAP).* The term "intelligence facilities" paints a more impressive picture than the reality. Housed in a small building were cells for the temporary confinement of detainees captured on Task Force raids, an interrogation room, and a decrepit office area. As I walked around asking questions and getting a sense of the operation, I opened the door to a supply closet. Inside was a four-foot-high mound of plastic bags and burlap sacks—evidence bags that our forward teams had been flying back. The bags were all piled up, unopened.

It turned out that when one of our forward-operating SEAL or Army Special Forces teams captured intelligence during a raid, they tossed

---

*Before his fall earlier that year, BIAP had been named after Iraq's dictator, Saddam Hussein.

everything—documents, CDs, computers, cell phones—into sandbags, trash bags, or whatever they had, typically tying a tag or affixing a Post-it note of explanation. Then they would throw those bags onto choppers returning to Baghdad, alongside mail, unneeded equipment, or even important detainees. The bags would not arrive for hours,* and the scribbled Post-its, many of which got lost on the way, never provided sufficient context for the rear-operating intel team to do its job.

The supervisor of the facility explained that, lacking dedicated translators, he used the interrogators' translators during their spare time, and there wasn't much spare time. Like ripe fruit left in the sun, intelligence spoils quickly. By the time the bags were opened, most of it was worthless: AQI cells would have moved or changed their plans. A map to Saddam Hussein's hiding spot could have lain among the documents and we wouldn't have known.

The operators, adept at their own roles but having little understanding of the nuts and bolts of intel analysis, could not anticipate what sorts of explanations would be meaningful, what sort of context was relevant, or which material had to be turned around instantly and which could wait. To many, the intel teams were simply a black box that gobbled up their hard-won data and spat out belated and disappointing analyses. They did not know the analysts personally and saw them as removed and territorial. The operators preferred to hold on to captured materials to give their less-expert, underresourced, but *familiar* team member trained in analysis a couple days with it in the hope that the small fraction of material he or she had time to comb through would yield insights of value. As on Flight 173, everybody was doing his or her job, but nobody was checking the fuel gauge.

On the intel side, analysts were frustrated by the poor quality of materials and the delays in receiving them. And without exposure to the gritty details of raids, they had little sense of what the operators needed. To them, every cell phone or dirty piece of paper they received was just another assignment handed down by a manager. Many saw operators as arrogant and ignorant of intelligence analysis: tools for breaking down doors who had no appreciation for the intelligence war. In their opinion,

---

*This may not sound like a long time, but relative to the lightning-fast timescale on which AQI operated, it was practically an age.

the operators were fighting the wrong fight; the operators had the same view of the analysts.

The teams were operating independently—like workers in an efficient factory—while trying to keep pace with an interdependent environment. We all knew intuitively that intelligence gathered on AQI's communications and operations would almost certainly impact what our operators saw on the battlefield, and that battlefield details would almost certainly represent valuable context for intel analysis, but those elements of our organization were not communicating with each other.

That evening, I stood at a whiteboard with a colleague to discuss the problem. I drew an hourglass figure to depict the organizational distance and relationship between the teams, the forward operating teams at the top of the glass and our rear analysis teams on the bottom. I placed my hand over the bottom half of the hourglass and asked, "Would removing this half affect the forward team at all?" The answer was no. Both were working as diligently as they knew how, but they were connected only through a choke point.

The unopened bags of evidence were symptomatic of a larger problem. We could try to solve it with a triage plan for relaying and processing data, but that would be like responding to United 173 with a specific technical procedure for landing gear malfunction. At best, we would solve one particular problem; at worst we would increase paperwork, slowing things down further, and the moment circumstances shifted, we would be back to square one. The choke point existed not because of insufficient guidance from above, but because of a dearth of integration.

To fix the choke point, we needed to fix the management system and organizational culture that created it. As soon as we looked at our organization through the lens of the team structure—searching for weaknesses in horizontal connectivity rather than new possibilities for top-down planning—similar choke points became visible between all our individual teams. We referred to them as "blinks."

Stratification and silos were hardwired throughout the Task Force. Although all our units resided on the same compound, most lived with their "kind," some used different gyms, units controlled access to their planning areas, and each tribe had its own brand of standoffish superiority complex. Resources were shared reluctantly. Our forces lived a proximate but largely parallel existence.

The blinks were even worse between the Task Force and our partner organizations: the CIA, FBI, NSA, and conventional military units with whom we had to coordinate operations. Initially, representatives from these organizations lived in separate trailers, with limited access to our compound. Built in the name of security, these physical walls prevented routine interaction and produced misinformation and mistrust. The NSA, for instance, initially refused to provide us with raw signal intercepts, insisting that they had to process their intelligence and send us summaries, often a process of several days. They weren't being intentionally difficult; their internal doctrine held that only they could effectively interpret their collections. Passing out raw data invited misinterpretation with potentially disastrous consequences. But exquisitely accurate analyses of where the enemy had been three days earlier wouldn't enable us to intercept foreign fighters bent on suicide attacks.

Until we fixed the blinks we would not be fully effective. We needed operational teams to gather, organize, and relay data to analysts in Baghdad, Tampa, and Washington. These analysts would then need to examine the data and communicate conclusions to the original team for follow-on action. Simultaneously, we needed to disseminate the relevant takeaways to the thousands of people in our organization; and we needed administrative higher-ups to modify operations and allocate resources based on the analysis. All this would have to take place in the span of hours, not weeks, and each situation would be different from those that came before.

We had to find a way for the organization as a whole to build at scale the same messy connectivity our small teams had mastered so effectively.

O ur circumstances were unique, but the problem is not. Though teams have proliferated across organizations from hospitals to airline crews, almost without exception this has happened within the confines of broader reductionist structures, and this has limited their adaptive potential.

In treating victims of the Boston bombing, Brigham and Women's salvaged (as opposed to amputating) a much higher percentage of limbs than other hospitals, despite having equal or higher average levels of injury of incoming patients.* In a paper written with their colleagues

---

*There were of course many variables at play, and this is not a large enough sample size to be statistically significant, so it is not conclusive evidence. However, it does fall in line with their other outstanding track records.

after the bombing, Drs. Carty and Caterson credited their hospital's culture of "fostering preparation and teamwork through daily collaborative interactions." The medical staff had long-standing relationships, built over years in caring for routine patients. Thus, when crisis struck, "no decision was made in a vacuum," says Caterson, "meaning that there was no longer a single surgeon saying this lower extremity is mangled; I'm going to take this leg off . . . we would make decisions as a team." Yet even Brigham and Women's has admitted that the overall organization did not possess the ability to deal with such an unexpected event.

Problems existed on the fault lines—in the spaces *between* elite teams. Different departments in the hospital had different conventions for keeping track of unknown patients. As an unprecedented volume of patients were whisked between the ER, operating theaters, and burn units, the tracking system was overtaxed: a report noted that "a nurse or technician manually moved [each] patient's icon on a tracking board, so other staff members could find them. In the post-bombing chaos, the staff did not always move tiles in a timely manner, so they did not always know exactly where patients were located." Brigham and Women's accomplished tremendous things that day, but the larger an enterprise gets, the harder it is for it to think and act as one.

In a now famous 1999 Institute of Medicine study, "To Err Is Human," it was estimated that between 44,000 and 98,000 people died every year as a result of medical errors. Even if the lower estimate of the study is used, deaths due to medical errors would have been the Centers for Disease Control and Prevention's seventh-leading cause of death in 1998, meaning that more people died as a result of medical errors than from motor vehicle accidents (43,458 deaths), breast cancer (42,297 deaths), or AIDS (16,516 deaths).*

A new study published in September 2013 asserts that the number of deaths due to medical error is dramatically higher: 210,000 to 400,000. Either estimate would have put medical errors as the third-leading cause of death in the CDC's 2011 ranking. If the estimated 100,000 deaths due to hospital-acquired infections are included, this loss is equal to twenty Boeing 747 airliners going down every week.

---

*CDC rankings don't include medical error as a separate cause/category of death.

COMMAND OF TEAMS

The quandary faced by Brigham and Women's in 2013, like that faced by our Task Force in 2004, was that of what we might call a "command of teams": adaptive small teams operating within an old-fashioned rigid superstructure. In a response to rising tactical complexity, many organizations in many domains have replaced small commands with teams. But the vast majority of these organizations have to be much larger than a single team; they consist of multiple teams, and these teams are wired together just like a traditional command. This stifles the teams' adaptive potential: when confined to silos like those of our Task Force, teams might achieve tactical adaptability, but will never be able to exhibit those traits at a strategic level.

The proliferation of the command of teams is not unique to mission-critical endeavors. A study of some seven hundred manufacturers by MIT economist Paul Osterman found that most were using work teams, and that almost half had the majority of their employees working in teams. A survey by the Work in America Institute of a hundred leading companies found that 95 percent of respondents ranked "teamwork: creating and sustaining team-based organizations" as the research topic that would have the greatest value for their organizations. Of course, office teams may be cohesive and adaptable or they may be teams in name only—the result of a manager putting up some posters, giving a pep talk, and then retreating to his corner office. Teams, like many of the topics studied in this book (trust, purpose, the need for adaptability, etc.), can easily devolve into a "bumper sticker solution"—rhetoric parading as real transformation. Nonetheless, studies at large companies with robust data sets such as Xerox, Ford, and P&G have found that the implementation of teams often leads to leaps in productivity as well as improvements in morale.

Teams can bring a measure of adaptability to previously rigid organizations. But these performance improvements have a ceiling as long as adaptable traits are limited to the team level. As the world grows faster and more interdependent, we need to figure out ways to scale the fluidity of teams across entire organizations: groups with thousands of members that span continents, like our Task Force. But this is easier said than done.

Small teams are effective in large part because they are small—people know each other intimately and have clocked hundreds of hours with each other. In large organizations most people will inevitably be strangers to one another. In fact, the very traits that make teams great can often work to *prevent* their coherence into a broader whole.

How does one build a team with seven thousand swim buddies?

"THE POINT AT WHICH EVERYONE ELSE SUCKS"

Anybody who has taken an introductory microeconomics course has learned of "diminishing marginal returns." With most goods and services, each additional unit brings less value or gratification than the one before: a sandwich will bring a very hungry man great satisfaction. The second sandwich will bring some happiness, the third a little less, and the tenth will probably be difficult to eat and might make you sick.* As it relates to manpower, this is known as the problem of "too many cooks in the kitchen."

How many "cooks" is too many? It depends. In a small kitchen or office, four might be the ideal number. For a company with operations the size of Walmart, the break point is much higher. For some activities, like having an engaging conversation, diminishing marginal returns sets in after a few people. For other tasks, like producing a mechanical item via assembly line, you can add just as much value with the hundredth employee as with the first.

For teams, this range is considerably narrower. Athletic teams, for instance, usually consist of fifteen to thirty people. Army Ranger platoons are composed of forty-two soldiers. SEAL squads contain between sixteen and twenty people. Beyond such numbers, teams begin to lose the "oneness" that makes them adaptable. As the proverbial kitchen fills up, communication and trust break down, egos come into conflict, and the

---

*There is a difference between diminishing *marginal* returns (when each additional unit adds less value than the previous one—this probably sets in after the first sandwich) and diminishing *total* returns (when each additional unit adds *negative* value—the sandwich that makes you feel *worse* than before eating it). For our purposes, the difference is not important: the point is that the positive attributes of labor do not always increase with scale.

chemistry that fueled innovation and agility becomes destructive. In many cases, this loss of adaptability dooms the enterprise.

Though any given SEAL was, like the entirety of our Task Force, on paper fighting the same fight, he was really fighting for his squad. The men on a squad prepare, deploy, and operate together. They spend four-month rotations in the alien, hostile deserts of Iraq or the arid plains of Afghanistan, and they rarely have meaningful, friendly interaction with anyone outside this circle. Imagine the closest roommate relationship you've ever had and multiply that by one hundred. The bonds within squads are fundamentally different from those between squads or other units. In the words of one of our SEALs, "The squad is the point at which everyone else sucks. That other squadron sucks, the other SEAL teams suck, and our Army counterparts definitely suck." Of course, every other squad thought the same thing.

Here, we run up against a fundamental constraint in the empathetic bandwidth of the human mind. British anthropologist Robin Dunbar theorized that the number of people an individual can actually trust usually falls between 100 and 230 (a more specific variant was popularized by Malcolm Gladwell as the "Rule of 150" in his book *Outliers*). This limitation leads to a kind of tribal competitiveness: victory as defined by the squad—the primary unit of allegiance—may not align with victory as defined by the Task Force. The goal becomes to accomplish missions better than the team that bunks on the other side of the base, rather than to win the war. In other words, the magic of teams is a double-edged sword once organizations get big: some of the same traits that make an adaptable team great can make it incompatible with the structure it serves.

Thousands of fledgling businesses have sunk because of an inability to scale their teamwork. Joel Peterson, a professor at the Stanford School of Business, says the rigidity that sets in with scale is one of the main causes of start-up failure. And the late J. Richard Hackman, a Harvard sociology professor, found that teams are much trickier to build and maintain than we like to think. The issue is not that teams never work, but that team dynamics are powerful but delicate, and expansion is a surefire way to break them. "[It's a] fallacy that bigger teams are better than smaller ones because they have more resources to draw on," he explains. "As a team gets bigger, the number of links that need to be managed among members goes up at an accelerating, almost exponential rate." In his handbook *Leading Teams,* Hackman reminds us of "Brook's Law": the adage that adding staff to speed up a behind-schedule project "has no better chance of working . . . than would a scheme to produce a baby quickly by assigning nine women to be pregnant for one month each . . . adding manpower to a late software project makes it later."

It was not possible to make the Task Force one big team, but we also could not stick with our command of teams compromise; stacking our small teams in silos had made us unwieldy. At the same time, we couldn't simply remove the reductionist superstructure and leave each team to its own devices; we needed coordination across the enterprise. Somehow we would have to scale trust and purpose without creating chaos.

TEAM OF TEAMS

Millennia-old behavioral patterns, the neurological constraints of the human brain, and the history of American special operations were against us as we tried to move beyond the point where "everyone else sucks." We needed to spread the oneness—and the accompanying adaptability—that infused individual Ranger platoons, Army Special Forces units, or SEAL squads across a task force of thousands.

As we sat in our makeshift command center in Balad, reading reports of AQI bombings, we realized that our goal was not the creation of one massive team. We needed to create a *team of teams*. It may sound like a kitschy semantic distinction, but it actually marked a critical structural difference that turned the aspiration of scaling the magic of the team into a realizable goal.

On a single team, every individual needs to know every other individual in order to build trust, and they need to maintain comprehensive awareness at all times in order to maintain common purpose—easy with a group of twenty-five, doable with a group of fifty, tricky above one hundred, and definitely impossible across a task force of seven thousand. But on a team of teams, every *individual* does not have to have a relationship with every other individual; instead, the relationships between the constituent *teams* need to resemble those between individuals on a given team: we needed the SEALs to trust Army Special Forces, and for them to trust the CIA, and for them all to be bound by a sense of common purpose: winning the war, rather than outperforming the other unit. And that could be effectively accomplished through representation.

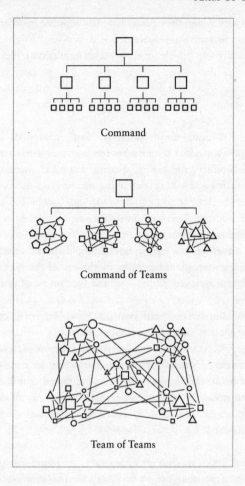

Command

Command of Teams

Team of Teams

We didn't need every member of the Task Force to know everyone else; we just needed everyone to know *someone* on every team, so that when they thought about, or had to work with, the unit that bunked next door or their intelligence counterparts in D.C., they envisioned a friendly face rather than a competitive rival. We didn't need everybody to follow every single operation in real time (something just as impossible as building lifelong friendships with seven thousand people). We needed to enable a team operating in an interdependent environment to understand the butterfly-effect ramifications of their work and make them aware of the other teams with whom they would have to cooperate in order to achieve strategic—not just tactical—success.

Time pressure was intense, and the stakes kept getting higher.

ALMOST

Throughout 2004 Iraq steadily and disturbingly unraveled. Fallujah fell. Under Zarqawi's shadow the city became an insurgent stronghold. By June, jihadists policed the streets, shutting down hair salons and movie theaters, torturing and killing Iraqi policemen and "spies." Foreign fighters streamed into Iraq at a rate that we estimated to be 100 to 150 each month. Each additional person—usually a suicide bomber or fanatically committed fighter—represented scores of civilian deaths to come. Fallujah became a staging area for increasingly sophisticated attacks, like the September 30 sewage plant bombing. By the end of the year, attacks on American forces averaged 87 per day, and the American death toll had passed 1,000.

AQI's momentum continued into 2005 as Zarqawi orchestrated a campaign of violent intimidation against January's parliamentary elections. Only 3,775 people voted in all of Anbar Province—about 2 percent of the population. Zarqawi's taunting claims that he regularly passed through American checkpoints with ease, combined with his mounting stature as an insurgent leader, further highlighted our apparent impotence. Stopping Zarqawi was an operational imperative for the Task Force, and for me it felt like an obsession.

In February 2005, we had an opportunity to target Zarqawi. It had been fourteen months since we first confirmed his presence inside Iraq. A combination of intelligence sources confirmed that he was traveling in a sedan, and a Predator,* ten thousand feet above the ground, spotted the vehicle moving across a lightly populated area west of Baghdad. A flurry of communications sparked across the Task Force as we mobilized strike forces for immediate movement, and requested conventional units to prevent escape of his vehicle.

---

*A standard unmanned aerial vehicle or drone capable of providing real-time transmission of full motion video of objects on the ground.

As the Predator operator tracked the sedan, it moved into a cul-de-sac, stopped momentarily, and then drove out. The operator, to maintain surveillance, had to adjust the camera, and through sheer bad luck, missed Zarqawi jumping from the vehicle and moving away on foot. We captured his computer and carbine, but it was a bitter disappointment. The man with the $25 million bounty on his head had eluded us yet again.

Although we knew that finding the man would not destroy his organization—especially given how resilient and decentralized AQI was—we also knew it was a strategic and symbolic victory that we needed. Every missed opportunity to capture or, if need be, kill AQI operatives—especially one as valuable as Zarqawi—would cost U.S. military or Iraqi civilian lives down the line. Since I had taken command at the helm of the Task Force, the situation in Iraq had only grown worse, and this showed no signs of relenting.

That June I was summoned to the White House to brief the president on the status of our efforts to capture or kill Zarqawi. Sitting between Secretary of Defense Donald Rumsfeld and Secretary of State Condoleezza Rice in the cramped confines of the Situation Room, I provided George W. Bush and his assembled national security team with an overview of our efforts to date, and my genuine confidence that ultimately, we would stop him. But the real question was whether it would be soon enough to prevent his setting all of Iraq aflame.

By this point I knew that defeating Zarqawi and his organization could not be accomplished by a traditional command—even a command composed of teams as capable as our own. We would have to match AQI's adaptability while preserving our traditional strengths, and this would necessitate an unprecedented transformation—it would require a true team of teams. Accomplishing this would involve a complete reversal of the conventional approach to information sharing, delineation of roles, decision-making authority, and leadership.

RECAP

♦ Although our Task Force's constituent teams exemplified adaptability, a commandlike superstructure constrained the organization at large. This "command of teams" approach was more flexible than a conventional command, but was still not adaptable enough to deal with the complexities of the twenty-first century and battle AQI.

♦ Although teams have proliferated across many sectors, they have almost always done so in the confines of broader commands. More and more organizations will need to overcome this hurdle and become more adaptable.

♦ Unfortunately, many of the traits that made our teams so good also made it incredibly difficult to scale those traits across our organization. We were also up against some fundamental constraints. Building a single team the size of our Task Force would be impossible.

♦ The solution we devised was a "team of teams"—an organization within which the relationships between constituent teams resembled those between individuals on a single team: teams that had traditionally resided in separate silos would now have to become fused to one another via trust and purpose.

PART III

SHARING

In January 2000, Khalid al-Mihdhar obtained a visa to enter the United States. Two days earlier, he had been the subject of a joint CIA-FBI meeting. A CIA analyst present knew that Mihdhar had connections to suspected terrorists, but "as a CIA analyst, he was not authorized to answer FBI questions regarding CIA information." When, later that summer, the FBI grew suspicious of Mihdhar, internal divisions at the Bureau hampered efforts to locate him, and an interested "criminal" FBI agent assigned to the case of the USS Cole bombing was erroneously told that since he was not an "intelligence" FBI agent, he could not pursue Mihdhar. The following September, Mihdhar piloted American Airlines Flight 77 into the Pentagon.

In July 2001, an FBI agent in Phoenix sent a memo to FBI headquarters suggesting the "possibility of a coordinated effort by Usama Bin Laden" to send terrorists to flight school in the United States, and noting the "inordinate number of individuals of investigative interest" who were enrolled in flight schools in Arizona. Though they were addressed on the memo, members of the FBI's Usama Bin Laden unit did not read the memo until after September 11.

And with regard to Khalid Sheikh Mohammed, the man masterminding the attacks, the "pieces of the puzzle arrived in the spring and summer of 2001," but "they were not put together." In April, the CIA learned that someone named "Mukhtar" was coordinating a plot against the United States, and later that spring they learned that a known terrorist—Khalid Sheikh Mohammed—was actively recruiting operatives to travel from Afghanistan to the United States for an attack. In August, the CIA learned that Khalid Sheikh Mohammed's nickname was "Mukhtar," but the chatter from April about a "Mukhtar" who was engineering an attack had cooled off.

The U.S. intelligence system was "blinking red," as The 9/11 Commission Report *would later put it. "Systems," plural, would be a more accurate description, as these roadblocks to sharing prevented the kind of integration that could have averted the attacks.*

Nobody connected the dots.

CHAPTER 7

SEEING THE SYSTEM

It was October but by late morning the heat was shimmering off the Baghdad pavement. A twenty-six-year-old intelligence analyst with a scruffy beard and a Columbia camping shirt squinted as he left the Task Force's screening facility. He was carrying seven pages of paper: the printout of a PowerPoint analysis he had assembled, and the brief biography of an Iraqi car dealer turned AQI operative.

Time was critical. The analyst had been tracking this target for several weeks, but he had only confirmed the man's role and identity the day before questioning. Signals intercepts indicated he had recently been active inside the capital. AQI was using lethal VBIEDs (vehicle-borne improvised explosive devices) to kill civilians in neighborhoods across the city—targeting this man was crucial to stopping the terror campaign.

In a bunker fifty yards from the screening facility, the analyst presented his conclusions to colleagues seated around a table in the Situational Awareness Room (SAR). Based on this analysis, the onetime car dealer became a priority. Our targeting machine digested this new intelligence and added him to the list of individuals we were tracking. The man in question did not know it, but his life had become much more dangerous.

Soon, analysts identified the man's dwelling and vehicle, as well as two associates with whom he spoke and met. Shortly after 9:00 p.m. on the fourth day, intelligence assets located him in a house in the Hurriya neighborhood. A Predator unmanned aerial vehicle was requested. Intelligence surveillance and reconnaissance (ISR) assets were in high demand and the team using the Predator did not want to hand it over, but after a few tense conversations the vehicle was rotating in a gyre seventeen thousand feet above the target's house, providing constant real-time full-motion video of the site. The man had been *found*. The next stage of our F3EA assembly line—*fix*—clicked into gear as the intel analysts passed the case to their operational counterparts and began work on their next target.

Within minutes, an Army Special Forces assault team was assembled, briefed, and on the move. They traveled in a small convoy of South African–made armored vehicles designed for street warfare. These had been procured after the bitter experience of street combat in Mogadishu eleven years earlier.*

The operators were focused and calm. It was not their first rodeo, nor was it an exceptionally challenging operation. The men in the car had done this more or less every day throughout their deployment. The Predator's slowly rotating video feed streamed down to their vehicles, and as the operators watched they refined their plan to secure the immediate area around the house to prevent his escape, then enter the building. The basic outline was the same as ever: if he surrendered, he would be captured and interrogated; if he fought, he would die. The vehicles arrived on target. The AQI operative remained inside, oblivious. He had been *fixed*. Next came the *finish*.

At the objective, the streets were quiet. Once, Iraqis wandered at night to enjoy the cool evening air, but these days that was a rare sight. The operators posted vehicles at three corners and sent two of their number to a fourth. Dogs barked, as they always do, but the noise produced no discernible reaction from local residents. Cautiously, the operators approached a metal gate that controlled entry to the house's driveway and carport. They placed two expanding ladders against the courtyard wall. Soon, laser-aiming lights mounted on M4 carbines were darting around the courtyard, ready to engage any resistance.

The breach was not dramatic. There was no explosion or gunfire, just some muffled rattles as bolt cutters provided entry for operators who quickly followed, secured the courtyard, and approached the house. A few minutes later, the car-dealer-cum-aspiring-terrorist appeared in the doorway, flex-cuffed and blindfolded. He had been *finished*. Next came *exploitation*.

---

*Famously, this episode was commemorated in the book and movie *Black Hawk Down*.

An operator accompanied by an interpreter led the man to one of the armored vehicles while a rapid search of his home gathered a computer, a phone, and some documents. In half an hour he was at the unit's base—a now run-down Saddam Hussein–era villa. The operators, like the analysts, had performed superbly. They had delivered the honed efficiency that had, over the years, earned them their reputation as the world's finest. The team now handed the detainee and materials over to interrogators and intelligence experts who would *analyze* the man and the data. Like the intel team before them, the operators now moved on to the next target passed to them by the Task Force's assembly line. Whether or not the car dealer yielded intelligence of value was no longer the soldiers' problem. For most, the intelligence side of the war was to them a black box. They saw themselves as shooters; anything that distracted them from their priorities of *fixing* and *finishing* was a waste. This was what the awesome machine had taught them to do. They prepared to strike a new target.

Meanwhile, screening and exploitation of the files found at the car dealer's house began: new grist for the awesome machine.

But . . . the car dealer's name was imprecisely recorded (a common occurrence among Westerners dealing with unfamiliar naming conventions), and though the intelligence gathered had the potential to identify follow-up AQI targets, by the time it had navigated the labyrinth of security clearances, and made its way back to our Task Force, four days had passed. The car dealer's network had vanished; when AQI operatives were captured, the network quickly ensured that everyone connected to the target would disappear. Our information had become useless.

Our operation was a success at the level of each individual team, but it was also rife with opportunities left unrealized for our Task Force at large. This was the frustration of operating a command of teams where information wasn't clearly shared.

A t its heart, F3EA was a rational, *reductionist* process. It took a complex set of tasks, broke them down, and distributed them to the specialized individuals or teams best suited to accomplish them.

When we started falling behind in the fight against AQI, we tried to do what we had always done, only better: meticulously construct schedules, increase our intelligence structure, add interrogators, analysts, and technicians by the score, and sharpen our focus. If we each did our tasks better than ever, we thought, our machine would be unstoppable.

"We came from a background where if you were losing, you just weren't trying hard enough," recalls a SEAL commander who operated in Baghdad, "so we started going all out—timing how long it took us from the moment we fixed a target to get out of our cots, get our gear on, load choppers."

F3EA got tighter, faster, and more focused. By August 2004 we were running eighteen raids a month—a higher pace than we had thought possible. But it wasn't enough. By focusing on the component parts rather than the overall process, we were missing the fundamental problem. Speeding up the individual elements of the system did nothing to eliminate the blinks between them that most stymied our efforts. There were geographical blinks and technological ones: the distance between Washington and Baghdad could slow decisions, and occasionally bandwidth problems obstructed the transfer of data. More often, though, the blinks were social. Cultural differences between the Task Force's different tribes got in the way of communicating. Overcoming this would require completely rethinking the conventional organizational approach to distributing information.

THE "NEED TO KNOW" FALLACY

Any aficionado of action movies has heard the line "That's on a need-to-know basis, and you don't need to know," uttered by a broad-shouldered, square-jawed caricature of a Special Operations commando or serious-faced intelligence agent. Though we rarely use that phrase in real life, it is an accurate depiction of military and broader organizational sentiments about the value of information: given the overwhelming volume of, and myriad sensitivities around, information, the default is not to share.

As the different components of the F3EA process were executed, each team tended to view its role in splendid isolation. Their ability to specialize in their own domains *necessitated* ignorance of the process at large—for operators, time spent learning about the "black box" of intelligence was a distraction that took them away from their proper duties. But this limited definition of efficiency meant that they passed on information that was often less useful than it should have been, late, or lacking context.

Had each of our teams been an individual at BUD/S, he would have gotten booted in week one. They took pride in their *own* team's performance, like the prima donna slugger who touts his high batting average as his team consistently loses. Instinctively, the silos of our organization looked inward, where they could see metrics of success and failure.

The habit of constraining information derives in part from modern security concerns, but also from the inured preference for clearly defined, mechanistic processes—whether factory floors or corporate org charts—in which people need to know only their own piece of the puzzle to do their job. One of the oldest and most famous examples of specialization—and the compartmentalized ignorance that such specialization encourages—can be found in Adam Smith's 1776 description of a pin factory in his classic work, *The Wealth of Nations*:

> One man draws out the wire, another straights it, a third cuts it, a fourth points it, a fifth grinds it at the top for receiving the head; . . . the important business of making a pin is, in this manner, divided into about eighteen distinct operations . . . I have seen a small manufactory of this kind where ten men only were employed, and [those ten persons] could make among them upwards of forty-eight thousand pins in a day . . . But if they had all wrought separately and independently, and without any of them having been educated to this peculiar business, they certainly could not each of them have made twenty, perhaps not one pin in a day; that is, certainly, not the two hundred and fortieth, perhaps not the four thousand eight hundredth part of what they are at present capable of performing, in consequence of a proper division and combination of their different operations.

The pin factory benefits from putting blinders on each individual worker, as have many operations since. A man moving pig iron did not need to know where that iron came from before it arrived at the factory, or what the man who received it after him did with it; the assembly line worker building his small portion of a ship did not need to understand how the final product came together. But come together it would, thanks to the aggregation of these discrete efforts, and the intricate designs of managers. Things, in comforting simplicity, were the sum of their parts. The economic success of reductionist efficiencies in the twentieth century inspired increasingly fundamentalist adherence to Smith's doctrine of specialization.

But as technology has grown more sophisticated and processes more dispersed, the way component parts of a process come together has become far less intuitive, and in many cases impossible for a cadre of managers to predict fully. In a pin factory, a holistic understanding of the product is self-evident: Making pins is simple, and a worker in Smith's manufactory could easily see how his labor interacted with that of his peers. Even if each worker performed only one task, he still understood, at least in some way, the entire pin-making process and could probably explain the tasks of his fellow workers. Such is no longer the case in many factories. As technology has grown more sophisticated and processes more dispersed, the way component parts of a process come together has become far less intuitive. The man who fixes a valve on the landing gear of a passenger jet probably can't explain the details of the complete jet assembly.

Taylor saved money by firing the paper pulp chemist and replacing him with an uneducated laborer and a chart. Time and money spent learning the whole process would be time away from the job and money not spent on supplies. In the short run, this kind of education may not seem worth the opportunity cost.

In military, governmental, and corporate sectors, an increased concern for secrecy has caused further sequestering of information. We have secrets, and secrets need to be guarded. In the wrong hands, information may do great damage, as the recent Snowden and WikiLeaks scandals have shown. In the absence of a compelling reason to do otherwise, it makes sense to confine information by the borders of its relevance.

As growing volumes of data flood institutions divided into increasingly specialized departments, the systems for keeping information safe have become more and more complicated. More protocols have to be satisfied, more tests have to be conducted, more badges have to be swiped before information can be shared.

Over the decades, America's military and intelligence institutions have developed intricate matrices of clearances and silos to ensure that, as a Hollywood general might put it, people don't know what they don't need to know. In early 2003, when I served as the vice director for operations on the Pentagon's Joint Staff, the United States Central Command

(CENTCOM)* initially *prohibited* the Pentagon staffs from viewing their internal Web site out of a (common) fear of giving "higher headquarters" visibility into unfinalized planning products. Such absurdities reflect the truth that most organizations are more concerned with how best to control information than how best to share it.

The problem is that the logic of "need to know" depends on the assumption that *somebody*—some manager or algorithm or bureaucracy—actually *knows* who does and does not need to know which material. In order to say definitively that a SEAL ground force does not need awareness of a particular intelligence source, or that an intel analyst does not need to know precisely what happened on any given mission, the commander must be able to say with confidence that those pieces of knowledge have no bearing on what those teams are attempting to do, nor on the situations the analyst may encounter. Our experience showed us this was never the case. More than once in Iraq we were close to mounting capture/kill operations only to learn at the last hour that the targets were working undercover for another coalition entity. The organizational structures we had developed in the name of secrecy and efficiency actively prevented us from talking to each other and assembling a full picture.

Effective prediction—as we have discussed—has become increasingly difficult, and in many situations impossible. Continuing to function under the illusion that we can understand and foresee exactly what will be relevant to whom is hubris. It might feel safe, but it is the opposite. Functioning safely in an interdependent environment requires that every team possess a *holistic understanding* of the interaction between all the moving parts. Everyone has to see the system in its entirety for the plan to work.

A FABLE: THE FAILURE OF THE KRASNOVIAN SOCCER TEAM

Let's imagine that our fictional war game adversary, Krasnovia, liked the mechanical era too much to leave it. We can envision it as a country of Rube Goldberg–like contraptions engineered to do everything from

---

*CENTCOM is the combatant command responsible for the geographic theater of the Middle East, North Africa, and Central Asia. At this time, notably, this included preparation for the then-upcoming Iraq war.

getting people dressed in the morning to ironing their evening papers. The country's president (recently "elected" to his seventh term with 97 percent of the popular vote) does not believe in complexity. The economy is centrally planned, down to every family's daily food choices. Even the ecosystem is regulated: instead of exposing the state to the nonlinearity of evolution, government scientists laboring in concrete towers have devised schedules for breeding and then releasing (neutered) animals into the wild—starlings in April, toads in September.

Like his president, the coach of the Krasnovian soccer team—Coach T—worships at the altar of determinism, and on graduating from the National Academy of Planning, he resolves to bring reductionist management to the world's greatest game. Coach T's players don't know one another's names. They've never even seen each other. The men train separately, in one-on-one sessions with their coach. In these daily meetings, Coach T has his players focus on honing their personal fitness and rehearsing their respective portions of the 712 plays that he has designed. Once a year, the team assembles to rehearse. For these occasions, Coach T has developed an ingenious, lightweight piece of headgear similar to the blinders worn by horses. The contraption is designed to minimize distraction. When wearing it, players see only their individual patch of grass. Many of them, raised from a young age in one of the dedicated soccer camps developed by Coach T for each individual position, have never seen the entire field.

The annual practice is a beautiful thing to watch. The players' physical condition is unrivaled. They execute their plays flawlessly. Their archrival, Atropia, is nowhere near as fit, fast, or disciplined, and every four years, when the teams meet in the qualifying rounds of the World Cup, Krasnovian hopes run high. Usually around minute five, however, something happens that diverges from any of Coach T's 712 plans. The Krasnovians continue to execute their immaculate choreography, but they are kicking at the air and passing to nobody. The Atropians, without a plan but with awareness of the entire field, run circles around them.

After each loss, Coach T goes back and devises another plan, and by the next match, he has a flawless solution to the expired Atropian plays.

Contemporary environments now present too many equivalent likelihoods for top-down Krasnovian planning. Errors like misrecording a name could easily be corrected with some training and a memorandum, but that would do nothing to prevent the thousands of other tiny deviations, any one of which might also generate outsized impacts. Like the landing gear failure that ultimately doomed United 173, the root cause lay not in the lack of a specific procedure, but in the inability to correct in real time in response to unexpected inconsistencies. Task Force leadership was playing whack-a-mole: we could pick off problems as they arose, but we would never be able to predict and prescribe exactly what analysis would be relevant to specific operational teams, or what types of materials our operators should seek to help our analysts.

In situations of unpredictability, organizations need to improvise. And to do that, the players on the field need to understand the broader context. At the team level, this is self-evident. But at the broader institutional level, it is more difficult to engineer structures that are both coherent and improvisatory.

The problem, at one level, was obvious: we were failing to create useful bonds between one team and the next. The work done by our operators and analysts was inextricably linked, and yet we had placed the two groups in separate organizational silos—we had given them blinders—in the name of efficiency. Our players could only see the ball once it entered their immediate territory, by which time it would likely be too late to react. With no knowledge of the constantly shifting perspective of their teammates, they would have no idea what to do with the ball once they got it. They were playing Krasnovian soccer.

Though our Task Force had never found itself in this quandary before, neither the challenge, nor the eventual solution, was new.

"NEW METAL ALLOYS, SOME OF WHICH HAVE NOT YET BEEN INVENTED"

In September 1962 at Rice University, an enthusiastic President Kennedy, shining with sweat, delivered a now-famous speech. He pledged that the United States would send humans

> *240,000 miles away from the control station in Houston [in] a giant rocket, more than 300 feet tall . . . made of new metal alloys, some of which have not yet been invented, capable of standing heat and stresses several times more than have ever been experienced,*

fitted together with a precision better than the finest watch, carry-
ing all the equipment needed for propulsion, guidance, control,
communications, food and survival, on an uncharted mission to
an unknown celestial body, and then return it safely to Earth, reen-
tering the atmosphere at speeds of over 25,000 miles per hour,
causing heat about half that of the temperature of the sun . . . and
do all this, and do it right, and do it first, before this decade is out.
We must be bold . . . as we set sail we ask God's blessing on the
most hazardous and dangerous and greatest adventure on which
man has ever embarked.

Kennedy enumerated the obstacles—the distance, speed, and heat—
not to dissuade, but to inspire. One can imagine the thrill that must have
pulsed through the audience of budding engineers as their president
pointed out that the metals necessary to achieve this feat *had not yet been
invented*. Earlier in the speech Kennedy uttered the memorable statement "We do these things, not because they are easy, but because they are
hard."

Less than seven years later, more than 600 million viewers around the
world tuned in to watch Neil Armstrong set foot on lunar soil and pro-
claim "one giant leap for mankind" before planting an American flag on
the moon. To the best of our knowledge, that flag, though toppled by the
lander's liftoff blast and likely bleached white from decades of unfiltered
sunlight, is still there. The ridged imprints from Armstrong's rubber
soles—tiny, perfectly geometric mountain ranges—still stand, preserved
in the windless stasis of our favorite celestial boulder. No matter what
happens on frenzied Earth, the traces of *Apollo 11* should serve as a tes-
tament to human ingenuity for millions of years.

Almost as significant as what happened in space exploration in July
1969, however, is what did not happen. Two weeks before the *Apollo 11*
launch, on the other side of the Atlantic, the F-8 rocket assembled by
ELDO, the European Launcher Development Organisation, failed on the
launch pad. It was ELDO's fifth consecutive total failure.

NASA and ELDO had similar ambitions and faced the same challenges. The success of one and the failure of the other had little to do with
differences in expertise or resources, and much to do with how the organizations distributed information. NASA was, thanks to an approach
known as "systems management," a more effective organization. NASA

administrators Robert Seamans and Frederick Ordway summarized the nature of their achievement as follows: "The Apollo project . . . is generally considered as one of the greatest technological endeavors in the history of mankind. But in order to achieve this, a managerial effort, no less prodigious than the technological one, was required."

In the years leading up to Kennedy's speech, the United States had lagged embarrassingly in the Space Race. The Soviet Union had produced the first Earth orbiter, the first animal in orbit, the first lunar flyby, the first lunar impact, and the first images of the far side of the moon. It would soon put Yuri Gagarin into orbit, the first man in space. In the meantime, the American space effort struggled.

NASA's first unmanned test flight, Mercury-Redstone I, lifted off on November 21, 1960, but it did not lift very far: The launcher rose four inches off the ground, then settled back down. The escape rocket on the tip, designed to break free once it reached space, shot off and instantly opened the parachutes that were meant to help it land on reentry. It played atmospheric tug-of-war with itself for a few moments, burning fuel while its chute prevented any real ascent, then fell into the sea.

Postlaunch analysis blamed a communication issue between the Atlas rocket—originally configured to carry warheads—and its new satellite cargo. This caused a slight delay in shutoff signals for the engines of the various stages, launching the escape rocket too early. An almost identical issue of structural incompatibility between a Mercury capsule and an Atlas rocket had occurred a few months earlier. These "interface failures" were breakdowns, not of any given component, but of the integration between them. They were the Space Race equivalent of our Task Force's "blinks," and they arose from a similar lack of information sharing.

Originally established as a research organization, NASA was a constellation of teams conducting largely independent work farmed out by administrators. This structure facilitated the innovation capacity of small groups, and many scientists felt comfortable performing experiments in the context of specialized departments akin to those in a university. The interface failures, however, exposed an inherent problem: independent small groups were very effective at exploratory work, but trouble erupted when the projects of the disparate teams had to be integrated into a vehicle going into orbit.

Without fluid integration, nothing would work. The massive forces and tremendous speeds involved in rocket travel led to unpredictable vibrations throughout the whole vehicle, creating systemic issues that transcended the individual fiefdoms of the teams developing the components, and the separate disciplines of the structural engineer, the propulsion expert, the electrical engineer, and other team members. There was also electromagnetic interference: never before had so much digital hardware been crammed so tightly into such a machine, and the signals from different computers often interfered with one another. And then there was gravity: on Earth, dust, fluids, and other contaminants fall to the bottom of vehicles, but in space these elements float freely; if a single floating metal particle happened to touch two adjacent wires simultaneously, a short circuit could cause a system-wide failure. The rocket's computers, body, and electrical systems might have worked perfectly in isolation, but under the interdependent stressors of space travel, they broke down.

Given these failures, in 1962 NASA leadership had doubts about the feasibility of Kennedy's goal. "Most of us in the Space Task Group thought [Kennedy] was daft," recalled a NASA executive. "I mean, we didn't think we could do it. We didn't refuse to accept the challenge, but God, we didn't know how to do [Earth] orbit determination, much less project orbits to the Moon."

Scientists would have to rethink the basic assumptions of engineering. "How do you get liquid out of a tank at zero-G?" one engineer observed. "Everybody said, 'oh, what's so hard about that? You just pressurize it.' Pressurize it, my ass. The pressure exerts on everything, and the damn liquid is just floating around. It's liable to be in globs someplace in the tank, and you don't even know where it is in the tank."*

No one knew whether the lunar surface would be able to support the weight of humans, let alone a spacecraft. They did not know how much radiation would be encountered on the voyage between Earth and the moon, which had the potential to render the entire project moot. Fuel cell technology, which would become a staple of space travel, had not been heard of in 1960. And these were just the building blocks.

This kind of fundamental invention and discovery is usually tackled

---

*This is now a fundamental of zero-G. You use a bladder or capillary action. But, as the official put it, "we didn't know that in 1958 and '59."

by small teams, and only later expanded at scale: think of the Wright brothers or Gottlieb Daimler and his partner Wilhelm Maybach or Alexander Graham Bell and Thomas Watson. But NASA did not have the luxury of starting small. It had to develop and perfect all of these individual technologies simultaneously. Like our Task Force in 2004, and so many other organizations struggling to keep pace today, NASA found itself thrust into a complex environment, and would have to find a way to exploit the innovative abilities of a small team at the scale of a large organization.

To put a man on the moon, the Apollo program would eventually employ 300,000 individuals working for 20,000 contractors and 200 universities in 80 countries, at a cost of $19 billion. The old management model was not built to integrate discovery and development at this scale. As Stephen B. Johnson writes in *The Secret of Apollo*, "The switch from research to development required strict attention to thousands of details. Properly building and integrating thousands of components was not an academic problem but an organizational issue." NASA would have to link its teams together by disregarding the "need to know" paradigm and widely broadcasting information.

In 1963, NASA brought in George Mueller to build the managerial foundation of the Apollo program, and he brought a sea of organizational change. His vision for NASA was that of a single interconnected mind—an emergent intelligence like the "joint cognition" that defines extraordinary teams. As NASA director Wernher von Braun framed it, Mueller brought the perspective of an electrical engineer who aspired to create a managerial "nervous system," whereas von Braun, a mechanical engineer, saw organizations as reductionist contraptions.

Mueller threw out the old org charts and required managers and engineers, who were used to operating in the confines of their own silos, to communicate daily with their functional counterparts at other field centers and on other teams. Gone were the tidy, MECE-like organizational divisions. As described by Stephen Johnson, this "wreaked havoc at NASA headquarters . . . [it] converted NASA engineers who monitored specific hardware projects into executive managers responsible for policy, administration, and finance. For several months after the change, headquarters was in turmoil as the staff learned to become executives." People complained about the "almost iron-like discipline of organizational communication." Gone were the days when they could attack their own problems in isolation. Von Braun and other senior administrators protested.

Previously NASA headquarters would collect data from field centers each month and have a handful of managers check for inconsistencies. Mueller insisted on daily analyses and quick data exchange. All data were on display in a central control room that had links with automated displays to Apollo field centers. These rooms buzzed with activity, constantly receiving updates from contractors and teams and in turn providing information to them. It was the Internet before the Internet: information was updated and shared widely and instantly. As the utility of this information became evident, more and more engineers who were initially opposed started to come around.

Administrators built a "teleservices network" to connect project control rooms with hard copy and computer data and provide the ability to hold teleconferences involving the various laboratories, manufacturing centers, and test sites. NASA engineering talent was temporarily redirected from building rockets to designing an enormous set of radio "loops" that allowed teams to communicate with one another fluidly. "I think we had 250 channels [on which people could talk] in Complex 39," one official at the Kennedy Space Center recalled. "You could tune into North American 2, and you'd be listening to the guys working the engine. If there was a problem there, you could hear how they were handling the problem." At launch time, every team was put on the same loop. "You got instantaneous communication up and down," the official marveled. "[It was] probably one of the biggest loops ever put together . . . instantaneous communication, instantaneous transmission of knowledge."

NASA's approach to outside contractors also changed. NASA had always preferred doing things "in house"—the complex interaction of parts meant that subcomponents farmed out to contractors not privy to the full context were likely to create problems when integrated. Von Braun observed, "You cannot simply write a contract on a stage of the Saturn V and let the contractors go." Often NASA employees would take apart and rebuild everything contractors sent them. But to get a man to the moon, NASA needed expertise and capacity beyond that offered by its own staff.

The solution was to bring contractors in-house. In place of a maze of silos and protocols legislating who could know what, von Braun created two states: in and out. Those who were in had to embrace and understand the Apollo project in its entirety. Specialists continued to do specialized work, but they needed an understanding of the project as a whole, even if establishing that understanding took time away from other duties and was, in some ways, "inefficient." NASA leadership understood that, when creating an interactive product, confining specialists to a silo was stupid: high-level success depended on low-level inefficiencies.

An administrator recounted the collaboration with one contractor: "The reason that it [eventually] worked and that we got it ready on schedule was because we had everybody in that room that we needed to make a decision . . . It got to a point where we could identify a problem in the morning and by the close of business we could solve it, get the money allocated, get the decisions made, and get things working."

What Mueller instituted was known as "systems engineering" or "systems management," an approach built on the foundation of "systems thinking." This approach, contrary to reductionism, believes that one cannot understand a *part* of a system without having at least a rudimentary understanding of the whole. It was the organizational manifestation of this insight that imbued NASA with the adaptive, emergent intelligence it needed to put a man on the moon.

In the two years after Mueller was brought on, Apollo transformed from a group of loosely organized research teams into a tightly run development organization. Even the engineers most ardently opposed to systems management found that many technical problems could be solved only by sharing information. As von Braun put it, "The real mechanism that makes [NASA] 'tick,' is . . . a continuous cross-feed between the right and left side of the house." In half a decade, a space program that had once been a national embarrassment became the best in the world.

LAUNCH TOWER OF BABEL

On the other side of the ocean, ELDO had also started out with similarly grand aspirations. Established soon after the European Coal and Steel

Community—the predecessor of the EU—it represented unity between countries that had nearly destroyed one another twice in fifty years. The initiative would encourage cooperation between nations, and Western European businesses, governments, and militaries would all gain technical expertise and credibility if the mission succeeded and put objects in orbit.

In 1961 European technology and expertise were on par with those of the United States. The Germans had been the first to develop military rockets; the United Kingdom had a successful program of developing air-to-surface, surface-to-air, air-to-air, and ship-to-air weapons; Italy, France, Belgium, and the Netherlands also brought significant resources to bear. But ELDO teams worked independently, users and manufacturers communicated rarely, and each nation assumed control of a different stage of the rocket: the United Kingdom produced the booster, France the second stage, Germany the third, while Italy made the satellite test vehicle. There was no single location for project documentation, no system for providing access to other groups' documentation, and no specifications for what documentation each entity should produce. Each country managed its part through its own national organization, and each sought to maximize its own economic advantages, which often meant withholding information. Contractors reported only to their national governments. In 1968, NASA's international programs chief described the ELDO members' "half-hearted and mutually-suspicious character of participation." This competitiveness might have been a boon to a less interdependent endeavor, but it was problematic for something as linked and complex as spaceflight.

ELDO's first launch failed because it used the wrong kind of bolts to connect the French and German stages. The next collapsed because of differences between connecting rings used by the Germans and Italians. The next attempt, in August 1967, made headway when the second stage successfully separated, but once free of the booster, it did not fire. An electrical ground fault had de-energized a relay in the first stage when the rocket was sitting on the launch pad, and this led to a failure of the second-stage sequencer. Four months later, another electrical interface issue brought down the next launch. In July 1969—a few weeks prior to the American moon launch—an interface error ignited a rocket's self-destruct system while it sat on the launch pad. ELDO's final launch attempt, in

November 1971, blew up ninety seconds into flight. The organization was dissolved three years later.

Internal and external analyses later concluded that all these problems stemmed from shortfalls of organizational communication—devastating "interface failures," or blinks. In his 1964 book *The American Challenge*, French journalist Jean-Jacques Servan-Schreiber argued that Europe's lag behind the United States in the Space Race was not a question of money but of *"methods of organization* above all . . . this is not a matter of 'brain power' in the traditional sense of the term, but of organization, education, and training." On the other side of the pond, Secretary of Defense Robert McNamara concurred that Europe suffered from a managerial deficit: "The technological gap was misnamed." It was a space age Tower of Babel: the countries' inability to speak to one another obstructed their joint effort to reach the heavens.

Like Taylor's world's fair exhibition in Paris, the success of *Apollo 11* and the concurrent shambles of *Europa I* shone a spotlight on the role of management in large-scale endeavors. Congress held hearings to study NASA's managerial secrets. The systems management put in place at NASA became a core process of aerospace research and development, essential to everything from the International Space Station to the Boeing 777.

NASA's success illustrated a number of profound organizational insights. Most important, it showed that in a domain characterized by interdependence and unknowns, contextual understanding is key; whatever efficiency is gained through silos is outweighed by the costs of "interface failures." It also proved that the cognitive "oneness"—the emergent intelligence—that we have studied in small teams *can* be achieved in larger organizations, if such organizations are willing to commit to the disciplined, deliberate sharing of information. This runs counter to the standard "need-to-know" mind-set.

NASA, at the vanguard of new technologies, was confronting complexity ahead of its time. A half century later, almost every organizational actor has become ensnared in the wayward swirl of complexity.

Some of NASA's innovations sound incredibly simple: take off the blinders and have people talk to each other. The basic concept requires only the *un*learning of fundamentalist approaches to efficiency, but the implementation requires constant maintenance: making sure that everyone has constantly updated, holistic awareness became a full-time job for many, and required commitment and time from everyone.

In fact, even for NASA, as historian Howard McCurdy has noted, "maintaining . . . organizational culture as practiced by the first generation of employees turned out to be most difficult to do." After Apollo, its well-integrated system of units slid into a competitive set of independent entities; its open communications calcified with bureaucracy. One employee characterized NASA in 1988 as "the Post Office and the IRS gone to space." The investigation after the *Challenger* disaster had especially harsh words for NASA's organizational practices, but the subsequent, efficiency-focused program ushered in during the 1990s, called "Faster, Better, Cheaper" (FBC), took NASA further down the path of carelessness, reducing the "inefficient" ties that had defined the Apollo approach. One famous interface failure occurred when a communication gap between two working groups resulted in the loss of the $125 million *Mars Climate Orbiter*: one system was built for metric measurements, one for imperial measurements. As McCurdy notes, FBC was the antithesis of systems engineering. Systems engineering was "formal, elaborate and expensive." It was inefficient. But it worked.

SETS AND SYSTEMS

Systems thinking has been used to understand everything from the functioning of a city to the internal dynamics of a skin cell, and plays a key role in deciphering interdependence.

Consider a doctor and her education. Doctors come in many varieties—pediatricians, ENTs, radiologists, etc.—yet while in medical school, all undergo the same rigorous overview of the way the human body works. It doesn't matter if, as a hand surgeon, you spend the rest of your life looking only at palms, wrists, and fingers. Because the human body is not a *set* of *independent* elements, but a *system* of *interdependent* elements, you need to understand how the metabolism of sugar works in order to understand how diabetes can cause the death of tissue in fingers, just as you need to understand how repeated pressure on the median nerve can lead to carpal tunnel syndrome. When we go under the knife, we want to know that the person holding it has a holistic understanding of the fundamentals of the body, not simply a Tayloresque instruction card.

A checklist is inadequate for surgery because of the quintillions of possibilities that interdependence generates. We would never call the rigors of medical school "easy," but it is more feasible to spend seven years learning about the complex cause-and-effect relationships in the human body than to attempt to record and memorize every possible event that can befall bodies.

This is the difference between "education" and "training." Medical school is education, first aid is training. Education requires fundamental understanding, which can be used to grasp and respond to a nearly infinite variety of threats; training involves singular actions, which are useful only against anticipated challenges. Education is resilient, training is robust.

Coleman Ruiz talks about BUD/S "taking individual performance out of the lexicon on day one." This emphasis on *group success* spurs cooperation, and fosters trust and purpose. But people cooperate only if they can *see* the interdependent reality of their environment. Trainees learn to work together during BUD/S "surf passage" only because they can see that one individual's failure will result in a flipped boat, and if that happens, the whole group will suffer.

In our Task Force, our specialized units had little insight into how their peer teams functioned, or how all the pieces fit together. Everyone knew the boat kept flipping, but without a clear view of what everyone else was doing, nobody could see why or how to change it.

Like NASA, we needed to promote at the organizational level the kind of knowledge pool that arises within small teams. This was the key to creating a "team of teams."

We did not want all the teams to become generalists—SEALs are better at what they do than intel analysts would be and vice versa. Diverse specialized abilities are essential. We wanted to fuse generalized *awareness* with specialized *expertise*. Our entire force needed to share a fundamental, holistic understanding of the operating environment and of our own organization, and we also needed to preserve each team's distinct skill sets. We dubbed this goal—this state of emergent, adaptive organizational intelligence—*shared consciousness*, and it became the cornerstone of our transformation.

RECAP

♦ Like NASA before it, our Task Force found itself confronted with a *complex problem that demanded a systems approach to its solution; because of the interdependence of the operating environment, both organizations would need members to understand the entire, interconnected system, not just individual MECE boxes on the org chart.*

♦ Harnessing the capability of the entire geographically dispersed organization meant *information sharing had to achieve levels of transparency entirely new* to both organizations.

♦ In traditional organizations, this constitutes culture change that does not come easily. It *demanded a disciplined effort to create shared consciousness.*

CHAPTER 8

BRAINS OUT OF THE FOOTLOCKER

I n July 2004, shortly before the El Amel sewage plant bombing, we had left the battered buildings at Baghdad International Airport, and moved our new headquarters to Balad Airbase, sixty-four miles north of the capital. Twenty years earlier, Soviet-built MiG-21s had screeched on and off Balad's tarmac to strafe Iranian troops during the bitter Iran-Iraq War. Later, those same aircraft postured as a threat to General Norman Schwarzkopf's "Hail Mary" juggernaut into southern Iraq in 1991. Now it was the roar of American jet engines that reverberated off the concrete.

The base lay near the lush Tigris River, but in the July heat its grounds were stark brown. Two runways sliced across the center, flanked on one side by administrative and maintenance buildings, and on the other by a smattering of decrepit concrete shelters. The Task Force occupied a special high-security compound abutting aircraft taxiways that gave us easy access to planes and helicopters. The compound consisted of prefab trailers, plywood huts, and a hodgepodge of tents clustered in close proximity. Living quarters, workspaces, equipment maintenance, and the mess hall were all nearby. My "commute" to work was an efficient forty-foot walk.

We were given three aging bunkers on the west side of the base, nicknamed "Yugos" after the Yugoslavian contractors who had built the hardened hangars to protect Iraqi combat aircraft. Medicine ball–size holes punched through the roofs testified to their failure against the precision weaponry of coalition aircraft during the 2003 invasion. The bunkers were the size of large circus tents, constructed of two thick layers of concrete separated by about a foot of sand. Long, low, arched garage door openings spanned each end. They were beige like the sandstone buildings around the compound, and the desert around them. Inside, sound reverberated harshly off the concrete. Our Task Force picked one as our headquarters and moved in.

Although the acres of Iraqi equipment destroyed in the invasion and an eternally smoldering garbage dump presented a depressing picture, for us Balad was a beautiful opportunity: a place to build something entirely new, the physical manifestation of the organizational system that might tilt the odds in our favor. One of my father's favorite admonitions, applied playfully when I did something dumb, was borrowed from an old sergeant: "Put your brains in your footlocker, I'll do the thinking around here." Our imperative was the opposite: at Balad we meant to get all the brains out of all the footlockers and working together.

We had analyzed the problem and we knew what needed to change. To become effective against AQI, we would have to dismantle our deeply rooted system of secrecy, clearances, and interforce rivalries, and in its place establish an environment of such transparency that every man and woman in our command understood his or her role within the complex system that represented *all* of our undertakings. Everyone needed to be intimately familiar with every branch of the organization, and personally invested in the outcome. This ran against the grain of the distinct specializations that we had spent the last century developing. Our hope was that—as with BUD/S, CRM, and NASA—sharing information would help build relationships and the two together would kindle a new, coherent, adaptive entity that could win the fight.

It was an enormous and risky experiment. At Balad, we set about building the lab.

Traditionally, the physical layout of military installations mirrored and supported reductionist efficiency. The Pentagon's unusual shape was originally chosen to fit into a specific piece of land below Arlington Cemetery, and though the project was relocated (to avoid desecrating Pierre L'Enfant's grand plan for America's capital) the five-sided design was maintained; it is supposedly possible to move between any two locations in the building in less than seven minutes. Today its seventeen and one-half miles of corridors still follow a logical and quickly grasped pattern, but thousands of doors on those corridors are now "access protected"—a euphemism for locked. Even if your clearance level gains you entry, you may find yourself in a further submaze of locked inner doors and access points. Offices are separate and sterile, and despite being in the same building as twenty-eight thousand others, people work largely in small, discrete groups—or alone. Built at the start of World War II to pull the military services, previously spread across separate office buildings in Washington, D.C., into cooperative proximity, the building has seen its original intent eroded. It is now a building in which individuals toil independently in accordance with top-down, need-to-know reductionist planning. They might as well be spread around the globe.

At our U.S. headquarters at Fort Bragg, a similar physical paradigm prevailed for the first twenty years of the organization's history. Built in the early 1980s with an emphasis on security, the windowless buildings were divided into hallways of small offices further segmented by cubicles. Few common areas existed to foster social interaction, and strict limitations on outside visitors further separated the Task Force from other organizations on the sprawling installation at Fort Bragg.

In the private sector also, physical space has for a century been used to facilitate and enforce efficiency and specialization. Along with factory assembly lines, the architectural frames of white-collar work have evolved to maximize efficiency. In the nineteenth century, "countinghouses" where partners and clerks worked side by side at identical rolltop desks began to disappear, replaced by subdivided offices. As the volume of clerical and administrative work grew, white-collar professions began importing the reductionist ideal of specialization from the factory floor. Management historian Alfred Chandler observed that the role of the merchant, which once embraced "exporter, wholesaler, importer, retailer, shipowner, banker and insurer," split—like Adam Smith's pin production—into multiple specialized businesses in the late 1800s.

Years later, in what Chandler referred to as "the Managerial Revolution," the specialized businesses were reunited when they merged into large, vertically integrated corporations with dozens of departments and hundreds of offices. Many functions were consolidated under centrally managed entities, instead of the sea of small actors responding independently to the forces of the market (Chandler dubbed this force "the visible hand" in contrast to Adam Smith's description of market forces as "the invisible hand"). The number of people working in "professional services" rose from 750,000 in 1860 to 2.16 million in 1890, and to 4.42

million by 1910, but the number of firms that employed them dropped: 4,000 firms collapsed into 257 combinations between 1897 and 1904. But consolidation did not signal a return to the shared space and understanding of countinghouse culture. Instead, companies went to greater lengths to preserve stratification.

New technologies enabled the construction of larger, taller buildings to house the increasingly complicated strata of the workplace. The "office building" took shape under the hand of architects such as Louis Sullivan, who envisioned structures composed of independent, standardized cells, which he likened to the hexagonal building blocks of beehives: discrete, MECE units, not to be merged.* Dictaphones and pneumatic tubes enabled discrete, directed communications at a distance without the messy inefficiencies of the countinghouse. Executives moved to separate rooms, then to plush suites, and finally to different floors to separate them from the "pools" of stenographers toiling away at desks arranged in grids, silent but for the clacking of typewriter keys. The "corner office" where a manager could separate himself from the rest of the workforce became a status symbol. (During the 2008 financial crisis it emerged that many executives commute to their offices in private elevators, further minimizing any potential interaction with employees.) It was in the early 1900s that the term "ladder" became common parlance for the corporate hierarchy.

These buildings—the forebears of the Pentagon and the glass slabs that make up today's urban skylines—were designed for the efficient flow of paperwork. This flow was often quite literally an assembly line. As a clerical worker explained in 1958,

> The girl at the end . . . opens and sorts mail. The next girl is our doer. She does whatever the mail calls for—a cancellation, a receipt or whatnot. Then I check the papers she hands me, and add whatever notations are necessary before I pass them along for copying to the first girl on my left, our team's typist. She, in turn, gives the whole batch to the last girl, our assembler, who puts the papers together in proper order and forwards them, maybe to another department, or to central filing, or possibly back to a policyholder.

---

*In fact, Sullivan coined the famous phrase "form follows function" in his 1896 article "The Tall Office Building Artistically Considered."

The goal, as in factories, was for processes designed by management to be executed in as efficient and specialized a way as possible. Management theorist R. H. Goodell noticed how visitors passing in a corridor distracted clerical workers. By turning their desks away from the door and facing them toward a blank wall, he could reduce disruption and at the same time play on the uneasy feeling that, at any given moment, their supervisor might be looking over their shoulders—both increased productivity.

How we organize physical space says a lot about how we think people behave; but how people behave is often a by-product of how we set up physical space. At Balad we needed a space that facilitated not the orderly, machinelike flow of paperwork, but the erratic, networked flow of ideas—an architecture designed not for separation, but for the merging of worlds. We weren't the only ones to be trying this—there was a growing movement in the private sector to organize offices for better cooperation, too.

Firms that value innovation and creativity have spent a lot of time searching for ways to inject interactivity into work environments. In 1941 Bell Labs famously broke with tradition, hiring Skidmore, Owings & Merrill to design a campus whose spaces promoted interaction: to move from an office to a lab, for example, employees had to walk through the cafeteria where they would bump into people. The hope was that such casual interactions with peers, managers, and even custodial staff might prompt unexpected insights. In the 1970s even staid IBM experimented with early "nonterritorial" offices where engineers could come in, grab their materials, and sit anywhere in the open plan space arranged to facilitate "serendipitous encounters" with team members. As with NASA, these changes were not initially welcomed, but grew in popularity. "I was skeptical before, but I'd hate to go back to a closed office now," said one engineer. Another was more succinct: "Don't fence me in again." In Silicon Valley, Google, Facebook, and other titans, as well as countless start-ups, use open plans that put different teams and different rungs of management in the same space.

When former mayor Michael Bloomberg moved into New York's City Hall, he turned down the building's fancy mayoral suites, and instead had the Board of Estimate Hearing Room—one of the most lavish ceremonial spaces in the historic landmark—converted into a "bullpen."* He

---

*In the fall of 2008, then–Major General Mike Flynn (my intelligence officer in four different assignments: XVIIIth Airborne Corps, the Task Force, the Joint Staff in the

filled the space with hundreds of cubicles—including one for himself—to maximize the cross-pollination of ideas. He had test-driven this model at Bloomberg LP, the financial and media conglomerate that made him a billionaire.

Bloomberg says, "I've always believed that management's ability to influence work habits through edict is limited. Ordering something gets it done, perhaps. When you turn your back, though, employees tend to regress to the same old ways. Physical plant, however, has a much more lasting impact . . . I issue proclamations telling everyone to work together, but it's the lack of walls that really makes them do it."

Bloomberg's hierarchy-flattening, silo-merging bullpen, his sociable workplace bagel bars, and his zero tolerance policy for executive dining rooms or reserved parking spots were inspired in part by his first employer, the investment bank Salomon Brothers: "Anyone could come up to [the CEO's] desk, anytime. He was on a first-name basis with as many people at the bottom of the corporate ladder as at the top."

This is not just about symbolic egalitarianism. The cultivated chaos of the open office encourages interaction between employees distant from one another on the org chart. Putting himself in the middle of it kept Bloomberg's finger on the pulse of the organization. "If you lock yourself in your office, I don't think you can be a good executive," he says. "It makes absolutely no sense to me." If his own mayoral career has been any measure, he is right: according to Bill Keller, the Pulitzer Prize–winning *New York Times* correspondent, "The great urban contraption that is New York City government has probably never been so well run."

The appreciation for serendipitous encounters embodied by Bloomberg's bullpen and Silicon Valley's open plans is a way of saying, "We don't know what connections and conversations will prove valuable."

At Balad, we attempted something similar: engineers gutted the inside of the main bunker. We burned the decrepit mess of debris, old partitions, and Soviet-era war matériel that had filled it, and we erected an open plan plywood endoskeleton. We ran all of our operations out of the

---

Pentagon, and finally at ISAF in Afghanistan) and I visited the Bloomberg bullpen after returning from Iraq. Although we had evolved the Task Force's physical and cultural ecosystem independently, we were struck by the similarity to what he used to run New York City and what we used to fight a complex war.

Joint Operations Center (JOC)—an expansive central space similar to Bloomberg's bullpen.

A wall of screens at the front of the space showed live updates of ongoing operations: video feeds of small skirmishes or ongoing raids, JOC log entries recording the outcomes of successful captures or "friendly" casualties, maps of our gains and losses in different regions of the country. Immediately in front of the screens, we arranged portable tables in a large U-shaped configuration where the Task Force commander and key leaders all sat, able to see and communicate with one another easily as they worked. Radiating outward were banks of long tables and chairs for the myriad functions of intelligence, air and artillery support, medical evacuation, liaison officers, and all the other capabilities germane to our operations.

Anyone in the room—regardless of their position in the org charts' silos and tiers—could glance up at the screens and know instantly about major factors affecting our mission at that moment. Personnel were placed strategically throughout the space, depending on their function—those with access to real-time information critical to ongoing operations were closer to the center of the room, those with a longer-term focus were on the fringes, so they could focus on other work. Any of them, however, could walk freely across the room for quick face-to-face coordination. With the touch of a button on the microphone, everyone's attention could be captured simultaneously.

We hoped the new architecture would elicit the emergent intelligence we believed resided in the force as a whole and give our teams a comprehensive view of the entire system. It was not enough to know just their own part (or that of one person they bumped into in the cafeteria).

In 2004 we had sixty or so people sitting in the space—intelligence analysts, operations officers, military liaisons, intelligence surveillance and reconnaissance (ISR) operators, airpower controllers, DOD lawyers, and medical staff. To eliminate one potential excuse for not collaborating, we designated the entire area a top secret security space. Almost any document or conversation relevant to our operations, many of them very sensitive,* could be discussed and debated on the open floor. It was an unprecedented move.

---

*Extremely sensitive activities such as management of intelligence agents, and personnel actions within our force, were appropriately conducted in more limited settings.

I had a small private office, but rarely used it. Instead, I worked from a space adjacent to the JOC, which we called the Situational Awareness Room (SAR), at the head of another U-shaped table. In this smaller replica of the JOC, I would work alongside my key staff (e.g., intelligence, operations, legal), and with the senior representatives in our force from multiple interagency organizations. In the JOC, the focus was Iraq. In the SAR, it was global. Here we created the network to overlay Al Qaeda's international network. My intelligence director, operations director, and senior enlisted adviser sat beside me and could see and hear everything I did.

LEARNING FROM THE CUBICLE'S FAILED REVOLUTION

Our new physical plant provided structure for our transformation, but we knew it was not enough. A new layout with an old culture can deliver the worst of both worlds: countless managers, eager to adopt the new trend that promises innovation but reluctant to abandon the org chart, have done away with cubicles only to produce a noisier, more distracting environment that is neither efficient nor effective.

The cubicle itself is a good example of management space gone wrong. Originally created by the visionary inventor Robert Propst to free workers from isolation, the cubicle has become a symbol of the impersonal culture it aimed to reform. The "Action Office II" was supposed to be customizable and reconfigurable for privacy, but also for cooperation, promoting interaction. It was designed to be arranged in organic clusters, reflecting a new conception of the office as an interconnected whole.

Put into production by Herman Miller in 1967, Propst's invention was immediately perceived as transformative. The *New York Post* ran an article about it titled "Revolution Hits the Office," which argued that the days of "the completely enclosed 'boxes' in which the bosses isolate themselves behind monster mahogany status symbols and the inhuman row upon rigid row of steel desks with their clumsy drawers at which you sit all day" would soon draw to a close. "The success of the concept seems assured," the article concluded.

Anyone who has set foot in a corporate office in the past thirty years can attest that the product was indeed successful, but the concept of an organic workplace defined by freedom and intellect was not. Instead, managers discovered that they could use the Action Office to squeeze more people into smaller spaces, using the same unforgiving grid that steno pools had featured since the turn of the century. The cubicle's very adaptability allowed it to become, in the rueful words of one Herman Miller employee, "the inevitable expression of a concept which views people as links in a corporate system for handling paper, or as input-output organisms whose 'efficiency' has been a matter of nervous concern the past half-century . . . the [Action Office] is admirable for planners looking for ways of cramming a maximum number of bodies."

Today, a staggering 93 percent of those who work in cubicles say that they would prefer a different workspace. As Propst put it two years before his death, reflecting on his greatest legacy, "The dark side of this is that not all organizations are intelligent and progressive. Lots are run by crass people who can take the same equipment and create hellholes. They make little bitty cubicles and stuff people in them. Barren, rat-hole places . . . I never had any illusions that this is a perfect world."

The structure and symbolism of the Task Force's new nonhierarchical space was critical, but our organization would not be reborn by just moving furniture around. We needed to renovate our organizational culture as well.

Cultures, however, are more resistant to designed change than bricks and mortar. Shared consciousness demanded the adoption of extreme transparency throughout our force and with our partner forces. This was not "transparency" in the sense that it is usually used in the business world, a synonym for personal candidness. We needed transparency that provided every team with an unobstructed, constantly up-to-date view of the rest of the organization. It is the type of transparency that those of us raised in the comfort of bureaucratic silos find uncomfortable. But it would be absolutely critical to our ability to coalesce and succeed as a team of teams.

Some pieces were simple: my command team and I added people to the "cc" line of e-mails whenever it seemed that even the second- or third-order consequence of the operation discussed *might* impact them. We had to acknowledge that we often could not predict who would and would not benefit from access to certain information. We took almost all phone calls on speakerphone—that included me, the commander in charge of our nation's most sensitive forces. This could make people uncomfortable, sometimes intensely so. But never once in Iraq did I see it hurt us nearly as much as it helped. We were trying to normalize sharing among people used to the opposite. Our standing guidance was "Share information until you're afraid it's illegal."

THE O&I

The most critical element of our transformation—the heart muscle of the organism we sought to create and the pulse by which it would live or die—was our Operations and Intelligence brief. The O&I, as it was commonly called, is standard military practice: a regular meeting held by the leadership of a given command to integrate everything the command is doing with everything it knows.

When I assumed command in 2003, the O&I was a relatively small video teleconference between our rear headquarters at Fort Bragg, a few D.C. offices, and our biggest bases in Iraq and Afghanistan. Quickly, though, that audience grew. We urged everyone from regional embassies to FBI field offices to install secure communications so that they could participate in our discussions.

When people think of cutting-edge military hardware, they usually picture weaponry, not a bulked-up version of Skype, but that was our main technological hurdle and point of investment for several months. We knew that forging the neural network that would facilitate our emergent analysis of complex problems was vital for our long-term success, so we designed prepackaged communication bundles that our teams could take into the field, wherever they were in the world. Like NASA, we invested in bandwidth to enable us to reach every component of our force and our partners, from austere bases near the Syrian border to CIA headquarters at Langley, Virginia. Satellite dishes, from small to huge, connected the force. Secure video teleconferences, chat rooms, a Web portal, and e-mail became key arteries of our circulatory system. Technically it was complex, financially it was expensive, but we were trying to build a culture of sharing: any member of the Task Force, and any of the partners we invited, could eventually dial in to the O&I securely from their laptops and listen through their headphones.

As the scope of the Task Force's global activities increased and we integrated more players into our network, the O&I became a bona fide institution. The meeting ran six days a week and was *never* canceled. We conducted it by video teleconference at 9:00 a.m. Eastern Standard Time. This made it a convenient start to the workday for the Washington-based departments and agencies we were trying to integrate ever more tightly into our operations. In Iraq, the meeting kicked off at 4:00 p.m., giving operators time to rise in the late morning, train, prepare, participate in the O&I, and then get ready for the raids and fights that would take them from dusk until dawn. That synchronized cycle—what we called our "battle rhythm"—was fueled by the O&I, which pumped information and context throughout our Task Force.

There were real risks in doing this. Opening a top secret video teleconference to a wide community exposed us to potential leaks—after all, the information we were discussing was secret for a reason. Also, broadcasting unfiltered accounts of our successes and failures risked misinterpretation of complex, in-process endeavors or statements being taken out of context. But I had no interest in, and we had no time for, painting a rosy picture of what was in reality a hellish scene. Anyone who wanted to beat us at a game of bureaucratic politics would have all the ammunition they needed, but that wasn't the fight we were focused on.

PUSHBACK

When we set up our new SAR at Balad, we put extra seats at the horseshoe table for the partner agencies that we hoped would come to augment our Task Force. In the early days, only the CIA liaison's seat was occupied. Intuitively, we knew that if we could generate enough success on the battlefield, others would want to participate. The problem was how to get their participation up front. We needed to bind everybody into a single enterprise, but we had no explicit authority to do so.

This was true even for the military forces that made up the operational arm of the Task Force. Throughout its history, the Task Force commander has led operators from each of the various branches of the armed services, but each of these subunits also had administrative commanders within their own branch of service. The Task Force commander, for example, did not oversee the selection of personnel, training, or maintenance of the Ranger regiment. That was the regimental commander's job, and in executing it he was answerable up a distinctly different chain of command to Army Special Operations Command and the Department of the Army. It is an awkward system. I would joke that commanding the Task Force is a bit like being a Formula 1 driver: you get to drive an incredible car, but you don't own it, and you don't pay for the repairs when you break something. Naturally, there is a bit of tension between the car's owners and the man driving it through a war zone every day.

Despite the difficulties, we placed SEALs alongside Army Special Forces alongside Army Rangers alongside intelligence analysts whose prior exposure to our operators had been limited to complaints about the speed and quality of the analyses they provided. Individual and organizational arrogance manifested itself in subtle ways as people tried to assert or maintain their preeminence. Ultimately, however, the press of the fight demanded expedience, and expedience demanded a meritocracy. If an individual or unit produced good intelligence, reliable coordination, or accurate and timely warnings, they rose in relevance and respect. Legacy accomplishments or bluster might work for a while, but eventually people either produced or faded in importance. No one wanted to hear what you'd done in the last war.

However dysfunctional the internal competition within our command, it was dwarfed by that between our organization and the CIA, NSA, FBI, and other external agencies. Much as von Braun found with NASA contractors, we realized that no group could be useful if it did not understand the full context. We could not simply ship our intelligence requirements out to these agencies and expect them to realize all the intricacies of what we wanted and needed. They had to sit with us, to understand exactly what was happening on the ground. We hoped that eventually they would reciprocate by giving us similar insights into how the war looked from their offices.

When filled, the SAR felt cramped and occasionally very loud. Many of the people sent to work with us found the environment distracting, or were uncomfortable in the participatory atmosphere. For bureaucrats who had built careers on discretion and never putting a toe out of line by oversharing, our way of working was anathema. One partner agency offered the same response every day for the first year of our experiment: "Nothing new to report on our end."

Just as our individual teams benefited from a shared sense of purpose that extended from the tactical situation on the ground to larger strategic goals, the elements of Task Force would need to share both an up-to-the-minute awareness of the battlefield and a belief that we were all fighting the same war, based on the same principles and with the same objectives. We hoped to lay the foundations for both, as NASA had done, by pressing holistic awareness and integration throughout the organization as a whole. If everyone had the same playbook, maybe we would get better at the game.

The critical first step was to share our own information widely and be generous with our own people and resources. From there, we hoped that the human relationships we built through that generosity would carry the day.

Information sharing had to include every part of the force. As soon as our operators completed a raid, we would rush the evidence to the nearest outstation, photograph every scrap, and use our new bandwidth to feed the data to imagery analysts, linguists, and other subject matter experts. It was choppy and unpolished, but instantaneous—no more trash bags and Post-it notes piling up in a closet. Moreover, as with our cc's and our speakerphone, we distributed our intelligence and analysis widely, without preconditions. This struck many as naïve. But, as the old adage goes, "knowledge is power," and we were throwing that power to the wind. Our thinking was that the value of this information and the power that came with it were greater the more it was shared.

SUCCESS

By 2005 at least one of our hypotheses had been confirmed: because the intelligence agencies got faster and more robust intelligence from the Task Force than from any other source, they dramatically increased their participation. Our process began to develop its own gravitational pull as more and more groups recognized what the speed and transparency we had put in place could offer. Our forces were in daily contact with Al Qaeda, the nation's highest counterterrorism priority, and we were offering to share whatever we were learning.

Many of the Joint Interagency Task Forces (JIATFs) we had formed in Iraq and Afghanistan grew as partner agencies began deploying more young analysts to serve "downrange" and gain access to the intelligence our operators and sources were producing. A Defense Intelligence Agency (DIA) analyst could walk from the JIATF over to our Temporary

Screening Facility, where we housed Al Qaeda detainees, and contribute questions to, or observe the interviews of, a detainee. The analyst could write a firsthand report for his headquarters with the most current information from the counterterrorism battlefield. That was good for the analyst, and good for the analyst's organization. It might also generate a response from the analyst's parent organization that could be valuable to us the next day, or be connected to another report from somewhere else in the world. One individual, properly empowered, became a conduit to a larger network that could contribute back into our process. We made sure that our operators interacted with the analysts; one Army Special Forces squadron commander mandated that his operators sit with intel analysts, taking notes on how they worked, how they thought, and what kinds of information they found most useful. As he put it, "To win, all of us would need to be knee deep in the fight, all of the time."

In time, people came to appreciate the value of systemic understanding. O&I attendance grew as the quality of the information and interaction grew. Eventually we had seven thousand people attending almost daily for up to two hours. To some management theorists, that sounds like a nightmare of inefficiency, but the information that was shared in the O&I was so rich, so timely, and so pertinent to the fight, no one wanted to miss it.

The O&I also became one of the best leadership tools in my arsenal. Our organization was globally dispersed and included thousands of individuals from organizations not directly under the control of the Task Force. The O&I could not replace a hand on a shoulder, but video could convey a lot of meaning and motivation. Our leadership learned, over time, to use this forum not as a stereotypical military briefing where junior personnel give nicely rehearsed updates and hope for no questions. Instead, it was an interactive discussion. If an individual had a four-minute slot, the "update" portion would be covered in the first sixty seconds, and the remainder of the time would be filled with open-ended conversation between the briefer and senior leadership (and potentially anyone else on the network, if they saw a critical point to be made). Instead of black-and-white lines of questioning ("How many x?"), our dialogue became interactive and broad ("Why are you thinking x?"). The responses to this type of interaction created new insights, deepened the group's understanding of a complex issue, and highlighted the deep levels of understanding of our personnel around the globe. Most important, it allowed all members of the organization to see problems being solved in real time and to understand the perspective of the senior leadership team. This gave them the skills and confidence to *solve their own* similar problems without the need for further guidance or clarification. By having thousands of personnel listen to these daily interactions, we *saved* an incalculable amount of time that was no longer needed to seek clarification or permission.

The fusion of operations and intelligence (O and I) was the essence of the meeting. An imagery analyst could report on recent activity at a location of interest during the meeting (say at 5:00 p.m. Iraqi time), and that house could be raided by Rangers within hours. At the next day's O&I, another analyst could then discuss the chemical makeup of the explosives found in the house's car-bomb workshop. The initial imagery analyst would get the visceral satisfaction that her work had saved lives and that her continued effort was impacting operations directly, not just generating a paper storm in D.C. Our organization was not just "getting smarter" or "doing more" in isolation. Instead, it was *acting* smarter and learning constantly, simultaneously.

The best moments in the O&I were when the briefing touched off a debate between different agencies, or teams, or departments. Perhaps two analytical silos had reached drastically different conclusions based on the same evidence, and we needed to reconcile them and understand why. Perhaps a team in Mosul had seen a tactic, or a group of individuals, eerily reminiscent of what a team in Tikrit had seen last week. The meetings allowed critical information to reach the right ears and eyes. The risk, of course, was that it might reach the wrong ears and eyes as well. The question was how that potential risk stacked up against the benefits.

WHAT ABOUT WIKILEAKS?

On January 5, 2010, a twenty-two-year-old Army specialist walked out of a secure—or supposedly secure—room on Forward Operating Base Hammer, forty miles east of Baghdad, with nearly 400,000 highly classified military reports from the war in Iraq, all saved on CDs he had marked "LADY GAGA." Three days later, he popped the CDs into his work computer and downloaded 91,000 reports on Afghanistan. Over the next several months, he repeated the same stunt, eventually gathering 250,000 classified State Department cables, which he passed on to WikiLeaks. By November, all had been released on the Internet to the global public.

The U.S. government went into convulsions. "This disclosure is not just an attack on America's foreign policy interests," said Secretary of State Hillary Clinton the day after the State Department cables leaked. "It is an attack on the international community." Never before in U.S. history had so much classified material been compromised in one blow. Since then, several similar incidents have unfolded, most notably the even bigger leak perpetrated by contractor Edward Snowden.

An investigation identified the soldier, who by then had been demoted to private first class, as Bradley Manning.* A Fox News op-ed asked with outrage how "all this leaked information was the work of a single 22-year-old enlisted man in the Army." The author was incredulous: "How could one individual gain such access to all that classified material? Clearly we have grossly under-prioritized information security."

Since *The 9/11 Commission Report* famously concluded that the U.S. intelligence community had all the pieces of the puzzle but had failed to put them together and protect the country, the national security community has seen a gradual but undeniable paradigm shift toward greater information sharing. Ten years after September 11, fact finders for the Senate Committee on Homeland Security and Government Affairs reported, "the attacks on 9/11 showed all of us that the Cold War 'need to know' system for managing classified and sensitive information drove a culture of information security that resulted in countless stove-pipes and secretive pockets of the nation's most valuable information." At the same time, the national security apparatus has ballooned in size. As of this writing, 854,000 people hold clearance at the top secret level and a third of them are private contractors. The result is that more secret information is more easily accessible by more people than has ever been the case.

Partly as a result of those changes, a very young soldier with a history of depression and erratic behavior was given access to a trove of secret documents. Stealing and disseminating those documents was as easy as using some elementary code work and a few compact discs.

Should better defenses have been in place to prevent this information from being copied by Manning? Certainly. Should blank CDs be disallowed in a Secure Compartmentalized Information Facility? Obviously.

---

*Upon arrest, Manning was further demoted to private, and has since changed her name to Chelsea.

Should superiors have intervened and prevented Private Manning from deploying to Iraq based on a history of behavioral issues in the Army? Without a doubt. Did Private Manning put lives at risk? Yes. But was it a mistake to design a system that gave privates and specialists access to extensive and valuable data? Absolutely not.

Massive leaks are *not* an inevitable consequence of the current level of information sharing, but even if they were, the benefits vastly outweigh the potential costs. The sharing of information within the U.S. intelligence community since 9/11 has saved many lives and done far more good than the damage from incidents like the Manning and Snowden leaks has done harm. We should not let the fact that the benefits are usually invisible—whereas the leaks make front-page news—blind our assessment. Our Task Force never experienced any serious leaks, but we knowingly ran that risk every time we held our O&I. Our experience was that shared information saved lives on an untold scale.

Brains in a footlocker benefit no one, and taking them out was a critical step. However, achieving teamlike levels of shared consciousness would take more than just sharing information.

RECAP

♦ Shared consciousness in an organization is either *hindered or helped by physical spaces and established processes*. Often, efforts to facilitate Taylor-inspired efficiencies have produced *barriers to information sharing and the kind of systemic understanding we needed to pervade our Task Force.*

♦ Creating transparency and information sharing at the scale we needed required not only a redesign of our physical plant, but also a rethinking of almost every procedure in our organizational culture. The daily O&I briefing lay at the core of our transformation: this pumped information about the entire scope of our operations out to all members of the Task Force and partner agencies, and also offered everyone the chance to contribute.

CHAPTER 9

BEATING THE
PRISONER'S DILEMMA

In one of the most memorable scenes from Ron Howard's 2001 movie *A Beautiful Mind*, the protagonist—mathematician John Nash, played by Russell Crowe—is sitting with three colleagues in a Princeton bar when four women walk through the door. One of them, referred to only as "the blonde," is breathtakingly beautiful. One sultry glance from her over to the mathematicians' table and the men are convinced that she is interested—but who is to be the lucky man? Jokingly, one asks, "Shall we say swords, gentlemen? Pistols at dawn?" Another says, "Every man for himself, gentlemen." Another provides academic context for their face-off, saying, "Recall the lessons of Adam Smith, the father of modern economics . . . ," to which the group replies, together, "In competition, individual ambition serves the common good." But Nash/Crowe, shuffling the stack of papers he brought with him to their night out, doesn't join in. Instead, he adopts the far-off look that moviegoers know signals revelatory contemplation and, as ethereal piano twiddling grows louder in the background, he says quietly, "Adam Smith needs revision."

"If we all go for the blonde," he explains, none will get her—determined to undermine one another, they will, driven by competition, destroy one another's chances. "Then," he says, "we will go for her friends," but scorned by being second choice, they will all give the men the cold shoulder. "What if no one goes for the blonde?" he suggests. If the four men each strike up conversation with one of her four friends, "we don't get in each other's way, and we don't insult the other girls." With a faint grin, he says, "It's the only way we win," then runs out of the bar to spend the night alone recording his epiphany.

This fictionalized episode provides a good introduction to one of the major ideas of game theory: while Adam Smith has led us to believe that, as movie-Nash summarizes it, "the best result comes from everyone in the group doing what's best for himself," movie-Nash adds that there are times when "the best result would come from everyone in the group doing what's best for themselves . . . and the group."

This basic tenet of game theory is also illustrated by the Prisoner's Dilemma. In this famous thought experiment, two criminals—coconspirators—are arrested. They are taken to separate cells and interrogated. Both are offered the same deal: if you stay silent you'll be sentenced to one year; if you rat on your partner you'll go free; but if your partner rats on you, you'll serve two years. From a competitive, personal-interest perspective, both prisoners are incentivized to rat. However, as the diagram illustrates, if *both* prisoners rat then they *both* end up with a worse deal—serving two years—than they would have had they cooperated (each serving one year).

Prisoner's Dilemma

		A	
		BETRAY	STAY SILENT
B	BETRAY	2 2	0 2
	STAY SILENT	2 0	1 1

The Prisoner's Dilemma has interesting management implications. First, it suggests that there are circumstances in which cooperation is better than competition. This may seem obvious, but many managers assume that the healthy competitiveness *between* companies (the lifeblood of the free market) should be echoed *within* companies. Some of the twentieth century's most fabled executives extolled this "competitive spirit," purposefully pitting individual workers and departments against one another. Jack Welch introduced the "stack ranking" system, where employees constantly saw themselves assessed relative to others, an approach that became popular with leaders in other industries. Encouragement to collaborate tends to be more of a bumper sticker slogan than an actual managerial practice. In an interdependent environment, however, collaboration may be necessary to survival.

We were a real-life Prisoner's Dilemma. Each agency feared that sharing intelligence would work against its own interests. Competition between agencies made them reluctant to provide information; what if a partner agency didn't reciprocate? If each agency would cooperate, we would have the best possible outcome, but we could achieve that outcome only if we overcame the dilemma.

Incentivizing collaboration, however, is easier said than done. For starters, both prisoners must be shown the entire decision-making system, not just their own choices. If shown only his own fate, each prisoner will choose to betray the other. It is only when they are shown the decision-making stakes of the accomplice that they understand the consequences. This was what we were trying to achieve with the participatory transparency of our physical plant and forums like the O&I.

There is something else at play as well. While systemic understanding gives each prisoner an intellectual reason to understand why cooperation *would be* beneficial, it does not provide an assurance that his or her accomplice will follow through. After all, each individual's "dominant strategy" is betrayal. Even with holistic awareness, the prisoners still have to take a leap of faith.

We needed true, not theoretical, collaboration, transparency, and trust. Putting everyone in the same room was a start.* But if we wanted instinctive, second-nature, teamlike trust, we would have to go much

---

*As a side note, the lesson of separating prisoners is one that we also learned quite literally: When we held detainees, we found that when they were kept in the same room,

deeper. The stronger the ties between our teams—as with the prisoners— the higher the likelihood we would achieve the level of cooperation we needed.

When we first began nurturing shared consciousness, we did not fully appreciate the strength of the cultural barriers we were trying to over- come. If our partner organizations came to the table at all, they came with decades-long histories and a particular telescope for viewing the problem—what happened outside that tube of vision was irrelevant. Intelligence agencies wanted to build networks of understanding ground truth—through human sources or information or technical collection means. Diplomatic agencies wanted to create long-term institutions and stability. Our counterterrorism forces wanted to solve the real-time problems they saw on the battlefield night after night. Each of these per- spectives had value, but none could succeed in isolation. Showing them abstractly was not enough.

In order to achieve cross-functionality, our bonds with our partner organizations had to become as strong as those between the individuals on our operational teams. Too often we viewed our partners solely in terms of what we could get and give. We began to make progress when we started looking at these relationships as just that: *relationships*—parts of a network, not cogs in a machine with outputs and inputs. The kinds of relationships we needed have roots that go deeper than simply barter- ing. If we could develop that kind of understanding between partners, then one day down the line in a particularly urgent moment, one side might be able to urge the other, "trust me here," and have it work out.

WALK A MILE IN AN ANALYST'S SHOES

One of our most controversial moves was our embedding program, an exchange system we began in late 2003 in which we would take an indi- vidual from one team—say, an Army Special Forces operator—and assign him to a different part of our force for six months—a team of SEALs, for example, or a group of analysts. Our hope was that, by allowing our operators to see how the war looked from inside other groups, and by

---

they never cracked. When they were separated, it became much easier to persuade them to provide information.

building personal relationships, we could build *between* teams some of the fluency that traditionally exists *within* teams.

Predictably, initial resistance was intense. "Our teams train in entirely different ways," I was informed. I was told that I needed to understand that the tight bonds inside assault teams came from working with trusted comrades over years—to insert an outsider is an unwise and unfair risk to operators already performing the most difficult of missions. Simply put, it was anathema to the entire history and tradition of special operations selection, training, and war fighting. But I, and some other leaders, were convinced that we would have to bring together the different elite forces across the Task Force to an extent never before required or envisioned. This fight could not be won by anything but a tightly connected team.

As we implemented these exchanges, what we saw would likely have been predicted by a social scientist. Although it was a "forced" initiative, once the mandate was in place, elite units were naturally incentivized to send their best operators and leaders. These individuals would be representing their organization, so unit pride would drive them to select the best examples from an already highly selective sample set. Many of these top-of-the-pack personalities were also the types that had a natural ability to connect with others—especially in an environment where leadership and one's capability as an operator were a critical measuring stick among peers.

For example, we would require that an Army Special Forces operator embed with a SEAL team. The Special Forces are characterized by exceptional discipline at the individual level, while SEALs pride themselves on creative thinking at the operator level and a strong sense of individuality. The points of tension were predictable. But the Special Forces operator would soon realize the cultural norms of the SEALs and, while remaining true to his home unit's ethos, find a way to work effectively within the new structure. Over time, he would also begin to see some of the positives of the alternative approach, ultimately learning from SEAL culture and finding strengths that he could bring back to his team. The SEALs, meanwhile, would see in the Army operator the strengths of the culture that he came from, realizing that the individuality promoted there clearly comes with strengths that they could learn from. As an added bonus, each unit wouldn't see the exchanged operator as a one-off example; rather, they would see their newfound friend as representative of the entire unit from which he came—and their feelings of trust and under-standing would expand to the other unit, even if they'd only really gotten to know a single operator. This connective tissue grew stronger. When these operators returned to their home unit, their positive comments on the rival unit would spread, deepening the ties between teams. Slowly, we grew the bonds of trust needed for us to overcome our Prisoner's Dilemma.

We also expanded and refined our system of sending liaison officers to our partner organizations. Liaisons are institutionalized ambas-sadors who serve to connect organizations—our Task Force would send a liaison to, say, the CIA, and they would send a liaison to us. Tradition-ally, this was a duty assigned to someone on their final tour before retire-ment or as a way to shuffle someone away from a squadron where they were not fitting in. Their duties were unenvied, and they were generally seen as a spy by the gaining organization—someone who was there sim-ply to sit through meetings and report back to their home organization. They brought very little to the plate, and were rarely trusted.

However, as interfaces became increasingly important, we realized the potential for bolstering our relationships with our partner agencies by way of a strong linchpin liaison officer (LNO). As it turned out, some of our best LNOs were also some of our best leaders on the battlefield. We started taking world-class commandos—men who could snipe, fast-rope, and skydive—and we placed them, attired in civilian suits, in embassies thousands of miles from the fight, because we knew we needed a great relationship with the ambassador and the other interagency leadership posted there. Everyone hated removing some of our best operators from the battlefield, but we reaped enormous benefits.

Our goal was twofold. First, we wanted to get a better sense of how the war looked from our partners' perspectives to enhance our under-standing of the fight. We saw one piece of AQI up close and daily, but we knew that they were part of a larger, global system of finance, weapons, and ideology about which other people knew much more than we did. Second, we hoped that if the liaisons we sent contributed real value to our partners' operations, it would lay a foundation for the trusting relation-ships we needed to develop between the nodes of our network.

We became LNO fanatics. I would spend hours with my commanders hand selecting the best personalities and skill sets for different jobs. The person we sent to liaise with the embassy in Amman needed to be one thing. The one sent to work with the chairman of the Joint Chiefs of Staff, another. We knew we always needed a superstar in certain key positions, such as our LNO to the CIA, and I would insist that these key locations be manned by someone who had proven effective elsewhere. If we looked at our global enterprise as an organism, with the heart in the middle of the combat zone, these LNOs were our nerve endings.

When asking for LNO nominations to fill critical positions, we used two criteria: (1) if it doesn't pain you to give the person up, *pick someone else*; (2) if it's not someone whose voice you'll recognize when they call you at home at 2:00 a.m., *pick someone else*. Previously, we might have made these decisions based on rank, position, or where people wanted to go in their careers. But to get this right, personal qualities trumped everything else. These were people who needed to enter an unknown, and sometimes hostile, bureaucratic environment, then build trust-based relationships with the leadership there—a very difficult proposition.

Once we had LNOs in place, they couldn't fall victim to the "out of sight, out of mind" syndrome. Nor could they be viewed as simply staff augmentation to the organization we'd sent them to. Instead, we considered them precious assets—but knew they could be that only if we had the right personalities, empowered with the right support from us.

Early on we learned that to be effective where we sent them, our LNOs needed to have access to senior leaders in that organization, and to be trusted. That didn't come easily.

CHICKEN SANDWICHES AND TRASH

Lieutenant Commander Conway's* reception was chilly. I'd secured grudging permission from the country team in the U.S. embassy in an unstable Middle Eastern country to place a single Task Force liaison with them to help coordinate the wider effort against Al Qaeda, but there were clear, understandable reservations when the battle-hardened SEAL officer appeared. Worries ranged from compromise of sensitive intelligence to concerns over Task Force combat forces appearing on the scene. Some were as mundane as the competition for physical space in the embassy, others more deeply rooted in the wide gulf between organizational

---

*Conway is a pseudonym.

cultures. Most qualms were as unfounded as they were natural, but all were real obstacles.

We'd chosen Conway carefully. He was a walking mass of extroverted energy, habitually upbeat and helpful. In his previous tour he'd worn body armor and night vision goggles to go toe-to-toe with Al Qaeda fighters in Anbar Province, but his new mission required him to be accepted by his new colleagues. Where Iraq had forced Conway to risk his life, now he decided he had to subordinate his ego.

At his new post, he was initially granted no access to intelligence and given nothing to do, so Conway volunteered to take out the trash. Each afternoon he went office to office gathering refuse and carrying it to the dumpster. When he found out that one embassy colleague loved Chick-fil-A sandwiches, Conway arranged for the next Task Force delivery to include several in its contents. A man the U.S. government had spent hundreds of thousands of dollars to train as a SEAL was, for three months, a glorified garbage man and fast food delivery boy.

But when the situation heated up in the country's capital and the ambassador came to our LNO and asked whether he knew anything about force protection and dealing with the growing Al Qaeda threat, our man was exactly where he needed to be. "I do," he said. "That's what I'm trained in. And I can do you one better—let me make a call." Soon, the entire weight of the Task Force enterprise was at the disposal of the interagency team at the embassy. Our LNO was there to serve the collective mission—from trash to terrorism. The Task Force's relationship with that country grew tighter nearly instantaneously. A new node in our network came online and began to thrive.

We found that it was essential that we make our LNOs key players at their host agencies. To some degree, like Conway, our men and women could accomplish much through force of personality and talent, but they also needed institutional support from the Task Force. I thought of my LNOs as old-school deep-sea divers, connected to the surface by an oxygen hose. Their effectiveness depended on our ability to pump resources and information to them, making them effective and desirable to their hosts. Nothing was more highly valued by many of our partners than insights into the shadowy counterterrorist fight we were waging. So we armed our LNOs with a constant stream of intelligence, and empowered them to share it as they felt appropriate. Information sharing was key, because ultimately, that was what we might one day turn around and request from the host agency in return. Ideally an LNO would develop such a fantastic relationship with the NSA or National Geospatial Agency (NGA), for example, that when we really needed sensitive signals or imagery intelligence on a target *urgently*, it would come quickly, fully, and without any bureaucratic friction—on a phone call.

As partner organizations came to appreciate our LNOs, they reciprocated by sending their own LNOs to us. The talent pool available to us steadily increased as our partners came to realize that the better their LNO, the more they could leverage the Task Force to help with their hardest missions. The empty seats around our SAR filled up. The JIATF swelled with analysts sent from across the United States. Just as BUD/S increases the horizontal bonds between aspiring SEALs, we found that this approach to collaboration was strengthening the ties not only among the Task Force's internal teams, but also between the Task Force and the partner agencies with whom we would have to cooperate in order to win the fight. As the liaising "ramped up," organizations signaled their enthusiasm about our Task Force by the quality of people that they sent us. Receiving a talentless functionary frequently meant that his home agency was planning to stonewall; a superstar showed they were eager to engage.

Steadily, in large part as a result of internal embedding and LNOs, and complemented by the growing O&I, we began to overcome internal competition and barriers to cooperation. Bonds of trust began to form. People from different tribes began to see increasingly familiar faces. Even strangers were now, by extension, part of a familiar and trusted unit entity, and received the benefit of the doubt. Being part of the network became an important form of capital. Most important, it was not a zero-sum game; the more you put into the system, the more it could serve you.

Nowhere was the elimination of territorialism clearer than in the exchange of our coveted air assets.

ISR

Under a pitch-black sky, thirty operators jogged toward idling helicopters. Rotor blades whirled, kicking hot desert air across the airfield runway. Ten minutes earlier, this team had received its final briefing on the night's mission. They would be in flight for thirty-five minutes, and then patrol for nearly an hour before hitting the target. They were out to capture a mid-level AQI operative. The target, they believed, had intelligence that would help them get one step closer to an upper-echelon enemy leader in the region. It would not be the most incredible mission of any of their careers, but it was the night's work, and an important step in their efforts to understand and dismantle the network.

The operators took their seats, and officers took final headcounts. The assault commander plugged into the helicopter radio. With the flip of a switch, he could speak with his team on the helicopters, the pilots up front, or his leadership at headquarters. He could also monitor communications between his headquarters and other assault elements around the country. His pilots were going through final checks when he heard the call.

"Lima 2-1, this is Lima 0-3." His senior officer, who sat five hundred yards from the helicopters in their operations center, was making contact. Perhaps, he hoped, it was a positive update from the target site which was currently being monitored by ISR (intelligence surveillance and reconnaissance) feed into the operations center.

"Go for 2-1," he replied.

"We just got word, 2-1, that ISR is being pulled for a priority target in Baghdad. That puts us below minimum requirements. We need to stand down."

The commander felt frustrated. His pilot, who also heard the call, looked over his shoulder and made eye contact with the assault team leader. The pilot slashed his hand across his throat to confirm what he'd just heard. The assault team leader nodded, then cued his radio. "Roger, 0-3. Shutting it down."

The pilot killed the rotors. "We lost our ISR, gents. We're standing down." In the dark, he could see helmets being removed and heads shaking. It was the second night in a row that they had lost their assets.

To a degree never before seen in warfare, ISR assets like Predator unmanned aerial vehicles or a small, prop-driven, manned aircraft, like the Beechcraft King Air we'd gutted and outfitted with surveillance equipment, became coin of the realm in our fight in Iraq and Afghanistan. ISR dramatically expanded our ability to gather intelligence on targets and develop new ones. In the conduct of raids the real-time FMV (full-motion video) coverage that was piped to multiple locations on the ground allowed commanders to pare assault forces to a minimum by providing security from enemy reinforcements that had before required us to place a cordon of troops around the target site. Without ISR, a raid might require an additional platoon or more of troops, more helicopters, and other support. Simply put, the more ISR a unit had access to, the more operations it could execute.

Competition for ISR within our task force was intense. Early in the war, one of the most time-consuming parts of senior leadership's job was determining where to deploy our limited assets. When a ground commander was forced to hand over an ISR asset, it could cause internal convulsions in the Task Force, and potentially serious loss of morale for the affected unit. The way our operators experienced it on the ground, one moment they had a helicopter or a Predator, the next moment it was gone. From their vantage point, someone else had taken it—it *was* a zero-sum game. All they knew concretely was that they couldn't do their mission.

When they understood the whole picture, they began to trust their colleagues. Much like the prisoners deciding whether or not to rat, our commanders' responsiveness to such demands grew as they came to understand the greater environment in which the decision had been made, and the people receiving what had been taken away. Previously, the world outside of a commander's domain looked like a black box; once an asset left, it was just *gone*. Once they could see *why* and *how* their assets were being used, however, and once they knew and respected the other individuals handling these tools, things changed.

Before, these decisions took place behind closed doors. Now, the resourcing conversations sometimes occurred right in front of them during an O&I. "When we started constantly talking at lower levels of the organization," explains an enlisted SEAL who worked with the Task Force in Iraq, "we could basically see where the fight was hot, where it wasn't, and where people needed ISR the most. Plus, we could see that it was actually to our benefit sometimes to surrender that asset." With that awareness came a faith that when theirs was the priority mission, they would get what they needed when they needed it. Holistic understanding of the enterprise now permeated the ranks.

As person-to-person relationships across the enterprise deepened, unit commanders gave away prized assets, often to the initial surprise and frustration of those below them, because they trusted that the asset would be used in a context even more critical than their current situation. Moreover, they began to see the favor being repaid in kind. This fostered trust in the other unit among even the most skeptical, hardened, competitive operators. Suddenly, we were overcoming our Prisoner's Dilemma.

We had worked out our solutions to the Task Force's Prisoner's Dilemma by trial and error, but we later learned that game theory scholars shared our conclusions. In 1980, Robert Axelrod, a professor of political science at the University of Michigan, solicited programs for an iterative computer Prisoner's Dilemma tournament. The fourteen entries in the original first round—submitted by leading game theorists across a spectrum of disciplines, including economics, psychology, mathematics, and political science—varied greatly in initial strategy and complexity of coding. However, the winning strategy contained just four lines of code. Submitted by University of Toronto professor Anatol Rapoport, the program was called Tit for Tat. The strategy always began with cooperating, and then simply did what the other player did on the previous move, cooperating if the other cooperated, defecting if the other defected. It did not hold a grudge: if its opponent began to cooperate again after defecting, Tit for Tat would also return to cooperation. A second round of the tournament was held, and many more entries were submitted. Again, Rapoport's simple strategy won out. The program succeeded because it defaulted to trusting, cooperative behavior, and punished the other player for selfish behavior. However, as one peace and conflict studies expert has since noted, "the punishment lasted only as long as the selfish behavior lasted. This proved to be an exceptionally effective sanction, quickly showing the other side the advantages of cooperating."

Daniel Kahneman, the Nobel Prize–winning cognitive scientist, believes that the human mind has two different decision-making tracks: "system 1" operates automatically and quickly, while "system 2" is deliberate and effortful. We tend to use system 1 frequently and reflexively—for instance, gauging the emotions on someone's face—and apply system 2 when weighing difficult decisions or attempting complex calculations. What we saw in the Task Force was that while cooperation began as a conscious system 2 decision ("they'll help me later if I help them now; cooperation is in my interest"), a track record of productive collaborations led to reflexive, system 1 cooperation—in other words, real trust. Furthermore, this trust had a viral effect: once it passed a certain threshold, it became the norm.

One of the best examples of this symbiosis was our newfound ability to hit "follow-on targets."

FOLLOW-ON TARGETS

AQI was organized as pockets of fighters spread geographically around the country. Key leadership moved constantly, bouncing between geographic hubs to share information and guidance with their network of fighters. If Al Qaeda was an organism, the hubs of fighters were the muscle, while the mobile leaders were the oxygen, providing energy for the muscles, and the roads of Iraq were the circulatory system through which this oxygen could flow. Movement over long distances was done during the daylight hours, since AQI knew that our night vision and overnight reconnaissance assets gave us an advantage over them in the dark. If we were to disrupt their network, we not only needed to own the night, we had to disrupt the oxygen flow during the day.

Daytime interdiction of AQI leadership was a simple and elegant concept, born on a whiteboard during a discussion between operators and intelligence officers. If life worked like the movies, the force would have launched an operation immediately. But on a real battlefield, such concepts are followed by a litany of logistical queries. How would we follow the vehicle in heavy traffic? How would we stop a vehicle? Could our helicopters get from our compounds to the vehicle's location fast enough? As operators approached the location, how could they be sure they were moving toward the correct car? The list went on. Success would require perfect choreography between our best ground operators, our helicopter pilots, our operational headquarters, and our overhead intelligence collection platforms, as well as fluid, iterative adaptation across our force.

A typical cycle ran like this: After we hit a target in the middle of the night, the assault element would return to base, debrief the mission, and ensure that intelligence analysts were tracking any key information they'd learned on the target. The operators would grab a hot meal before heading to bed just after sunrise. At this point, their work, for the night, is done. Meanwhile, the daylight-hour intelligence teams continue to monitor the target. The interaction between these operators and analysts, once uncomfortable and mechanical, is now fluid and natural; they trust one another and knew that cooperation is in their own interests, as well as for the greater good.

On one of our raids, the previous night's target building had been a safe house for a group of fighters. Just before noon, while our operators from the night prior are sleeping, overhead reconnaissance platforms identify a vehicle pulling up to the compound—the site of the gunfight a few hours ago. A blurry black-and-white video feed grabs the attention of the daylight intelligence team. They watch as the driver and two others park outside and walk into the courtyard, clearly unaware of the previous night's activities. All eyes focus on the three fuzzy figures on the large screens at the front of their operations center. The figures slow as they enter the courtyard—sensing that something isn't right. They stop and look around, probably unnerved by the lack of movement. They call out to their friends, but hear nothing in return. They move a bit more, now very cautiously. Perhaps they notice expended cartridges on the ground, or freshly broken window glass. All three stop cold, turn to each other, then sprint back toward their vehicles.

Instantly, a young intelligence analyst reaches for the secure phone on her desk. She is twenty-three years old, and on her second combat tour. No one is directing her actions, and no one would reprimand her if she did nothing. But she knows what to look for, and she has just seen it. She is aware of this particular compound's importance in the current fight, as she is in seamless contact with the intelligence team supporting nighttime operations. Most important, she knows exactly whom to contact. Her phone call is not being made to inform and is not a request for permission—its purpose is to create action, which is exactly what it does.

"There's movement at last night's compound. Vehicle arrived, three people exited, then hopped back in the vehicle and sped east after realizing there'd been a fight," she says to the operator on the other end of the line.

"Get it on!" he yells to his operators, who instantly reach for their gear. Sixty seconds have passed since the vehicle sped away.

"Okay, we're looking at it," he says, back on the line. He has now pulled up the same intelligence video feed in his operations room. He puts her on speakerphone so that her voice can help feed the thinking of the personnel in his team room. She explains what she's seen while he and the others on his team listen. They watch the vehicle's movement as the operations center goes from medium to full-octane in a matter of sixty seconds. Likely vehicle routes are mapped on displays at the front of the operations center. Helicopter engines start to whir. Operators move toward their staging area. Four minutes have passed since the vehicle sped away.

The car begins to move east, and the targeting team starts identifying locations along the likely routes that are feasible for an interdiction. They estimate they have a forty-minute window. If everything lines up per-fectly, they'll know soon enough who the three figures were.

After a quick update in the staging area, the operators jog toward the waiting helicopters some two hundred meters away. Already sweating in the 110-degree heat, they duck as they approach the spinning rotor blades and split up onto the various aircraft. Some strap themselves to the exter-nal benches of MH-6 Little Birds, others climb inside larger UH-60 Black Hawks. The helicopters lift up and the base disappears behind them. Eight minutes have passed since the vehicle sped away.

As they fly, a live video stream of the target vehicle is pushed to mul-tiple headquarters around the country. The operators in the helicopters receive real-time updates on the direction of the vehicle and any suspi-cious activity. As the vehicle chooses its route, the potential locations for interception narrow, and the pilots and assault team leader refine the plan. Finally, only one option remains. The helicopters head in that direc-tion and loiter over the horizon. Reconnaissance assets inform operators and intelligence teams that the vehicle is continuing to head to the inter-ception site; they estimate it is three minutes out. The entire assault team hears the information in real time; they do a final check on their weapons and prepare to insert.

"Vehicle is stopping." The voice on the radio belongs to an analyst in the operations center—a voice they now know and trust. "Original vehi-cle is stopped on the roadside . . . two kilometers from the interdiction site . . . another vehicle has pulled up alongside." The operators wait. "Okay . . . one passenger from vehicle one has gotten into vehicle two. Vehicles have departed in opposite directions. Vehicle one is two minutes from interdiction zone."

The assault team commander knows that the next move is his. Any hesi-tation and they could lose both opportunities. "Execute on vehicle one," he tells his helicopter pilots—and they make a beeline to the interception zone. Then, calling back to his operations center, the assault team leader tells them, "Cut one asset to follow vehicle two. Possible follow-on target." The entire team hears him as he passes these orders on the common radio net-work. There are nods from the people onboard his helicopter. Everyone from the pilots to the assaulters to the intelligence analysts in the opera-tions center shares an understanding of the situation and knows the plan.

Approaching the interception zone, overhead reconnaissance platforms seamlessly talk the helicopters onto the right vehicle. They land their aircraft in a perfect configuration to force the vehicle to stop. The dust from the rotor blades and noise of the engines confuse the driver and his passenger. Before they get their bearings, operators heave the doors open and the two suspects are secured. Though there are weapons in the car, neither individual had time to reach them. The vehicle is searched in a matter of minutes as the two are questioned about their activities. They quickly divulge that they're nobodies—local fighters—who'd been told to drive someone more senior for the day. That's all the operators needed to hear.

"It's the other guy, boss," states one of the operators over his interteam radio. It's the first time he's spoken since the mission began, but he has perfect context on the multiple changes that have taken place over the past twenty minutes. The assault team commander again moves without hesitation.

"Detain them on aircraft two," he states over his radio. "Reload the birds. We're taking vehicle two."

The entire mission is recalibrated. New plans are made, literally, on the fly. Intelligence teams at the operations center plot the direction of vehicle two, identify new cutoff points, and communicate these with the pilots. The attention of the Task Force shifts in unison to the new objective. Helicopters land for a second time. Operators sprint toward vehicle two. The senior member is taken into custody—and a bit of oxygen is taken out of the Al Qaeda network. Forty-six minutes have passed since the vehicle sped away from the compound.

No single supervisor had planned or even dictated in the operation in real time; the solution emerged from a dense knot of interactions at the ground level. My role in these situations was usually that of spectator. One key to the success of operations like this was the contextual awareness made possible by the O&I, but equally important was defeating the challenge of the Prisoner's Dilemma—the creation of strong lateral bonds through our embedding and liaison programs. Only with deep, empathetic familiarity could these different units function so seamlessly together—put their lives on the line for one another. What on the surface seemed like an inefficient use of time in fact laid the foundation for our adaptability.

Together, these two cornerstones—systemic understanding and strong lateral connectivity—grounded shared consciousness. Both diverged wildly from the MECE, reductionist doctrines we had spent most of our lives upholding, but, in this new setting, against this new threat, they worked.

The two strains of shared consciousness also paralleled the ingredients that, at a lower level, had ensured the success of our small teams for decades: "seeing the system" is essentially a macro version of the "purpose" that gives our operators the context and commitment to persevere in volatile situations, and the interteam bonds we used to beat the Prisoner's Dilemma are akin to the trust between team members. As we discussed in chapter 6, this—the realization of team traits at scale; the transformation into a team of teams—was exactly what we needed.

We were not the only ones in need of such solutions.

DECENTRALIZED OPERATIONS WITH COORDINATED CONTROL

On April 1, 2014, Mary Barra, the CEO of General Motors, stepped into a somber, wood-paneled room full of cameras and congressional representatives. Representative Tim Murphy, Republican of Pennsylvania, initiated the proceedings: "I now convene this hearing of the Oversight and Investigation Subcommittee titled 'The GM Ignition Switch Recall: Why Did It Take So Long?'"

This question had been on the public mind since GM had issued a recall of 800,000 vehicles two months earlier. A faulty ignition switch had been used in the Chevy Cobalt and the Pontiac G5; a weak spring meant that small amounts of force applied to the key when in the ignition—a bump by a knee or the tug of a heavy keychain—could cause the engine to turn off. The ignition shutoff also disabled airbag deployment, significantly increasing the danger of the fault.

The costs had been high. The inexpensive Cobalt and G5, thought to be safe, were parents' frequent choice for children's first cars, so many of the deaths that resulted from this design error were of teenagers. What the public found most shocking, however, was not the existence of the ignition switch issue or even the age of its victims, but the time it had taken GM to address the problem.

"As soon as the Chevy Cobalt rolled off of production lines in 2004," an incredulous Representative Murphy read to the packed hearing room, "customers began filing complaints about the ignition switch. In 2004 and 2005, GM engineers twice considered the problem, and even developed potential solutions to fix it. But GM decided that 'the tooling cost and piece prices are too high,' and that 'none of the solutions represent a business case' . . . it wasn't until December 2013 that the company finally put the pieces together . . . almost 10 years after customers first told GM the Cobalt ignition switch didn't work." In those ten years, at least thirteen people died.*

GM appeared to be the ultimate evil corporation. Representative Diana DeGette, a Colorado Democrat, marveled that "the piece [that was responsible for the crashes] cost pennies," yet GM had not replaced it. For four hours, righteously indignant politicians alternately questioned and berated Barra. Press coverage highlighted GM's greed.

The reality, however, was more complex. What seemed like a cold calculation to privilege profits over young lives was also an example of institutional ignorance that had as much to do with management as it did with values. It was a perfect and tragic case study of the consequences of information silos and internal mistrust.

Forty-one-year-old Alfred P. Sloan, already an experienced executive, joined General Motors in 1918. GM founder William C. Durant had snapped up the United Motors Company, Sloan's previous employer, in a spree of corporate acquisitions. It was an exciting time for American business, especially the nascent auto industry. Eight-year-old GM had already established itself as a market leader and was growing fast. But Durant's binge mergers created problems. Though a visionary, he was unable to bind this sprawl of companies together in an orderly fashion. Alfred D. Chandler later described the company as lacking "any effective over-all administrative structure—clear lines of authority and communication [or] accurate information about the corporation's operations." The brink of bankruptcy loomed on more than one occasion and there was no central view of how its many acquisitions were operating. This led to a duplication of efforts, a lack of distinction between brands, and a fuzzy picture of the company's finances.

Early on, Sloan had a Taylor-at-Midvale epiphany. He saw that GM's problem lay in its organizational structure, or lack thereof. Things were too casual and associative; Durant was applying the old "countinghouse"

---

*GM officially acknowledges 13 deaths as a result of faulty ignition switches in Chevy Cobalts and Pontiac G5s, but 153 death claims have been submitted. GM's count includes only incidents involving head-on collisions with nondeploying airbags.

apprenticeship ways to an entity that was too large and complicated to be run that way. While GM may have had efficient assembly lines on the factory floor, at the managerial level mechanistic order was absent.

Sloan envisioned a MECE, top-down solution. He presented Durant with an "Organizational Study" that proposed a system of separate entities with clearly delineated purviews whose limited interaction would be controlled from the top by central executives. He called it "decentralized operations with coordinated control"—what we now call silos. As historian William Pelfrey notes, "None of it sounds . . . revolutionary today, [but] it was all untested theory back in 1920."

Durant ignored the plan. A few years later, however, when the founder's frenetic leadership style finally lost him control of the company, the board placed Sloan in charge. He inherited a company whose growing pains had left it overextended and financially weak. As with our Task Force in 2004, however, desperation made those in charge much more willing to take a gamble on a wild proposal.

What followed has been described as "the largest turnaround and the most thorough transformation in business history." Mess was out, and silos were in. Things became standardized, rational, and MECE. The changes saved the company. As Pelfrey summarizes, "Alfred Sloan institutionalized a new culture, one never before attempted in a systematic way in any corporation . . . a hierarchical, command-and-control culture."

The results were indisputable. From 1921 until his retirement in 1956, Sloan's tenure at the helm of GM saw unparalleled growth even through the Great Depression (GM was the only automaker for whom this was true). From near bankruptcy, GM saw net sales grow fivefold from 1921 to 1929, moving from a net loss of $38.7 million to a net profit of $248.3 million, and becoming the first company in history to earn a billion dollars in a single year. Its market share "grew from less than 10 percent in 1915 to over 40 percent in 1939." By the time Sloan retired, his firm was producing more than *half* of all the cars sold in America—double the output of Ford and triple that of Chrysler (both of which had led GM before Sloan stepped into the top job).

The efficacy of Sloan's silos was clear. The plan that Durant had rejected "was eventually copied by most corporations and even governmental and nonprofit organizations . . . forever chang[ing] the way large enterprises and institutions were administered."

Like other large endeavors, including our Task Force, however, GM discovered that what worked in the twentieth century could not hold forever.

Fast-forward to 2013 and GM's silos have a very different legacy. In the decades after Sloan, the company went into decline—in the 1970s it proved unable to react creatively to new competition from Japan, or to respond as technologies and customer preferences changed. With its rigid silos, "GM couldn't keep up," journalist Alex Taylor writes. "As effective as the structure had been in its prime, it was not suited to the changing competitive realities of the 1980s and 1990s, where speed and agility were much more crucial."

Internal rivalries—the consequence of separate divisions and a competitive culture—inhibited communication. Each division maintained its own design and marketing operations and mistrusted other teams. This was one of the problems the silo system had been put in place to solve, and Sloan's solution had worked well to a point; but like other command-and-control structures, it failed at the threshold of complexity.

The company had little cross-silo information flow. One former executive recounted that at a particular executive meeting, Richard Gerstenberg, GM CEO during the 1970s, requested the formation of a task force to come up with a report on the problem that the executives were currently discussing, only to be told (after an awkward silence) that the meeting he was currently in was the result of a task force he had appointed to investigate the very same issue several months prior.

Ultimately, GM's failures didn't just ding profits—they cost lives. The internal investigation GM finally commissioned in 2014 into the deaths caused by GM's faulty ignition switches exposed deep failures in the organization. Riddled with a lack of contextual awareness and trust, GM's divisions were playing Krasnovian soccer and they were losing at the Prisoner's Dilemma. And customers—largely young drivers—were paying the price.

At a technical level, the core of the ignition switch problem lay in a simple interface failure: a faulty ignition switch that could sometimes disable the engine while the car was in motion, which would in turn prevent airbags from inflating. Understanding and correcting this issue would have been remarkably simple—on par with landing a plane with a faulty gear piston—had the engineers been able to see it. What ended up costing lives, as in the case of United 173, was organizational. At GM, airbags and ignition systems were overseen by two different teams. It would take a decade of demonstrated road failures and tragedies before the organization connected the dots.

In the fall of 2002, engineers noted that the ignition switch would sometimes inadvertently rotate out of the "run" position, but this group was unaware that such rotation would cause airbags not to deploy. On their own, ignition shutoffs were classified as "non-safety issues," and placed on the back burner.

Once reports of accidents began coming in, various divisions held meetings, but no meaningful action was taken. An internal report later concluded that "the engineers . . . did not know how their own vehicle had been designed. And GM *did not have a process in place to make sure someone looking at the issue had a complete understanding* of what the failure of the Ignition Switch meant for the customer."

Other communication problems pervaded the company. For instance, though the ignition switch had failed some preproduction tests, the information was not passed on to the authorities who signed off on putting the part into production. Later, when a critical internal component connecting the ignition switch and the airbags was changed, this information was not shared. It was not even added to the central database that tracked alterations, so it took years for engineers and investigators to pinpoint the interface failure. And when GM finally opened an investigation into airbag nondeployments, nobody told the chief investigator about GM's prior work on the Cobalt issues. The relatively easy-to-fix ignition issue "passed through an astonishing number of committees" without ever being addressed. Like the unopened bags of potential intelligence at our old base in the Baghdad airport, people flagged it, then forgot about it once it was passed on.

This was inextricably linked with the general culture of efficiency and internal competitiveness. Perhaps some employees would have tried harder to relay these issues up the chain of command, or perhaps senior leaders would have investigated the mysterious crashes more thoroughly, had the slogan "cost is everything" not dominated decision making. Like the "Faster, Better, Cheaper" approach that encouraged poor decision making at NASA in the 1970s, this drive to cut out fat inhibited systemic understanding. An engineer interviewed said that the emphasis on cost cutting "permeates the fabric of the whole culture," leading to a privileging of timing over quality, and a resistance to raising issues. No team wanted to be the group that lagged in efficiency or took too long to fix a problem on account of being overly cautious. An avoidance of responsibility had become known as the "GM nod"—a staple of survival and job security at the company.

The silos and competitiveness that once made GM the world's most successful company now resulted in spectacular failure. Incredibly, GM's CEO and general counsel did not *learn* about the ignition switch safety issues until January 2014—a full twelve years after the problems were first raised.

As the truth behind the danger of these cars, the ease of the technical fix, and the duration of GM's inaction came to light, the company was vilified. Senator Ed Markey told a press conference, "Two dollars. That's how little this ignition switch could have cost to repair . . . That was apparently two dollars too much for General Motors." But casting GM's leaders as cold, calculating misers who ran the numbers and determined that the lives lost were worth the profits made—like blaming Captain McBroom for the crash of Flight 173—oversimplifies the situation. GM's byzantine organizational structure meant that nobody—venal or kindly—had the information to make those calculations.

The internal report concluded that from 2006 to 2010, GM demonstrated a "failure to take basic steps." As we've discussed, top-down coordination of siloed efforts works only if those on top actually understand how everything will interact. At GM they no longer did. The products, markets, and supply chains they dealt with had crossed the threshold from complicated to complex. Like NASA before it, GM was running up against the constraints of reductionist management.

On the other side of Detroit, at Ford Motor Company's "Glass House," the towering headquarters in Dearborn, a very different story took shape. As the twentieth century closed, the company was struggling with similar issues to GM's: stiff competition from foreign automakers compounded by a dysfunctional internal culture of need to know and competitiveness. Engineers and designers were rivals; executives and labor hated each other; C-suite leaders felt that their success could come only at the cost of their peers. It was rife with "the other guy sucks" sentiment.

In 2005, Bill Ford saw the writing on the wall: "We can continue to cut costs and improve our efficiency, but we cannot win the hearts and minds of a new generation with efficiency alone." The board brought in Alan Mulally as CEO. Mulally had been in charge of Boeing's commercial airplanes division and had overseen the development of the 777, one of the safest, most advanced, most financially successful passenger planes ever created. He attributed the project's success to a management approach called "working together" that involved forcing interaction between previously separate groups and cutting-edge technological platforms for ensuring constant, systemic transparency. Boeing deployed a state-of-the-art computer system to maintain a live-updated 3D model so that engineers could see immediately, for instance, whether a hydraulic tube being considered by one design team would interfere with the modification of door hinge components. The ten thousand people on the project were put into "design build teams" (DBTs). Previous projects had been plagued by communication problems; executives who had been at the company for decades lamented the fact that these issues seemed to skyrocket as the company's operations expanded and its products grew more complicated. But Mulally's "working together" system created the old-school, teamlike oneness across an enterprise of ten thousand. This was a man who saw the imperative of beating the Prisoner's Dilemma.

At Ford, Mulally ushered in a campaign he dubbed "One Ford." As Ford had grown and followed the example set by Sloan's GM, it had undergone mitosis into hundreds of subdivisions and cliques. Mulally eschewed internal competitiveness, and demanded honesty and transparency. He saw that there were too many small meetings that fractured the organization. He replaced them with a single weekly corporate-level meeting—the "business plan review" (BPR). He allowed no side discussions, secrets, BlackBerry use, or even jokes at others' expense. As Bryce Hoffman writes in *American Icon: Alan Mulally and the Fight to Save Ford Motor Company*, "The BPR . . . would shine a light into the darkest corners of the company . . . in a company like Ford, the weak went to the wall; only the strong survived. Now they were being told they were all on the same team, and Mulally expected them to act like it."

Mulally took efforts to rope nonexecutive employees into these discussions, people who had "tried unsuccessfully to draw management's attention to inefficiencies in their departments, shortcomings in Ford's business strategy, or ways its products and processes could be improved." Willing to listen, Mulally found himself "inundated with e-mails but responded personally to every message." Mulally's goal at Ford, like ours in Iraq, was to wire all his forces together to produce an emergent intelligence and create shared consciousness.

He forcibly integrated engineers and designers. Japanese automakers had long integrated these disciplines, but at Ford they were separate tribes. As a result, "A designer who knew nothing about thermodynamics might create a great-looking grille only to discover that it did not allow enough air to flow into the engine compartment. An engineer with no knowledge of ergonomics might develop an exhaust system that worked perfectly but was impossible to install." Mulally brought them together, and explicitly emphasized "shared purpose." He extended his embrace of cooperation to Ford's historically fraught relationship with the labor unions, and he worked with rivals GM and Chrysler to make sure the suppliers they all depended on—many of which were struggling—stayed in business. Mulally recognized that the interdependence of the market meant that keeping these suppliers alive would benefit Ford. So antithetical to the cutthroat auto industry was such behavior, Hoffman compares it to "Protestants and Catholics coming together to work on a downtown development plan for Belfast."

As at Boeing, Mulally's solutions worked wonders. While GM and Chrysler were filing for bankruptcy in 2009, Ford, which had been in the most dire straits of the big three automakers, was turning a profit. In Hoffman's words, "Mulally had done what many inside Ford believed was impossible: He had figured out a way to profitably produce cars in the United States."

Morale hit an all-time high. Though Mulally shared much *more* information across the organization, there were no leaks to the press for the first time in memory. Detroit celebrated Mulally's magic: he was the Automotive Hall of Fame's "Industry Leader of 2009"; *Automobile* magazine's "2010 Man of the Year"; *Fortune*'s "Businessperson of the Year"; and the *Detroit News*' "Michiganian of the Year" (despite the fact that he had only moved there to work with Ford, and spent what free time he had with his family back in Seattle). Jim Cramer, the hyperbolic host of *Mad Money*, declared him "the greatest turnaround artist of all time—not *our* time, *all* time." Wall Street bankers said that "the biggest threat to Ford Motor Company is that Alan Mulally steps off the curb tomorrow and gets nailed by a bus . . . [the company] can manage everything else."

In his own way, he became as fabled as Sloan—by doing exactly the opposite. The approach worked just as well at Ford as it had at Boeing. As Mulally put it, "Working together always works. It *always* works. Everybody has to be on the team. They have to be interdependent with one another."

Mulally's belief in the universal utility of rejecting silos and embracing interdependence is backed up by Sandy Pentland, an MIT professor who studies the effects of information flow on organizations and communities. Looking at very large data sets, Pentland has found that sharing information and creating strong horizontal relationships improves the effectiveness of everything from businesses to governments to cities. His research suggests that the *collective intelligence* of groups and communities has little to do with the intelligence of their individual members, and much more to do with the connections between them.* "The best ideas," he writes, "come from careful and continuous social exploration . . . it is the *idea flow* within a community that builds the intelligence that makes it successful."

"Idea flow" is the ease with which new thoughts can permeate a group. Pentland likens it to the spread of the flu: a function of susceptibility and frequency of interaction. The key to increasing the "contagion" is trust and connectivity between otherwise separate elements of an establishment. The two major determinants of idea flow, Pentland has found, are "engagement" within a small group like a team, a department, or a neighborhood, and "exploration"—frequent contact with *other* units. In other words: a *team of teams*.

Looking at the influence of idea flow on trading Web sites and social networks, Pentland found that collective intelligence stems from unsiloed dissonance: "when the flow of ideas incorporates a constant stream of outside ideas as well, then the individuals in the community make better decisions than they could on their own." Tuning such networks to expose users to more diverse voices could increase returns by more than 6 percent—doubling profitability for all of the social traders.

He has conducted similar studies at a number of companies, outfitting employees with badges that produce detailed, quantitative measures of how people interact (tone of voice, whether people face one another, how much they gesture, rates of interruption, etc.). At a Chicago-area IT consultancy, he collected a billion measurements in one month—1,900 hours of data—and found that engagement was the central predictor of productivity, exceeding individual intelligence, personality, and skill. At a German bank, Pentland examined five teams in the company's marketing division for one month, collecting 2,200 hours of data and sequencing 880 e-mails.

---

*In fact, the worst-performing groups he analyzed were those that were dominated by one or two hotshots.

The teams that had the highest levels of internal engagement and external exploration had much higher levels of creative output—something that was reinforced by an internal study of his labs at MIT. When Pentland surveyed a number of R&D labs, he found that he could predict the labs' creative output with an extraordinary 87.5 percent accuracy by measuring idea flow. In the more than two dozen organizations he has studied, Pentland found that interaction patterns typically account for almost half of all the performance variation between high- and low-performing groups.

This is true even in work not seen as requiring creativity and innovation. In 2008, Pentland studied a Bank of America call center. Such centers tend to be standardized and reductionist—up there with manufacturing in terms of the degree to which things are prescribed. Success is measured by AHT (average call handle time), which ideally should be as low as possible. Pentland gave workers sociometric badges all day for six weeks, and measured levels of interaction and engagement. When he shifted the coffee break system from being individual to being team based, interaction rose and AHT dropped, demonstrating a strong link between interaction and productivity. As a result, call center management converted the break structure of all call centers to the same system, and saved $15 million in productivity.

But fostering such engagement is more easily said than done. Almost every company has posters and slogans urging employees to "work together," but simply telling people to "communicate" is the equivalent of Taylor's telling his workers to "do things faster," and stopping there. GM, in addition to the "cost is everything" slogan, had posters everywhere reading "QUALITY ABOVE ALL"—but it was the former, not the latter, that was practiced.

It is necessary, we found, to forcibly dismantle the old system and replace it with an entirely new managerial architecture. Our new architecture was shared consciousness, and it consisted of two elements. The first was extreme, participatory transparency—the "systems management" of NASA that we mimicked with our O&I forums and our open physical space. This allowed all participants to have a holistic awareness equivalent to the contextual awareness of *purpose* we already knew at a team level. The second was the creation of strong internal connectivity across teams—something we achieved with our embedding and liaison programs. This mirrored the *trust* that enabled our small teams to function.

Shared consciousness is emphatically non-MECE and, at low levels, inefficient. But it is vastly more effective than its predecessor—not just for us, but for the other organizations we have examined. And if it could work in the military (in many ways the archetypal stratified, "need-to-know" domain) and the auto industry (pioneers of assembly lines and silos), it can work almost anywhere.

Alfred Sloan described his system as "decentralized operations with coordinated control." We found that we benefited from the opposite. First, we needed *coordinated operations*, something that necessitated emergent, adaptive intelligence. Shared consciousness achieved this, but it was only the first half. As we would soon find, keeping pace with the speed of our environment and enemy would require something else as well: *decentralized control*. Creating it would be just as taxing, radical, and necessary as shared consciousness. Where shared consciousness upended our assumptions about information and responsibilities, this next step—which we called "empowered execution"—would transform the way we thought about power and leadership.

RECAP

♦ *Cooperation across silos would be necessary for success*, and while systemic understanding was a valuable first step, we needed to build more trust if we were to achieve the fluid, teamlike cooperation that we needed across our force; we had to overcome the challenge of the Prisoner's Dilemma.

♦ To this end, we used embedding and liaison programs to create *strong lateral ties* between our units, and with our partner organizations. Where systemic understanding mirrors the sense of "purpose" that bonds small teams, this mirrored the second ingredient to team formation: "trust."

♦ Together, these two elements completed the establishment of *shared consciousness*, something that was vital to our success. As is evidenced by the failures of GM and successes of Ford, the same innovations are sorely needed by many organizations still using rigid silos in an interdependent world.

PART IV

LETTING GO

No captain can do very wrong if he places his ship alongside that of the enemy.

—Admiral Horatio Nelson's instruction to
his captains on the eve of the Battle of Trafalgar

CHAPTER 10

HANDS OFF

I am a light sleeper, so even if I had lain down only an hour earlier, I would hear the dulled thump of hard rubber boots on the wooden walkway outside our hooch. The door would creak open and a couple of knocks would be followed by: "Sir, are you awake?"

"Sure, come on in," I would reply as I sat up in the metal-frame bunk that spanned the width of my room. Daylight would flood in as the door opened—we worked nights, and I would usually go to sleep soon after dawn. Two people—usually a commander of one of the Task Force's subordinate units (the SEALs, Army Special Forces, Rangers, etc.), along with operations, or intelligence officers or sergeants—would enter.

I would know from their expressions whether they were notifying me of friendly casualties—comrades, often friends, killed or seriously wounded. More often the news was welcome—the capture of a long-pursued AQI leader, or a positive location for one of our "high-value targets."

Such news would often be followed by a request for a decision to strike—in daylight that often meant a precision airstrike. Procedures required me, as the commanding general, to approve such airstrikes when U.S. forces were not already engaged in an ongoing firefight because we might risk losing men or endangering civilians.

"Tell me about it," I would say. The officers would present several pages—printed maps, photographs, and background intelligence on the intended target. I would judge the validity of the case against the individual, the strength of the intelligence that convinced us of his current location, and whether or not an airstrike was the only viable option.

After a few minutes of reading and questions, I would ask my visitors if they wanted me to approve the strike. They would respond with a "why do you think we woke you up?" look and nod yes. I would usually approve their recommendation.

Being woken to make life-or-death decisions confirmed my role as a leader, and made me feel important and needed—something most managers yearn for. But it was not long before I began to question my value to the process. Unless I had been tracking the target the previous night, I would usually know only what the officers told me that morning. I could ask thoughtful questions, but I had no illusions that my judgment was markedly superior to that of the people with whom I worked. As much as I would like to think otherwise, I only rarely had some groundbreaking insight. Most of the time I would simply trust the recommendations made by those who came to get me, as they knew the most about the issue. My inclusion was a rubber stamp that slowed the process, and sometimes caused us to miss fleeting opportunities.

Shared consciousness helped us understand and react to the interdependence of the battlefield where we faced off against AQI. But interdependence was only half of the equation—the other half was speed, and that was still an issue. We had become vastly more thoughtful, integrated, and insightful, but the Task Force still was not fast enough.

A big piece of why we lagged AQI lay in our need to relay decisions up and down the chain of command. Decisions that senior leaders a few decades prior would have been *unable* to oversee now required senior approval. Walking down the hall to grab me might take only a few minutes, but in a fast-paced environment, that could be the difference between operational success and failure—between capturing AQI operatives or letting them slip through our fingers, or between life and death for our operators and for Iraqi civilians. The requirement to consult me for strikes was symptomatic of a bureaucracy that, over the years, had grown slower and more convoluted as the world around it had become faster.

Paradoxically, the seemingly instantaneous communications available up and down the hierarchy had *slowed* rather than accelerated decision making. Leaders who could be contacted in moments felt compelled to withhold authority on decisions of significant importance (or for which they might ultimately be held responsible). Repeatedly we navigated approval processes that went all the way to the Pentagon or the White House for strikes against terrorist leaders we'd located, for the deployment of forces, or for the implementation of information campaigns. Communications may have been instantaneous but decisions never were. The aggregate effects were crippling.

Within the Task Force, thanks to radical information sharing, we had come a long way with regard to Drucker's exhortation to "do the right thing" rather than "do things right": people at every level of the organization had the information and connectivity to determine what the right thing was, in real time. But, held back by our internal processes, they lacked the ability to act on that determination. We had gotten halfway to transcending Krasnovian soccer and then stopped: we had built an outstanding team bound together by the oneness of trust and purpose and capable of devising, in real time, brilliant, emergent solutions to complex problems, but we still required every player to get written permission from the coach before passing the ball. Meanwhile, senior leaders from Iraq to Washington had in-boxes overflowing with requests to do things that they knew less about than the people on the ground and about which they were often unable to judge effectively.

This organizational impediment, like so many that we had already dismantled, had its roots in the practical problem solving of another era. In this case, it was the age-old relationship between visibility and control.

"ALL UNDER THE GUNS OF HIS SHIPS"

In November 1852, Matthew Calbraith Perry pushed off from the beaches of Norfolk, Virginia, and set sail for Japan. Behind him glided the largest naval force the United States had ever sent overseas. Commodore Perry was endeavoring to "open up" the island nation, which had for two centuries maintained the self-imposed isolation of *sakoku*: no foreigner could enter Japan, nor could any Japanese leave, on penalty of death.

Perry was a lifelong military man. The younger brother of the War of 1812 hero Oliver Hazard Perry, Matthew enlisted in the Navy at age fourteen. For four and a half decades, he fought pirates, policed smugglers, and performed diplomatic duties on behalf of the United States. He commanded the Gulf Squadron during the Mexican War, assisted colonists in West Africa, and served on a Mediterranean tour that aimed to convey American goodwill to the Ottoman Empire. But the trip to Japan was the mission that would make him famous.

Around the time of his promotion to captain in 1837—then the highest rank in the Navy—Perry began to develop an interest in Japan. A forward-looking man, he had campaigned for the widespread adoption of steam-powered ships, and believed in America's potential as a naval power. But steamships, unlike sailing vessels, required refueling. Perry recognized Japan's strategic importance as a way station en route to China, and in 1851, he made an official proposal for the expedition.

As it happened, President Millard Fillmore also saw opportunity. The opening of Japan would enable the United States to establish a Pacific steamship line, allowing faster communication and increased trade between Asia and the United States. California had become a state in 1850 and Pacific trade was on the rise, increasing the number of American merchant ships in need of supply points and protection. In 1852, Perry set out from Virginia, empowered by Fillmore with an authority that would be unheard of today.

Simply put, Perry was allowed to do pretty much anything he wanted. As he recorded in his diary shortly before embarking:

> It is my duty and it certainly is a pleasure to say, that the President and every member of his Cabinet evinced the liveliest interest in the Expedition and extended towards me the utmost kindness and consideration, authorized me the most liberal equipment of the vessels, invested me with extraordinary powers, diplomatic as well as Naval.

He was not exaggerating. Secretary of State Daniel Webster told Perry that he could "write his own ticket," and a fellow diplomat confirmed that the secretary wished him not only to have "all the strength you desired, but that you should be clothed with full and discretionary powers."

The State Department and the Navy generated a list of U.S. priorities in Japan, including the protection of American sailors and any property that wound up wrecked on Japanese shores, permission for American ships to dock and resupply in Japanese ports, and permission to engage in trade with Japan. But the best way to pursue these aims was left to Perry's discretion. A letter of instruction explained:

> The Secretary of the Navy will . . . be pleased to direct the Commander of the Squadron to proceed, with his whole force, to such point on the coast of Japan as he may deem it advisable, and there endeavor to open a communication with the government, and, if possible, to see the Emperor in person, and deliver to him the letter of introduction from the President with which he is charged.

Deliver the letter he did, in large part thanks to the authority granted to him. He demanded to see only the highest officials, rebuffing Japanese attempts to trick and delay him, and threatening to open fire. Perry supposedly presented Japanese officials with a white flag, explaining that if they chose war over negotiation, they could raise the white flag when they wanted peace, as "victory would naturally belong to the Americans." His bold actions altered the course of Japanese, Asian, and world history.

Carl Builder, a military expert at RAND, summarized Perry's broad authority, writing: "Perry, halfway around the globe and months away from Washington, acted as presidential emissary, ambassador, commander in chief, secretary of state, and trade commissioner, all under the guns of his ships, as he threatened war and negotiated treaties with feudal Japan."

This freedom of action stood in marked contrast to the situation of Perry's peers in the Army. While Perry was preparing for his expedition in 1852 and pondering how best to use his "full discretionary powers," Ulysses S. Grant was serving as a first lieutenant assigned as the regimental quartermaster for the Fourth Infantry Regiment stationed in San Francisco. The commander of the Pacific Division, Brigadier General Ethan Allen Hitchcock, had been given—by Army standards—a fairly expansive mission and broad authority to reorganize federal troops in California and protect gold rushers and settlers from Indian attacks.

But the expeditionary nature of the mission did not prevent the Department of the Army from sending very specific instructions about how it wanted things done: The secretary of war told Hitchcock how to save funds, and ordered him to have his soldiers plant gardens instead of purchasing produce. The Department of the Army sent an inspector general to California in July 1852 to inspect the construction of new forts and hold junior officers accountable for expenses incurred.

By 1864, Grant was a lieutenant general commanding the Union Army. The command and control he exercised in a routine communication with Major General George Meade, his subordinate and the commander of the Army of the Potomac, is a world apart from the instructions given to Perry:

> *HEADQUARTERS ARMIES OF THE U. S.,*
>
> *May 7, 1864, 6.30 A.M.*
>
> *MAJOR-GENERAL MEADE, Commanding A. P.*
>
> *Make all preparations during the day for a night march to take position at Spottsylvania C. H. with one army corps, at Todd's Tavern with one, and another near the intersection of the Piney Branch and Spottsylvania road with the road from Alsop's to Old Court House. If this move is made the trains should be thrown forward early in the morning to the NY River.*
>
> *I think it would be advisable in making the change to leave Hancock where he is until Warren passes him. He could then follow and become the right of the new line. Burnside will move to Piney Branch Church. Sedgwick can move along the pike to Chancellorsville and on to his destination. Burnside will move on the plank road to the intersection of it with the Orange and Fredericksburg plank road, then follow Sedgwick to his place of destination.*
>
> *All vehicles should be got out of hearing of the enemy before the troops move, and then move off quietly.*
>
> *It is more than probable that the enemy concentrate for a heavy attack on Hancock this afternoon. In case they do we must be prepared to resist them, and follow up any success we may gain, with our whole force. Such a result would necessarily modify these instructions.*
>
> *All the hospitals should be moved to-day to Chancellorsville.*
>
> *U. S. GRANT,*
> *Lieut.-General.*

The difference between Perry's open purview and the specificity of instruction imposed on Meade was not a function of rank. As the commander of the Army of the Potomac, Meade would probably have outranked Perry,* and the force he commanded was more than two hundred times the size of Perry's.

What caused the divergence between Perry's freewheeling and the Army's regimented command and control? Varying levels of competence? Different approaches to discipline? The reason was actually much more pragmatic: The Army controlled its officers because it *could*. Army operations took place on land, and thanks to the postal service, Ulysses S. Grant could receive regular detailed updates and send actionable replies. He *could* give directions, so he did—transparency and communication together bred control. The Navy, on the other hand, couldn't reach its captains. As Joseph Conrad explained: "A ship at sea is a world in herself and in consideration of the protracted and distant operations of the fleet units the Navy must place great power, responsibility, and trust in the hands of those leaders chosen for command."

The variable separating Commodore Perry from Grant was the availability of information and communication. The inability to communicate with a far-off fleet demanded that Perry be given levels of autonomy he would never have realized as a commander of land forces.

Predictably, advances in live communications have significantly curtailed the powers and responsibilities enjoyed by Navy commanders. Although there remain vestigial cultural differences between the forces,† Perry's contemporary equivalents are kept under Grant-like wraps. This is for seemingly good reason: Why have an admiral act on behalf of the president when the president can pick up the phone and call any leader in the world? Why have a ship's captain make decisions in a vacuum when

---

*It is hard to make a direct comparison, as this was before the U.S. Navy had expanded to include admirals. Perry's rank of commodore put him at the top of the naval hierarchy, but still with considerably fewer men and resources under his control than Meade.

†"Command by Negation," a concept unique to naval command and control, allows a subordinate commander the freedom to operate as he or she thinks best, keeping authorities informed of decisions taken, until the senior overrides a decision. The Navy is the only service that uses the acronym UNODIR (UNless Otherwise DIRected), by which a commanding officer informs the boss of a proposed course of action, and only if the boss overrides it will it not be taken. The subordinate is informing the boss, not asking permission.

you can have his (presumably older, wiser, more experienced) superiors monitor his actions and provide instruction?*

In short, when they can *see* what's going on, leaders understandably want to *control* what's going on. Empowerment tends to be a tool of last resort. We can call this tethering of visibility to control the "Perry Principle."

Taylor's contemporary Henri Fayol enumerated the "five functions of management" as "planning, organizing, commanding, coordinating, and controlling." The last three become much easier to attend to when you have more information, creating a cycle of seeking ways to gather and centralize more information in order to push more and more efficient directives to the organization. The function of workers is to feed this cycle and await the next commands.

Today's managers have access to all kinds of information about their employees that they lacked just a few years ago. Communication and monitoring technologies like those we used in Iraq, or Sandy Pentland used in his experiments on idea flow, enable higher-ups to analyze macro trends in their markets to keep tabs on how many minutes an individual employee spends resting versus working. Automated systems at restaurants monitor waiters' movements, tracking every ticket, dish, and drink, searching for patterns that suggest efficacy as well as those correlated to theft. All of this enables the habitual centralization of power.

In Iraq, senior leaders like me enjoyed unprecedented insight into every second and square foot of our Task Force's endeavors. I could watch operations in real time and speak to operators in the middle of a firefight (although I never did, for reasons that will be explained later in the chapter). On many occasions we were able, almost instantly, to link together Naval Headquarters in Bahrain, ships operating off the Horn of Africa, Central Command in Tampa, Florida, the Pentagon, our teams on the ground in Africa, and other supporting elements to coordinate sensitive actions. This led us to tighten our grasp on decision making. But as we continued to watch and learn from AQI, we asked ourselves whether perhaps something had changed. We had access to more real-time information than any force in the history of warfare, but to what end?

---

*Similarly, the advent of the telegraph in the late 1800s took away what little expeditionary authority Army officers in the West once had.

While military leaders a century ago yearned for the ability to see and control more of their battlefield, their heirs today have been inundated with too much of a good thing. At our headquarters, I had simultaneous access to live updates and real-time video from offices and operations across the world, and was connected to almost every decision of consequence. This was great for establishing holistic awareness, but it also created a nightmare of paperwork and approvals—time that could otherwise have been spent solving real problems.

Like other staples of managerial thinking, the Perry Principle made sense in a world that no longer exists, but offers little help when the velocity and volume of decisions needing to be made so exceed the capabilities of even the most gifted leaders that empowerment of those on lower rungs is simply a necessity.

In Iraq, we could see that our sharing of information was an effective tool. But the centralization of control that came with such access to tactical data was another question entirely. Centuries of technological and managerial developments suggested that the Perry Principle of extending control, and empowering only as a last resort, was a good rule. But the rules of engagement had changed.

I began to reconsider the nature of my role as a leader. The wait for my approval was *not* resulting in any better decisions, and our priority should be reaching the best possible decision that could be made *in a time frame that allowed it to be relevant*. I came to realize that, in normal cases, I did not add tremendous value, so I changed the process. I communicated across the command my thought process on decisions like airstrikes, and told them to make the call. Whoever made the decision, I was always ultimately responsible, and more often than not those below me reached the same conclusion I would have, but this way our team would be empowered to do what was needed.

The practice of relaying decisions up and down the chain of command is premised on the assumption that the organization has the time to do so, or, more accurately, that the cost of the delay is less than the cost of the errors produced by removing a supervisor. In 2004 this assumption no longer held. The risks of acting too slowly were higher than the risks of letting competent people make judgment calls.

We concluded that we would be better served by accepting the 70 percent solution today, rather than satisfying protocol and getting the 90 percent solution tomorrow (in the military you learn that you will never have time for the 100 percent solution).

I did not expect a bad outcome, but I watched to see how we would do.

"USE GOOD JUDGMENT IN ALL SITUATIONS"

The Ritz-Carlton hotel chain has spent a century building a reputation for quality, luxury, and reliability. Through recessions, depressions, corporate mergers, and world wars, the brand—originally a restaurant operated on high-end cruise ships, then a hotel that earned founder César Ritz the sobriquet "king of hoteliers and hotelier to kings"—has remained at the top of the food chain. Today, the company operates eighty-five hotels in thirty countries and regularly tops the Zagat lists for its hotels and dining. In particular, it has earned a reputation for offering outstanding service. It is César Ritz who is credited with the line, now a universal law in the hospitality industry, that "the customer is always right." Nearly fifty thousand executives from other companies have traveled to the Ritz-Carlton Learning Institute and Ritz-Carlton Leadership Center to learn how they too can achieve such quality of service.

One might think that this is a result of careful oversight and exacting requirements drilled into the Ritz's customer-facing employees—that outstanding service arises from a set of painstakingly detailed protocols. In fact, the company's approach to HR is famous for the freedom it grants. Employees can spend up to $2,000 to satisfy guests or deal with issues that arise. A Harvard Business School case study detailed this and other extraordinary policies, such as the fact that the Ritz trains all its employees to "break away" from their duties if a guest needs something special, and encourages employees to "use their empowerment." One of the basics that employees are given is "Instant guest pacification is the responsibility of each employee. Whoever receives a complaint will own it, resolve it to the guest's satisfaction, and record it."

A similar approach was taken at Nordstrom, the department store chain known for its "almost mythic levels of assistance" to customers. New employees are issued a card that reads:

WELCOME TO NORDSTROM.

We're glad to have you with our Company. Our number one goal is to provide outstanding customer service. Set both your personal and professional goals high. We have great confidence in your ability to achieve them, so our employee handbook is very simple. We have only one rule.

Flipping the card over reveals the company's single rule:

Our One Rule: Use good judgment in all situations.
Please feel free to ask your department manager, store manager, or Human Resources officer any question at any time.

Since the 1980s, when companies began experimenting with "empowerment"—the buzzword that summarizes what we called "decentralization of decision-making authority"—myriad studies in the social sciences have concluded that this psychological difference of empowerment has a very real impact. Jay Conger and Rabindra Kanungo's 1988 paper "The Empower Process: Integrating Theory and Practice" noted that empowerment improved employee satisfaction. Kenneth W. Thomas and Betty A. Velthouse identified the decentralization of authority as creating "intrinsic task motivation." Studies have found this effect in domains ranging from nursing in China to five-star hotels in Turkey.

The "scientific management" model, by contrast, was described by one of Taylor's disciples as resting "primarily upon two important elements":

1st: *Absolutely rigid and inflexible standards throughout your establishment.*

2nd: *That each employee of your establishment should receive every day clear-cut, definite instructions as to just what he is to do and how he is to do it, and these instructions should be exactly carried out, whether they are right or wrong.*

Today, even the most clockwork of tasks—like factory floor labor and other mechanical tasks—can benefit from some degree of innovation and creative thinking. The less people's jobs can be automated, the more you need them to take initiative, innovate, and think creatively. But despite the evidence of all these studies, few managers are willing to take this leap: today, only 20 percent of workers feel empowered and act resourcefully; most feel disenfranchised or locked down.

With rising interdependence and unpredictability, the costs of micromanagement are increasing. Rosabeth Moss Kanter of Harvard Business School, a pioneer in the study of empowerment in the workplace, sums up the imperative of extending authority downward: As world events become ever more disruptive, "the number of 'exceptions' and change requirements go up, and companies must rely on more and more of their people to make decisions on matters for which a routine response may not exist." She concludes, "The degree to which the opportunity to use power effectively is granted to or withheld from individuals is one operative difference between those companies which stagnate and those which innovate."

In other words, as our environment erupts with too many possibilities to plan for effectively, we *must* become comfortable sharing power. In a *Harvard Business Review* article, Josh Bernoff and Ted Schadler argue, "In a world where one angry tweet can torpedo a brand, corporations need to unleash their employees to fight back." Citing United Airlines' sluggish response to Dave Carroll's broken guitar, both before and after he posted his video, they assert that a new approach is needed—one in which team players do not have to consult with the coach before taking a shot. United is just one of many companies to suffer "viral" scandals: blogger Heather Armstrong took to Twitter to vent her frustration with Maytag; Greenpeace assaulted Nestlé's Facebook page about their environmental policies; Comcast found itself in the midst of unwanted attention after a subscriber posted a recording of his conversation with a representative who refused to let him cancel his service. The Internet has made individual consumers vastly more powerful—as Bernoff and Schadler observe, "anyone with a smartphone or a computer can inflict lasting brand damage." But for the most part, employees charged with responding to consumer complaints remain more restricted than ever by the Perry Principle; the organization has, in most cases, not evolved to mimic its protean environment. The asymmetry is a recipe for disaster.

If the first United representative Carroll had spoken to had had the authority to address his issue, the company could have avoided embarrassment, and might have acquired an advocate. Electronics chain Best Buy has tried to do just that. Using a system called Twelpforce, employees were enabled to respond on Best Buy's behalf on Twitter. When an iPhone bought from Best Buy broke and the consumer started tweeting that the in-store staff did not do him justice (instead of offering him a replacement iPhone they gave him a BlackBerry), a customer service representative saw the tweet, swooped in, responded, and arranged for him to have an iPhone the next day.

Best Buy, Bernoff and Schadler write, was

> just as susceptible to online customer complaints as any other company, but because it's run differently, it can respond differently. . . .
> Far better than trying to prevent such activity is to acknowledge that your employees have technology power . . . armed with technology, your employees can build solutions at the speed of today's connected customers.

Kanter foresaw that increased disruption and unpredictability would necessitate increased agility and adaptability which could be achieved only by loosening control. AQI had empowered its operatives, not only with technology, but with decision-making authority, while our operators struggled to respond under codes designed to align with the Perry Principle. This is just what we wanted in the Task Force: we accepted that divergences from plan were inevitable—we wanted to improve our ability to respond to them. We needed to empower our teams to take action on their own.

"AS LONG AS IT IS NOT IMMORAL OR ILLEGAL"

As an instinctive perfectionist, it pained me to do it, but I began pushing authority further down the chain of command. Empowerment did not always take the form of an overt delegation; more often, my more self-confident subordinates would make decisions, many far above their pay grade, and simply inform me. My response, often very publicly conveyed during our O&I, typically endorsed their initiative, and created a multiplier effect, whereby more and more people, seeing the success of their peers, would begin taking more matters into their own hands.

Like the directors of Ritz-Carlton and Nordstrom, I found that, by ignoring the Perry Principle and containing my desire to micromanage, I flipped a switch in my subordinates: they had always taken things seriously, but now they acquired a gravitas that they had not had before. It is one thing to look at a situation and make a recommendation to a senior leader about whether or not to authorize a strike. Psychologically, it is an entirely different experience to be charged with *making* that decision. Junior officers, instead of handing the decision to me and providing guidance, were now entrusted with the responsibility of a decision that was, quite literally, often a matter of life and death.

Eventually a rule of thumb emerged: "If something supports our effort, as long as it is not immoral or illegal," you could do it. Soon, I found that the question I most often asked my force was "What do you need?" We decentralized until it made us uncomfortable, and it was right there—on the brink of instability—that we found our sweet spot.

There were growing pains. Some subordinate leaders tried to hold authority at their level, and on a number of occasions I had to confirm to partner agencies or units that a decision voiced by someone in the Task Force had my approval. Often, I was hearing about the decision for the first time, but I cannot remember a time when I failed to support it.

On the whole, our initiative—which we call "empowered execution"*— met with tremendous success. Decisions came more quickly, critical in a fight where speed was essential to capturing enemies and preventing attacks. More important, and more surprising, we found that, even as speed increased and we pushed authority further down, the *quality* of decisions actually went *up*.

We had decentralized on the belief that the 70 percent solution today would be better than the 90 percent solution tomorrow. But we found our estimates were backward—we were getting the *90 percent solution today* instead of the *70 percent solution tomorrow.*

This took us by surprise and upended a lot of conventional assumptions about the superior wisdom of those at the top. Understanding the underlying causes of this unexpected outcome proved essential to sustaining and enhancing it.

---

*Like "shared consciousness," this term was coined not during the Task Force years, but during the course of our subsequent research at CrossLead.

A piece of this is the psychology of decision making. An individual who makes a decision becomes more invested in its outcome. Another factor was that, for all our technology, our leadership simply did not understand what was happening on the ground as thoroughly as the people who were there. The ability to see video footage and hear gunfire from an operation as it unfolded was a tremendous asset, but a commander on the ground can comprehend the complexity of a situation in ways that defy the visual and audible: everything from temperature and fatigue to personalities. I had been a baseball pitcher in my youth and knew that often the man on the mound knows what he's best postured to throw.

But the key reason for the success of empowered execution lay in what had come *before* it: the foundation of shared consciousness. This relationship—between contextual understanding and authority—is not new.

"EVERY CAPTAIN WAS A NELSON"

During this period I found myself pondering an exceptional example of the Navy's traditional embrace of empowerment, and asking myself what exactly made it work. On my daily runs parallel to Balad's long runway, I would listen to the audiobook of Adam Nicolson's *Seize the Fire* about Admiral Nelson. Nelson's genius as a leader had been his nurturing of the independent decision-making abilities of his subordinates—described by Nicolson as "entrepreneurs of battle." As we discussed in chapter 1, Nelson's wily perpendicular attack at Trafalgar created the chaos in which his force could thrive and his enemies—trained to follow flags and bearing little knowledge of the overall strategy—flailed. Nelson had told his commanders, "No captain can do very wrong if he places his ship alongside that of the enemy," but that broad authority could have gone terribly wrong if he had not spent decades cultivating their individual qualities as decision makers, and if they had lacked an overall understanding of the force and the battle as a whole. This was Nelson's equivalent of shared consciousness, and it was only because of it that his captains could thrive as empowered agents in a chaotic mêlée.

For most of my career in the Army, my mess dress uniform bore light blue lapels that signaled I was in the infantry. Artillery wore red,

Special Forces wore green, tankers wore yellow. Our uniforms—stripes, badges, tabs, and insignia—announced our rank, qualifications, and experience, our box in the org chart. They also bolstered our sense of identity. Of course, I believed that every branch mattered, but for twenty-four and a half years after I graduated from West Point, I *knew* blue mattered a bit more.

But when I was promoted to brigadier general in January 2001, my lapels changed to black—indistinguishable from those of generals who had ascended through the medical corps, engineers, or aviation. A general is expected to have *general knowledge* of the army—blue, red, green, and everything in between. It is *because* they have this general knowledge that leaders can be trusted to make major decisions.

In 2004 we were asking every operator to think like someone with black lapels—in other words, like Nelson's captains. We were working to pump general-officer information and awareness throughout our ranks, giving people used to tight orders and limited visibility the insights once reserved for people at the top. In the old model, subordinates provided information and leaders disseminated commands. We reversed it: we had our leaders provide information so that subordinates, armed with context, understanding, and connectivity, could take the initiative and make decisions. Shared consciousness meant that people at every level on our org chart now enjoyed access to the kind of perspective once limited to senior leaders.

The term "empowerment" gets thrown around a great deal in the management world, but the truth is that simply taking off constraints is a dangerous move. It should be done only if the recipients of newfound authority have the necessary sense of perspective to act on it wisely.

At Trafalgar, Nelson's redistribution of authority was put to the ultimate test: A few hours into the battle, a sharpshooter on the *Redoutable*—the enemy ship with which Nelson's *Victory* had locked masts—fired a shot that hit Nelson in the shoulder and became lodged in his back. The wound was incapacitating and clearly fatal. While Nelson's men carried their dying admiral belowdecks, the battle reached its climax. In the raging noise and violence, few noticed his absence. He died about three hours later, having lived just long enough to know of his victory.

"To any other Nation the loss of a Nelson would have been irreparable," said French vice-admiral Villeneuve, after the battle, "but in the British Fleet off Cadiz, every Captain was a Nelson."

We wanted our force to exhibit the entrepreneurial mind-set of those British captains, so we nurtured holistic awareness and tried to give everyone a stake in the fight. When we stopped holding them back—when we gave them the order simply to place their ship alongside that of the enemy—they thrived.

THE VISIBLE MAN MODEL OF DECISION MAKING

He was just fifteen inches tall and made of plastic, but he left an enduring impression on me. The brainchild of Marcel Jovine, a former Italian soldier who came to America as a POW in World War II, the Visible Man was a plastic anatomical toy introduced by the Renwal Products Company in the fall of 1958. He cost $4.98 and his clear plastic body held a skeleton and organs that could be removed and replaced.

My older brother Scott had one and I remember concluding that because we could see through the transparent "skin" of the body, we could get a general idea of what was going on inside. I thought about how much easier doctors' jobs would be if real humans were similarly designed; seeing might save a lot of exploratory surgery.

Though I never caught anyone, I suspect that eye rolling was common when I referred time and again to the Visible Man during the Task Force video teleconferences. I told subordinates that if they provided me with sufficient, clear information about their operations, I would be content to watch from a distance. If they did not, I would describe in graphic terms the "exploratory surgery" necessary to gain the situational awareness I needed. They were free to make all the decisions they wanted—as long as they provided the visibility that, under shared consciousness, had become the standard.

By 2006 we had transformed the way we observed, assessed, acted, and interacted in all our operations.

At Balad, our screens usually streamed FMV (full-motion video) transmitted down from a Predator UAV or manned surveillance aircraft

218 · TEAM OF TEAMS

providing a real-time view of somewhere in Iraq, Afghanistan, or elsewhere in the region. Sometimes instead they would display an operations log or chat room reflecting the latest updates provided by Task Forces across the region. We would watch our helicopters land in a cloud of dust and operators move swiftly toward their targets. Explosions could temporarily "white out" the screen and small arms fire looked like fireflies briefly illuminating the night. Logs would mirror what we saw: "Aircraft on ground," "Target contained (surrounded)," and hopefully "Jackpot," which indicated that the individual targeted on the mission had been captured, or sometimes killed.

My laptop had special software that enabled me to monitor (and speak to) any part of our force on internal radio nets. In real time I could see what was happening, hear the operators' internal discussions, and read their ongoing reporting. For a closet micromanager, it was a new opportunity to pull the puppet strings from great distances.

But I did not do that. I never told operators what to do on a raid; it would have been a mistake. I'd learned that seeing the conditions on the ground, hearing the tone and content of a radio call—having situational awareness of what was happening, and why—helped me do my part of the task better—not to reach in and do theirs. It was counterintuitive, but it reflected exactly the approach to decision making that we needed to pervade our force: "Eyes On—Hands Off."

I was most effective when I supervised processes—from intelligence operations to the prioritization of resources—ensuring that we avoided the silos or bureaucracy that doomed agility, rather than making individual operational decisions.

When we tried to do the same things tighter and faster under the constraints of the old system, we managed to increase the number of raids per month from ten to eighteen; by 2006, under the new system, this figure skyrocketed to three hundred. With minimal increases in personnel and funding, we were running *seventeen times faster*. And these raids were more successful. We were finding a higher percentage of our targets, due in large part to the fact that we were finally moving as fast as AQI, but also because of the increased quality of decision making.

"Eyes On—Hands Off" represented a complete reverse of the Perry Principle: if we could see it, we would *not need* to try to control it. As it turned out, this would also require a rethought approach to personal leadership.

RECAP

♦ Traditionally, organizations have implemented *as much control over subordinates as technology physically allowed*.

♦ New technologies offer today's leaders unprecedented opportunities to gather information and direct operations, but because of the speed necessary to remain competitive, centralization of power now comes at great cost. While shared consciousness had helped us overcome the *interdependence* of the environment, *speed*, the second ingredient of complexity, still posed a challenge.

♦ Effective adaptation to emerging threats and opportunities requires the *disciplined practice of empowered execution*. Individuals and teams closest to the problem, armed with unprecedented levels of insights from across the network, offer the best ability to decide and act decisively.

CHAPTER 11

LEADING LIKE A GARDENER

T he cramped bridge of the *Red October*, a new Soviet nuclear submarine with stealthlike capability, is tense with anticipation as a
torpedo knifes through the water toward it. Impact means instant
death.

FIRST OFFICER VASILI BORODIN: Torpedo impact, 20 seconds.

His serious but utterly calm commander, Captain Marko Ramius,
played by Sean Connery with a distinguished beard and tailored black
navy tunic, seemingly ignores Borodin's warning. He turns to CIA analyst Jack Ryan (Alec Baldwin):

RAMIUS: *[to Ryan]* What books?

RYAN: Pardon me?

Talking about books at this moment seems like lunacy.

RAMIUS: What books did you write?

RYAN: I wrote a biography of, of Admiral Halsey, called *The Fighting Sailor* about, uh, naval combat tactics . . .

RAMIUS: I know this book!

Ramius appears totally engrossed with the book.

BORODIN: Torpedo impact . . .

Amazingly, Ramius continues the discussion.

RAMIUS: Your conclusions were all wrong, Ryan . . .

BORODIN: . . . 10 seconds.

RAMIUS: . . . Halsey acted stupidly.

Predictably, though others on the bridge assume they are doomed, at the last second Ramius cleverly prevents their demise by steering his submarine directly toward the oncoming torpedo, causing it to strike before its warhead is armed. It is the apogee of heroic leadership—omniscient, fearless, virile, and reassuring. It is also almost entirely unrealistic. While some leaders possess extraordinary gifts and project a charismatic presence, in a career alongside accomplished leaders, I never met a Marko Ramius—or anyone remotely close to the character author Tom Clancy created in *The Hunt for Red October*.

WHY TRADITIONAL LEADERS STRUGGLE

We gravitate toward "heroic leaders" who combine qualities we associate with leadership, such as wisdom and physical courage. For a generation after his 1815 triumph over Napoleon at the Battle of Waterloo, Arthur Wellesley, the Duke of Wellington, embodied this concept. Images of Wellington on horseback, deftly maneuvering troops, established an ideal: the leader as all-knowing puppet master, crafting brilliant strategies and distributing precise commands.

The organization as a rigidly reductionist mechanical beast is an endangered species. The speed and interconnected nature of the new world in which we function have rendered it too stupid and slow to survive the onslaught of predators. In some cases, it simply lumbers into tar pits, lacks the strength to free itself, and slowly dies. The traditional heroic leader may not be far behind. Yet even in our new environment, we still retain high, often unrealistic, expectations of leaders. We publicly demand high-level strategic vision and an unerring ability to anticipate broad market trends, but we simultaneously celebrate CEOs for encyclopedic mastery of every aspect of their business. We routinely ask government leaders if they knew the smallest details of an issue, and if not, why they didn't. We expect our leaders to know everything, knowing full well that the limits of technology and the human brain won't allow it.

As we saw with Commodore Perry and General Grant, leadership techniques have traditionally varied with physical proximity. Up close, as long as things moved at a reasonably slow speed, a competent manager could control a military formation or an assembly line. As distances grew greater, even energetic leaders found it impossible to micromanage what they couldn't see. Railroads, telegraph, automobiles, and radio made it easier for leaders to influence developments from afar, but real control remained elusively out of reach. Even at the pace of horses or steamships, local events could develop faster than distant decision makers could monitor, assess, decide, and act.

Recent technology might appear to have closed the gap between leaders and subordinates. Armed with unprecedented amounts of data, CEOs, politicians, and bureaucrats can peer into what is happening almost as it occurs. As we discussed, this information can seduce leaders into thinking that they understand and can predict complex situations—that they can see what *will* happen. But the speed and interdependence of our current environment means that what we cannot know has grown even faster than what we can.

The doctrine of empowered execution may at first glance seem to suggest that leaders are no longer needed. That is certainly the connection made by many who have described networks such as AQI as "leaderless." But this is wrong. Without Zarqawi, AQI would have been an entirely different organization. In fact, due to the leverage leaders can harness through technology and managerial practices like shared consciousness and empowered execution, senior leaders are now more important than ever, but the role is very different from that of the traditional heroic decision maker.

In the Task Force, we found that, alongside our new approach to management, we had to develop a new paradigm of personal leadership. The role of the senior leader was no longer that of controlling puppet master, but rather that of an empathetic crafter of culture.

Within such complexity, leaders themselves can be a limiting factor. While the human capacity for thought and action is astounding, it is never quite enough. If we simply worked more and tried harder, we reason, we could master the onslaught of information and "urgent" requirements.

But of course we can't. Author Dan Levitin explains:

> In 2011 Americans took in five times as much information every day as they did in 1986—the equivalent of 175 newspapers. During our leisure time, not counting work, each of us processes 34 gigabytes or 100,000 words every day. The world's 21,274 television stations produce 85,000 hours of original programming every day, as we watch an average of 5 hours of television each day, the equivalent of 20 gigabytes of audio-video images.

Where once an educated person might have assumed she was at least conversant with the relevant knowledge on a particular field of study, the explosion of information has rendered that assumption laughable.

One solution to information overload is to increase a leader's access to information, fitting him with two smartphones, multiple computer screens, and weekend updates. But the leader's access to information is not the problem. We can work harder, but how much can we actually take in? Attention studies have shown that most people can thoughtfully consider only one thing at a time, and that multitasking dramatically degrades our ability to accomplish tasks requiring cognitive concentration. Given these limitations, the idea that a "heroic leader" enabled with an über-network of connectivity can simultaneously control a thousand marionettes on as many stages is unrealistic.

CHESS MASTER TO GARDENER:
THE LEADERS WE NOW NEED

Considered by many to be the ultimate strategic contest between two players, the game of chess originated in eastern India in the sixth century. Once considered a game for nobility, chess was thought to be an effective tool for teaching strategic thinking to future leaders.

The various pieces—king, queen, rook, knight, bishop, and pawn—behave differently. The pawns, the most numerous, are the least maneuverable. The queen is the most maneuverable and thus the most lethal. The king, while relatively weak, is the figure that must be preserved. None can think or act for themselves. None eye the board from their unique vantage point and suggest moves. None cry warnings of danger. The chess player is all by herself to observe, decide, and act.

From a distance, the Task Force's fight in Iraq in 2004 looked like chess, more particularly the rushed *bullet* version of the game, where players have time constraints for each move. Empowered with an extraordinary ability to view the board, and possessing a set of units with unique capabilities, I was tempted to maneuver my forces like chess pieces against AQI. I could be Bobby Fischer or Garry Kasparov, driving my relentlessly aggressive campaign toward checkmate.

But the chess metaphor quickly broke down. Even in its most rapid form, chess is still a rigidly iterative game, alternating moves between opponents. War in 2004 followed no such protocol. The enemy could move multiple pieces simultaneously or pummel us in quick succession, without waiting respectfully for our next move.

They did so with such speed that it was soon apparent that their changes were not the outcome of deliberate decision making by seniors in the hierarchy; they were organic reactions by forces on the ground. Their strategy was likely unintentional, but they had leveraged the new environment with exquisite success.

Our teams were crafted to be chess pieces with well-honed, predictable capabilities. Our leaders, including me, had been trained as chess masters, and we hoped to display the talent and skill of masters. We felt responsible, and harbored a corresponding need to be in control, but as we were learning, we actually needed to let go.

I leaned back on what I'd learned—not in a classroom at West Point, or on a range at Fort Benning, but much earlier.

In the summer of 1966, soon after my father returned from his first tour in Vietnam, my parents bought a new house. The large, early-1900s brick home gave my parents, the six kids, Noche the dog, and a constant stream of visitors room to spread out. My mother, Mary, a perpetual motion machine, used part of the yard to take up gardening. No flowers— Mom was about measurable output. She grew fruit and vegetables. Beans were aligned with military precision, tomatoes on the right flank, lettuce in reserve. Napoleon would have approved, though Taylor would have moved the compost pile (my responsibility) near the fig tree, slightly closer to the squash lines, to shave seconds off labor.

There were challenges. The first year my mother overestimated the number of zucchini plants she needed and the family suffered through every permutation of zucchini dish except ice cream. But overall the garden was a rousing success. My contribution was spotty and occasional, but I did watch and learn.

If the garden is well organized and adequately maintained, and the vegetables are promptly harvested when ripe, the product is pretty impressive. The gardener creates an environment in which the plants can flourish. The work done up front, and vigilant maintenance, allow the plants to grow individually, all at the same time.

Years later as Task Force commander, I began to view effective leadership in the new environment as more akin to gardening than chess. The move-by-move control that seemed natural to military operations proved less effective than nurturing the organization—its structure, processes, and culture—to enable the subordinate components to function with "smart autonomy." It wasn't total autonomy, because the efforts of every part of the team were tightly linked to a common concept for the fight, but it allowed those forces to be enabled with a constant flow of "shared consciousness" from across the force, and it freed them to execute actions in pursuit of the overall strategy as best they saw fit.

Within our Task Force, as in a garden, the outcome was less dependent on the initial planting than on consistent maintenance. Watering, weeding, and protecting plants from rabbits and disease are essential for success. The gardener cannot actually "grow" tomatoes, squash, or beans—she can only foster an environment in which the plants do so.

THE GARDENER

Although I recognized its necessity, the mental transition from heroic leader to humble gardener was not a comfortable one. From that first day at West Point I'd been trained to develop personal expectations and behaviors that reflected professional competence, decisiveness, and self-confidence. If adequately informed, I expected myself to have the right answers and deliver them to my force with assurance. Failure to do that would reflect weakness and invite doubts about my relevance. I felt intense pressure to fulfill the role of chess master for which I had spent a lifetime preparing.

But the choice had been made for me. I had to adapt to the new reality and reshape myself as conditions were forcing us to reshape our force.

And so I stopped playing chess, and I became a gardener. But what did gardening actually entail?

First I needed to shift my focus from moving pieces on the board to shaping the ecosystem. Paradoxically, at exactly the time when I had the capability to make more decisions, my intuition told me I had to make *fewer*. At first it felt awkward to delegate decisions to subordinates that were technically possible for me to make. If I could make a decision, shouldn't I? Wasn't that my job? It could look and feel like I was shirking my responsibilities, a damning indictment for any leader. My role had changed, but leadership was still critical—perhaps more than ever.

Creating and maintaining the teamwork conditions we needed—tending the garden—became my primary responsibility. Without my constantly pruning and shaping our network, the delicate balance of information and empowerment that sustained our operations would atrophy, and our success would wither. I found that only the senior leader could drive the operating rhythm, transparency, and cross-functional cooperation we needed. I could shape the culture and demand the ongoing conversation that shared consciousness required.

Leading as a gardener meant that I kept the Task Force focused on clearly articulated priorities by explicitly talking about them and by leading by example. It was impossible to separate my words and my actions, because the force naturally listened to what I said, but measured the importance of my message by observing what I actually did. If the two were incongruent, my words would be seen as meaningless pontifications.

Communicating priorities and cultural expectations to our team of teams spread across multiple continents was a challenge. Written guidance was essential, but memos competed with the flood of text that engulfed all of us every day. To post brief updates and observations, I used a secure Web-based portal accessible to everyone, carefully composing each memo to ensure that it reflected not only my thoughts, but also my "voice." I tried to remember "less is more," and stuck to a few key themes. Experience had taught me that nothing was heard until it had been said several times. Only when I heard my own words echoed or paraphrased back to me by subordinates as essential "truths" did I know they had been fully received.

As a leader, however, my most powerful instrument of communication was my own behavior. As a young officer I had been taught that a leader's example is always on view. Bad examples resonate even more powerfully than good ones. In situations where senior leaders can cloister themselves behind walls or phalanxes of aides, emerging only when their ties are straight, their hair coiffured, and their words carefully chosen, controlling the signal might be possible. But in a world of tweets and 24/7 news coverage, it is not. I didn't even attempt to hide.

Instead, I sought to maintain a consistent example and message. Our daily Operations and Intelligence (O&I) video teleconference became key to my overall communications effort. Although the information exchanged was the baseline "product," the O&I served as my most effective leadership tool as well, because it offered me a stage on which to demonstrate the culture I sought.

Early in the fight I recognized that although I could theoretically command from any location, remaining deployed and appearing at the O&I while wearing my combat uniform against an austere plywood backdrop communicated my focus and commitment. I could demand effort from the force, or support from Washington, D.C., with greater legitimacy than from any other vantage.

I also demonstrated this new paradigm of leadership by demanding free-flowing conversation across the force during the O&I. The technical hurdles of creating a video teleconference for more than seventy locations, many of them isolated, bandwidth-starved bases, were huge, but the meetings had to be seamless. In the early days I saw that interruptions in connection or other glitches undercut the perceived importance of the forum, and I could not allow that. For the same reasons, the O&I was never canceled and attendance was mandatory. I felt that if the O&I was seen as an occasional event not always attended by key leaders, it would unravel.

The rules for any meeting are established more by precedent and demonstrated behavior than by written guidance. I wanted the O&I to be a balance of reporting of key information and active interaction. That didn't come naturally, particularly across a digital medium. The participants came from different organizational cultures, were thousands of miles apart, and had never met in person. Getting candor under those conditions was not easy, but we made it work. When necessary, I would preplan questions or comments and plant them with trusted partners to help demonstrate to everyone what I wanted the O&I to be.

Although the O&I had to be a briefing to the entire force, my role as commander remained central. Our system worked such that the person giving the brief was shown on the screen from wherever he or she was located, but the default returned to me when the brief finished. As a result, I was on live TV in front of my entire force and countless interagency partners every day for an hour and a half. If I looked bored or was seen sending e-mails or talking, I signaled lack of interest. If I appeared irritated or angry, notes such as "What's bothering the boss?" would flash across the chat rooms that functioned in parallel to the video teleconference. Critical words were magnified in impact and could be crushing to a young member of the force. I learned that simply removing my reading glasses and rubbing my temple was an action that was interpreted on several continents.

There were constant opportunities to lead. Each day several intelligence analysts, typically young people I hadn't yet met in person, would be tasked to give short updates from their locations—places like the U.S. embassy in Sanaa, Yemen, the National Security Agency headquarters at Fort Meade, or a small base along the Afghanistan-Pakistan border. Sitting in a small room, often alone, they would have the daunting experience of giving a televised presentation to a fifty-plus-year-old general and an intimidating group of experienced warriors and intelligence professionals. Few slept the evening before, and it would have been simple for me to unintentionally, even unconsciously, make it a terrible experience for them.

When their turns came and their faces suddenly filled the screen I made it a point to greet them by their first name, which often caused them to smile in evident surprise. They were eight levels down the chain of command and many miles away—how did the commanding general know their name? Simple: I had my team prepare a "cheat sheet" of the day's planned briefers so I could make one small gesture to put them at ease.

As they briefed me I tried to display rapt attention. At the conclusion, I'd ask a question. The answer might not be deeply important, and often I knew it beforehand, but I wanted to show that I had listened and that their work mattered. Some were flustered by the question—they would sigh in relief when they made it through their briefing—but it also gave them a chance, in front of the entire command, to show their knowledge and competence.

For a young member of the command, even if the brief had been terrible, I would compliment the report. Others would later offer them advice on how to improve—but it didn't need to come from me in front of thousands of people. When we did it right, the analyst left the O&I more confident about, committed to, and personally invested in our effort.

"Thank you" became my most important phrase, interest and enthusiasm my most powerful behaviors. In a small room with trusted advisers, frustration or anger can be put into context and digested. But the daily O&I was large enough that petulance or sarcasm could be disastrous. More than anything else, the O&I demanded self-discipline, and I found it exhausting. But it was an extraordinary opportunity to lead by example.

I adopted a practice I called "thinking out loud," in which I would summarize what I'd heard, describe how I processed the information, and outline my first thoughts on what we should consider doing about it. It allowed the entire command to follow (and correct where appropriate) my logic trail, and to understand how I was thinking. After I did that, in a pointed effort to reinforce empowered execution, I would often ask the subordinate to consider what action might be appropriate and tell me what he or she planned to do.

Thinking out loud can be a frightening prospect for a senior leader. Ignorance on a subject is quickly obvious, and efforts to fake expertise are embarrassingly ineffective. I found, however, that asking seemingly stupid questions or admitting openly "I don't know" was accepted, even appreciated. Asking for opinions and advice showed respect. The overall message reinforced by the O&I was that *we* have a problem that only *we* can understand and solve.

Gardeners plant and harvest, but more than anything, they *tend*. Plants are watered, beds are fertilized, and weeds are removed. Long days are spent walking humid pathways or on sore knees examining fragile stalks. Regular visits by good gardeners are not pro forma gestures of concern—they leave the crop stronger. So it is with leaders.

The military term is "battlefield circulation" and it refers to senior leaders' visiting locations and units. I found that these trips, like almost everything, benefited from careful planning and focused execution. Most of these visits had multiple objectives: to increase the leader's understanding of the situation, to communicate guidance to the force, and to lead and inspire. A good visit can accomplish all three, but a bad visit can leave subordinates confused and demoralized.

Visits offer an opportunity to gain insights absent from formal reports that have passed through the layers of a bureaucracy. I found it helpful to communicate before the visit the primary questions I had and to ask for background information I could review before arriving. On-site, briefings from the local leadership were appropriate, but they needed to be accompanied by less formal interaction with individuals further down the chain. It was pointless to bring junior members to big meetings in front of their entire chain of command and expect candor, but I found that creating the right venues was easy to organize.

There's an art to asking questions. Briefings are valuable but normally communicate primarily what the subordinate leader wants you to know, and often the picture they provide is incomplete. Thoughtful questions can help fill in the blanks. Early in 2005 my intelligence officer, then–Colonel (later Lieutenant General) Mike Flynn, taught me a great technique. We were visiting a unit that boasted of having more than 250 intelligence sources (Iraqi civilians recruited to pass information to U.S. forces). I was deeply impressed. Mike then asked a simple question: "Can you describe your very best source? I'll assume that all the others are less valuable." The unit admitted that the best was new and unproven, and in an instant it was clear that their source network had little real substance.

I later used a specific question when talking to junior officers and sergeants in small bases in Afghanistan: "If I told you that you weren't going home until we win—what would you do differently?" At first they would chuckle, assuming I was joking, but soon realized I wasn't. At that point most became very thoughtful. If they were forced to operate on a metric of task completion, rather than watching the clock until they went home, the implications would be significant. Almost all were good soldiers and leaders, but they had been shaped into thinking in terms of their tour of duty, a time horizon that rarely predicted successful mission completion.

Once they recalculated, their answers were impressive. Most adjusted their approach to take a longer view of solving the problem. You might expect them to seek a quicker solution and an earlier ticket home. But they were experienced enough to know that real solutions demand the long view—simple fixes are illusory. Although I couldn't change the troop rotation policy, as I left, I'd ask each soldier to execute his or her duties with that mind-set.

Communicating during visits is nonstop. From small group meetings with leaders to "town hall" talks to larger groups, I found it essential to let members of the command hear directly from me. I'd often start by standing in front of them and asking them to look into my eyes and decide over the next hour if they trusted me. I told them I was doing the same with them. "You have the right to judge in person the leader who represents you—and I have the right to size you up as well." I avoided talking down to them, and I tried to understand and respect their perspective. It was often difficult. Soldiers fighting a daily battle under frightening conditions can feel their leaders are far removed from their reality. There's no magic cure for this challenge, and soothing words that aren't backed up by action encourage cynicism. If, after hearing their problems or concerns, I couldn't do anything about them, I found it far better to state that directly than to pretend I could change things. Simple honesty shows, and earns, respect.

It is important to be realistic. Visits are often planned by well-intentioned, energetic staff members who plan more activities than can be accomplished. Hurried "drive-by" interactions leave subordinates frustrated—if you come to ask questions, leave enough time to listen to the answers. And remember that even senior leaders are human. Congressional delegations would often arrive in Iraq so exhausted by the long flight and their jammed schedules that they would doze off as we tried to explain what we were doing. It is hard to learn or express support for the force if you are asleep.

Over my career I'd watched senior leader visits have unintended negative consequences. Typically schedules were unrealistically overloaded and were modified during the visit to cancel parts of the plan. On the surface it might be the necessary decision, but invariably soldiers who had spent days preparing a briefing or demonstration for the "great man's" visit were informed at the last minute that all their work had been for naught. It was not a good way to improve morale.

I would tell my staff about the "dinosaur's tail": As a leader grows more senior, his bulk and tail become huge, but like the brontosaurus, his brain remains modestly small. When plans are changed and the huge beast turns, its tail often thoughtlessly knocks over people and things. That the destruction was unintentional doesn't make it any better.

THE WAY FORWARD

Leading a team of teams is a formidable task—much of what a leader must be, and do, has fundamentally changed. The heroic "hands-on" leader whose personal competence and force of will dominated battlefields and boardrooms for generations has been overwhelmed by accelerating speed, swelling complexity, and interdependence. Even the most successful of today's heroic leaders appear uneasy in the saddle, all too aware that their ability to understand and control is a chimera. We have to begin leading differently.

Creating and leading a truly adaptive organization requires building, leading, and maintaining a culture that is flexible but also durable. The primary responsibility of the new leader is to maintain a holistic, big-picture view, avoiding a reductionist approach, no matter how tempting micromanaging may be. Perhaps an organization sells widgets, and the leader finds that he or she loves *everything* about widgets—designing, building, and marketing them; that's still not where the leader is most needed. The leader's first responsibility is to the *whole*.

A leader's words matter, but actions ultimately do more to reinforce or undermine the implementation of a team of teams. Instead of exploiting technology to monitor employee performance at levels that would have warmed Frederick Taylor's heart, the leader must allow team members to monitor *him*. More than directing, leaders must exhibit personal transparency. This is the new ideal.

As the world becomes more complex, the importance of leaders will only increase. Even quantum leaps in artificial intelligence are unlikely to provide the personal will, moral courage, and compassion that good leaders offer. Persuading teams to network with other teams will always be difficult, but this is a culture that can be planted and, if maintained, can flourish. It just requires a gardener: a human, and sometimes all-too-human, leader displaying the willingness to accept great responsibility remains central to making an ecosystem viable.

RECAP

♦ Although we intuitively know the world has changed, most leaders reflect a model and leader development process that are sorely out of date. We often demand unrealistic levels of knowledge in leaders and force them into ineffective attempts to micromanage.

♦ The temptation to lead as a *chess master, controlling each move of the organization, must give way to an approach as a gardener*, enabling rather than directing.

♦ A *gardening approach to leadership is anything but passive*. The leader acts as an "Eyes-On, Hands-Off" enabler who creates and maintains an ecosystem in which the organization operates.

PART V

LOOKING AHEAD

The first duty imposed on those who now direct society is to educate democracy; to put, if possible, new life into its beliefs, to purify its mores; to control its actions; gradually to substitute understanding of statecraft for present inexperience and knowledge of its true interests for blind instincts; to adapt government to the needs of time and place; and to modify it as men and circumstances require.

—Alexis de Tocqueville

CHAPTER 12

SYMMETRIES

The funeral of the high-level AQI leader Abu Zar followed a familiar pattern; a wakelike outdoor gathering and then burial. In the late summer of 2005 we watched the event through Predator surveillance and accepted his death with mixed feelings. Removing an operative as effective as Abu Zar from the battlefield reduced the threat of VBIEDs (vehicle-borne improvised explosive devices) in Baghdad, but it eliminated our opportunity to question him on AQI's Baghdad network and operations. The fact remained, however, that he was dead.

Or so we thought. On January 6, 2006, one of our liaison officers reported that Iraqi forces had captured an individual they believed was Abu Zar—very much alive. The funeral had been an elaborate ruse to throw us off his trail. Alive and in our control, Abu Zar began to cooperate in our search for Zarqawi.

Intelligence reporting on Zarqawi had varied in volume and specificity through the summer and fall of 2005. We had monitored rumors that he was badly wounded and recovering in Syria, we listened to his broadcasts to various insurgent groups inside Iraq, and we even tracked a young Iraqi reported to be his latest wife, hoping for a lead. But in the spring of 2006 the young thug from Zarqa was free and more effective than ever.

Still, I was increasingly confident that his days were numbered. Our understanding of his organization, and of Zarqawi himself, had grown dramatically. More significant, so had the Task Force's effectiveness. Our pathetic intelligence abilities of October 2003 were a far cry from the sophisticated organization we had become. Despite events like the February 2006 AQI bombing of the Shia Golden Mosque in Samarra, which ignited a hurricane of sectarian violence across Iraq, the Task Force was vastly more effective than it had been, with greater abilities than ever before for targeting Zarqawi and destroying his network.

A curious incident reinforced my confidence. Through some adept technical work, we captured the raw digital footage of a propaganda film AQI was making. It showed Zarqawi, clad in his signature black, shooting weapons amid some nondescript dirt berms. The video reflected a catch-me-if-you-can cockiness crafted to enhance his warrior-leader image. But, before AQI could release its edited version, we released the outtakes: Zarqawi fumbling amateurishly with an automatic weapon, one of his henchmen grabbing a white-hot barrel with predictable results. More important, through some stunningly impressive work, analysts in D.C. were able to pinpoint the location where the scenes had been filmed. Our team of teams was now able to network its expertise quickly and effectively.

In early April, tipped off by back-from-the-dead Abu Zar, an intelligence sergeant major named Walter began watching a farmhouse in a rural area west of Baghdad. After weeks of surveillance, he saw indications of an AQI meeting. No order or plan had directed his surveillance of the location he labeled NAI (Named Area of Interest) 152, but after years in Iraq, he intuitively connected the dots.

Within minutes of seeing what looked to him like an AQI gathering, Walter passed the information to the Task Force, recommending an immediate strike.

A daytime raid was not a decision taken lightly. Flying in hostile airspace and landing close enough to the target that the suspects could not escape put our forces at risk.

Because the operators trusted Walter's expertise and instincts and were themselves immersed in the intelligence process, they assessed the risk and made a decision almost instantaneously.

The operators struck at 1:56 p.m. The resulting firefight killed five insurgents and revealed an arsenal of weapons, suicide vests, and other munitions. While the operation was still ongoing, surveillance noted activity at a farmhouse a short distance away. Walter and other analysts judged that it warranted targeting as quickly as possible.

As soon as the firefight at NAI 152 concluded, the operators "called an audible" and brought in Night Stalker helicopters to raid the suspected meeting at the neighboring farmhouse, now named Objective MAYERs. There was no time to get approval from Task Force headquarters, no time for a rehearsal, and no written operations order. The seasoned teams simply stood by the choppers, listened to the sergeant major's assessment over the radio, developed a plan, and flew to the objective within minutes. They landed on target two hours and fifteen minutes after beginning the firefight at NAI 152. The halting mechanics of 2003 seemed a lifetime ago.

No shots were fired in the second raid as the raid force captured twelve Iraqi men. But red flags became apparent immediately. The men were obviously not farmers, and in a country where everyone seemed to carry a phone, we found only one between them. Either they had deliberately not brought them or had thrown them into a nearby canal when they heard the helicopters. The men were detained and brought in for interrogation.

A statement in the following afternoon's Operations and Intelligence video teleconference made me take immediate notice: "This is not just a bunch of fighters. These guys are different."

Like the Old West scouting report that things are "too quiet," the statement carried tremendous significance. The briefer was one of our most experienced intelligence officers, a veteran of operations against the Abu Sayyaf (Al Qaeda–associated) insurgent movement in the Philippines, as well as years of operations in Afghanistan and Iraq. He knew what was normal, so different stood out.

Within days our analysts had identified several of the men as midlevel AQI operatives. Our teams also began a deliberate effort to determine if any was a senior leader or directly connected to one. They compared the men's stories for inconsistencies and asked each of the men to identify who among them was the most important.* Earlier in the fight such a guileless approach would have appeared stupidly simple to us. But we had learned that "if it's stupid and it works, it isn't stupid."

Initial suspicions bounced from one man to another until we focused on a confident middle-aged man we will call Allawi. In the days ahead,

---

*Interestingly, all twelve identified the same man—including the man himself. While a significant AQI operative, he did not turn out to be the man who led us to Zarqawi.

as the fight against AQI raged on across Iraq, we worked to understand who Allawi was.

Allawi's interrogation team wasn't the only group focusing on him, nor were the intelligence analysts working around the clock in adjacent plywood-walled rooms. Our entire network—our teams across Iraq, intelligence agencies back in the United States and in the United Kingdom, headquarters of partner units across the region, and more than seventy liaison teams that the Task Force had positioned in headquarters, offices, and other critical locations—joined in the effort. Across the network, teams coordinated the questions asked, shared the answers received, proffered suggestions, and exchanged insights. It was a battle of wits, and we now had harnessed thousands of minds—nobody's brain had been left in the footlocker.

In mid-May, after dozens of patient interrogation sessions, Allawi decided to give us what he knew we wanted: a connection to Zarqawi. He told us that he knew the identity of Zarqawi's spiritual adviser, a man named Sheikh Abd al-Rahman, who had regular face-to-face interaction with our target. It was the critical piece of the puzzle: all we had to do was to find Rahman and follow him to Zarqawi.

Easier said than done. Rahman lived in Baghdad, which in May 2006 was becoming a postapocalyptic shell of its former self. AQI-driven violence, highlighted by horrific car bombs, had already drenched the capital in blood when Shia rage over the Golden Mosque bombing erupted. Moving around the streets on operations, or conducting surveillance, became remarkably difficult. Sunnis were stopped at Shia checkpoints, pulled from vehicles, and executed on the spot. In raided AQI safe houses we found medieval-like torture chambers with photographs and videos documenting sectarian sadism.

We located a man we believed to be Rahman living with his family in a Baghdad neighborhood, and we readied both ground and air teams to maintain unblinking surveillance and PID, or "positively identify," the suspect up close. But keeping constant track of an individual who does not want to be found was challenging, even with our vastly improved technology.

An age-old quandary emerged: the decision to strike or hold. We felt we had eyes on Rahman, and hoped to watch him patiently until he led us to Zarqawi, but we knew the dynamic could change any day. If we struck immediately, we could probably capture Rahman, but unless he cooperated almost immediately, Zarqawi would be alerted and disappear. If we waited and watched, there was a greater chance we would spook the adviser, Zarqawi might move for other reasons, or any number of "black swans" might arise and disrupt our scheme.

To add further tension to our decision, massing enough surveillance assets to maintain unblinking surveillance of Rahman diverted us from other potential operations at a time when Baghdad was melting down. Information flowed; options were tabled and argued over. Patience is hard when people are dying. In the time before our creation of force-wide shared consciousness, tribal instincts would almost certainly have derailed our focus—teams not involved in the Zarqawi hunt would have made far more noise about their need for ISR assets. Thanks to the common purpose that suffused our Task Force, people understood, and we pressed on.

Finally, after seventeen days of round-the-clock surveillance, we saw the spiritual adviser relocate his family to another house in Baghdad. It was an indicator: Allawi had told us that such a move meant Rahman was about to depart the city to meet with Zarqawi. We stared harder.

Rahman's departure from Baghdad and journey to Zarqawi was pure drama. Watching from multiple command-and-control nodes, eyes straining to avoid missing even the smallest detail, we used our constellation of manned and unmanned surveillance aircraft to observe and record every move he made. I watched from Balad knowing that, eight time zones away in the United States, others were doing the same.

We saw Rahman get dropped off on the side of a road on the outskirts of Baghdad and be picked up almost immediately by a blue "bongo" truck.* This almost textbook "vehicle swap"—a move designed to confound anyone attempting to follow him—was oddly reassuring. Innocent civilians don't work to shake possible tails. A small restaurant in Baqubah, the capital of Diyala Province, was the scene of Rahman's next tactic. Entering a side door, he exited another a few minutes later to climb into a white pickup truck and drive off. The pickup had a surprisingly familiar look: Zarqawi was known to use multiple similar trucks to confound aerial surveillance. As we followed the pickup, we also maintained eyes on the original sedan Rahman had taken from Baghdad and on the restaurant, in case the man who left was not him. Had we been limited to a single aerial surveillance platform as we had been in 2003 or 2004, we

---

*A "bongo" truck is a flatbed pickup truck, produced by South Korean Kia Motors since 1980, that is popular in Iraq.

would have been forced to choose which to watch and left to hope our observation skills and luck were good. Now, thanks to our teams' willingness to pool resources, we were able to have different aircraft maintain their "constant stare" on each target. Throughout the process, we mapped out connections and plotted locations—targets we would strike after doing our best to get Zarqawi.

The house Rahman drove to was in an area called Hibhib. A driveway led from the main road, spanned a small canal, then dead-ended at a concrete and stone house that would have been a respectable addition to most American neighborhoods. The tree-lined road carried little traffic.

As Rahman drove up to the house, a man came out to greet him and escorted Rahman inside. The man then walked back out and moved down the length of the driveway to the road. He wore all-black robes, and cut a commanding presence. At the end of the driveway, he looked left and right, and turned before going back inside. Abu Musab al-Zarqawi.

We had talked for two and a half years about this moment, but decision time is never as neat and clean as you envision it. Going after him was a given, but the question was how. The unit that controlled our operations in Iraq operated about thirty feet from me inside our headquarters at Balad. Their commander and I spoke briefly as he confirmed his confidence that the man was Zarqawi and said he intended to strike.

He launched a raid force from Baghdad, but as a backup also had F-16s ready to bomb. He didn't ask permission and I didn't ask him to ask. I'd learned that trust was critical. Deviating from the modus operandi we had worked so hard to foster—even when the stakes were high—would be a mistake.

As always, events diverged from plan.

The Baghdad-based raid force was delayed by helicopter maintenance problems. We had a very limited time window in which to strike. Behind the house sprawled a grove of palm trees. Tracking someone who managed to flee into the palms, particularly as darkness approached, would require hundreds of soldiers and more luck than we wanted to bank on.

The commander turned to plan B—the F-16s—but one of the aircraft was off station for refueling. Critical minutes were ticking by.

Finally, a second F-16 made its way to the target. After a jaw-clenching delay of several minutes, it dropped its ordnance.

We watched the stone and concrete house containing the man who had masterminded AQI's reign of terror disappear in a cloud of smoke.

When the raid force landed, about twenty-eight minutes after the bombs, they found local Iraqi police on-site with an ambulance. Zarqawi lay on a stretcher, still alive. An American medic who understood the tremendous value of a live Zarqawi in custody worked to save him. But he died twenty-four minutes later of internal injuries.

They brought Zarqawi's body directly back to Balad. Lying on a mat on the concrete floor, the body showed no external injuries, and looked exactly as we'd seen Zarqawi in photographs. Still, to avoid any possibility of error, we passed the fingerprints back to the FBI in the United States and waited impatiently for them to confirm the identification before any leadership could announce the operation.

As we waited, we amassed intelligence on the targets we had identified during the chase. We also conducted a planned intercontinental farewell party for then–Rear Admiral Bill McRaven, a SEAL who had been a key element in the command for almost three years (he would later lead the Task Force and then United States Special Operations Command). That night he got the usual good-natured ribbing from people who admired him. We conducted his farewell digitally, Bill and his wife, Georgeann, gathered at Fort Bragg with staff and families there, while my command team from Balad, our other deputy commander from Afghanistan, and other members of the command from around the region participated by video teleconference. We joked, told stories, and passed gifts to Bill. To the uninitiated, it would have seemed a strange gathering, but by June 2006, our distributed network felt oddly normal. We had become a new command of a new age.

A s we celebrated, a staff officer walked in and whispered in my ear. My wife, Annie, told me later that as she watched my reaction on the screen, unaware of the operation, she knew something significant had happened, and prayed it was not more casualties. It wasn't. We had just received confirmation that Abu Musab al-Zarqawi was dead.

Now our task forces across Iraq swung into action. Over the course of the evening they struck targets as quickly as possible, including fourteen in Baghdad alone, hoping to hit each before word of Zarqawi's death prompted the AQI operatives to move. We had placed these strikes on hold before, concerned they could prompt Zarqawi to vanish. Such simultaneous strikes had the special potential to "shock" AQI's network, and at each target we gathered more intelligence, identified more connections, and prepared to maintain pressure.

In the moment, the operation against Zarqawi seemed like the most important thing in our lives—and perhaps at the time it was. The processes, relationships, and trust that underpinned that complex effort were by now things we almost took for granted. We used them every day and night as though they were the natural order of things. Inside, however, most of us knew just how much it had taken to bring that "natural order" into being.

THE *STAR WARS* BAR

The organization that pulled this off was a world apart from the organization that failed to prevent the sewage plant bombing in September 2004. Driven by the necessity to keep pace with an agile enemy and a complex environment, we had become adaptable. We had fused a radical sharing of information with extreme decentralization of decision-making authority.

In doing so, we had a structure unlike any force the U.S. military had ever fielded. Gone were the tidy straight lines and right angles of a traditional MECE org chart; we were now amorphous and organic, supported by crisscrossing bonds of trust and communication that decades of managers might have labeled as inefficient, redundant, or chaotic.

By 2007, the Task Force was winning the fight against AQI.* Our thinking had become smarter, and our execution more nimble. We were learning and adapting quicker than the enemy and—finally—hitting them faster than they could regenerate. We hit targets every night, but also started striking during the day—something we never could have done without the superior intelligence capabilities and trust between our operators and analysts that had been bred by our network.

A few years earlier, detainees would smugly dismiss our limited understanding of their organization. Now, they marveled at our intel, asking interrogators, "How are you doing this? How could you know that?" The answer was not some secret treasure trove of AQI data we stumbled across or a technological breakthrough in surveillance; it was the very

---

*Of course, this was only one piece of the war at large, and the fact that we had gained an edge over AQI, though it greatly behooved coalition forces, did not represent the be-all and end-all of the war. Nor, sadly, would our suppression of AQI outlast our presence in Iraq.

edge that AQI had once held over us: a revolution in the mundane art of management.

Our performance flowed naturally from the interconnected neural network that our force had become. Walking into the SAR, once a place of disciplined stratification, a visitor would now see a teeming assembly of experts from across our force and the intelligence community. An analyst would be next to an operator next to someone on rotation from one of our partner agencies, gathering information from Baghdad, Kabul, and D.C. We eventually dubbed it "the *Star Wars* bar," after the motley crew of aliens that populated George Lucas's extraterrestrial taverns.

Though the elimination of Zarqawi represented a pivotal moment in our fight against AQI, it was just one small piece of the puzzle. In fact, the decentralization of authority that AQI had engineered—and that we, in our own way, had adopted—meant that "decapitation" was no silver bullet. Our main strategy was to hollow out the middle ranks of the organization, which tended to be the most connected. An organization as regenerative and fluid as AQI would never possess a single point of failure, which was why it was important that we hit them relentlessly and accurately.

AQI was adaptable. But Zarqawi's death was a major victory in morale. At long last, we were better. We had become not a well-oiled machine, but an adaptable, complex organism, constantly twisting, turning, and learning to overwhelm our protean adversary.

In 1835, Alexis de Tocqueville published the first of two volumes of what is now considered one of the founding texts of political science: *Democracy in America*. He had just returned to his native France from a nine-month trip to the United States—at the time, a lazy backwater with a small economy whose chief relevance to Europe was its remarkable Revolutionary War a half century prior. Tocqueville, however, looked at America and saw the future. As revolutions spread across Europe, upending monarchies and ushering in republics and democracies, he turned to the United States as an example of how to do it right. Visiting bustling eastern cities and exploring the midwestern wilderness, Tocqueville was impressed by the "almost complete equality of conditions" in America. He was astounded by the high levels of civic participation in voluntary associations, writing that "in no country of the world has the principle of association been more successfully used or applied to a greater multitude of objectives than in America."

Tocqueville also wrote extensively on what he saw as America's vulnerabilities. Although people then and now tend to consider the essential tenet of democracy to be the political empowerment of the people, this alone does not produce a *successful* democracy—the people can be effectively empowered only if they have enough context to make good decisions. Tocqueville emphasized this point, noting that "in the United States the instruction of the people powerfully contributes to the support of the democratic republic."

Political scientist Brian Danoff explains that Tocqueville saw leaders as "charged with the task of educating democratic citizens, and providing their understanding of freedom with a sense of purpose, a sense of 'what freedom is for.'" This critical caveat to Tocqueville's predictions of American democratic success cuts to the heart of what makes democracy tick: a political structure in which decision-making authority is—in some ways—decentralized to the voters, rather than concentrated in a monarchic or oligarchic core, *requires* a high level of political awareness among the public in order to function. If people are not educated enough to make informed decisions at the polls, the feedback system on which democracy is premised will not work. The proliferation of democratic governments across the world over the past two centuries might suggest that the simple act of democratic decentralization itself is a recipe for success. But as Tocqueville points out, one cannot make good choices without proper context: a democracy such as America could remain free only with "a proper kind of education." In other words, a system requires shared consciousness before it can reap the benefits of empowered execution.

Tocqueville recognized that empowerment without context will lead to havoc. This is the risk run if traditional, hierarchical organizations just push authority down, *ceteris paribus* (think of the 2008 financial crisis, largely sparked by young, uninformed finance professionals being given far too much leeway and far too little guidance). An organization should empower its people, but only *after* it has done the heavy lifting of creating shared consciousness. This is much harder when you are trying to achieve something constructive: AQI could dole out empowerment with relatively little shared consciousness because, with destruction as their primary goal, precision and coordination were not always necessary; but for most human endeavors struggling to come to terms with a complex environment—everything from supply chain management to aid distribution to marketing to national governance—doing something *constructive* is essential to their mission. Empowered execution without shared consciousness is dangerous.

Similarly, shared consciousness on its own, as we learned, is powerful but ultimately insufficient. Building holistic awareness and forcing interaction will align purpose and create a more cohesive force, but will not unleash the full potential of the organization. Maintain this system for too long without decentralizing authority, and whatever morale gains were made will be reversed as people become frustrated with their inability to act on their new insights. Just as empowerment without sharing fails, so does sharing without empowerment.

Shared consciousness is a carefully maintained set of centralized forums for bringing people together. Empowered execution is a radically decentralized system for pushing authority out to the edges of the organization. Together, with these as the beating heart of our transformation, we became a single, cohesive unit far more agile than its size would suggest. Unlike the items in a MECE checklist, neither of these can be instituted alone; only when fused can they power an organization. As with team members, complex system components, and other dynamics we have discussed in the book, the union of shared consciousness and empowered execution is greater than the sum of their parts.

The speed and interdependence of the modern environment create complexity. Coupling shared consciousness and empowered execution creates an adaptable organization able to react to complex problems.

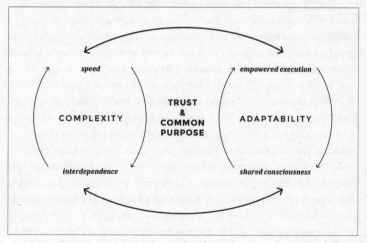

The relationship between context and authority is as ancient as it is intuitive, but it has usually been directed by improving the information given to senior leaders, thereby enhancing their decision-making purview (Tocqueville's application of this to the distributed governance of democracy is a historic exception).

We reversed this direction. We used shared consciousness to pump information out, empowering people at all levels, and we redefined the role of leadership ("gardeners"). What we did would not have been possible twenty, ten, maybe even five years prior—so essential to our approach were the information technologies we harnessed—nor would it have been necessary. Today it is.

A WORLD WITHOUT STOP SIGNS

This new world—the wayward swirl in which my granddaughter Emmylou will grow up—is equal parts exciting and frightening. Human interaction—not just in the context of management—is changing tremendously.

The University of Texas at Austin computer simulation on the future of automotive traffic provides a perfect reflection of these shifts. The program illustrates how a four-way intersection might look in an urban landscape dominated by self-driving cars communicating in real time. And watching it somehow just feels wrong. The intersection is huge—a ten-lane highway crossing over another ten-lane highway—but there are no traffic lights, no stop signs, and seemingly no sense of order. Vehicles don't queue up based on direction of travel to wait their turn before migrating to the other side en masse. Instead, cars going in all four directions zip past one another at full speed, constantly within feet of a horrific T-bone. The intersection is never empty; no vehicle ever stands still. It doesn't even look like they slow down. Their trajectories can be plotted in coordination with one another long before arriving at the intersection, so there is no need for the stopping and starting that characterize human behavior under similar circumstances. It looks like a death trap, but driverless cars promise to reduce traffic fatalities significantly. UT professor Peter Stone, one of the leaders of the project, notes that 25 percent of accidents and 33 percent of the thirty-three thousand auto deaths each year in America occur at intersections, and 95 percent are attributable to "human error." Early trials suggest that self-driving cars could save ten thousand deaths a

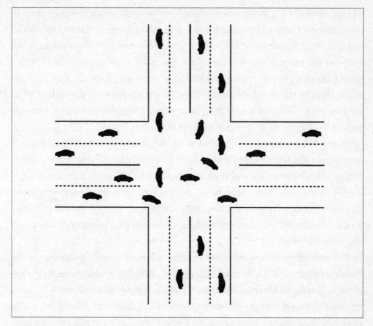

A computer simulation on how intersections could change in the future due to the innovation of self-driving cars.

year while making commutes faster and more comfortable. But for all the statistics and trials, the UT simulation still doesn't look right.

It looks unnatural because we have a strongly ingrained idea of how traffic *should* look, and it is governed by a mechanical rhythm of stops, starts, and turns. In contrast to these satisfying, machinelike motions, the fluid mess in the simulation seems like dangerous disorder. Psychologists and organizational theorists call these heuristics for how the world works "mental models." Mental models can be very helpful—they can provide shortcuts and keep us from reinventing the wheel. As *The Onion* put it tastefully, "Stereotypes are a real timesaver."

Problems arise when these models no longer reflect reality and when they inhibit creative thinking. We have to recognize that a mental model is *not* reality, it is just a representation of reality, and there are a near-infinite number of equally valid representations, almost all of which also leave something out in the interests of simplification. A subway map of

Washington, D.C., is no more "right" or "wrong" than a topographical map, but the former is useless for hiking and the latter is useless for catching a train. Nonetheless, we have to avoid the temptation to confuse the map for the terrain—to believe that subway lines are the only true representation of a city, or that lights and stop signs are the only way to manage traffic. In the words of Albert Einstein, "Our theories determine what we measure." When we urge people to think "outside of the box," we are generally asking them to discard mental models.

In the case of traffic, our mental model is one in a family of models about how the world around us should be run, most of which are mechanistic, with clear rules and demarcations and categories that are readily visible to the naked eye. Standards, norms, and rules of engagement make us comfortable. This is effective; this is efficient. Things should not look like a chaotic, self-organizing mess. And for the past century, those models served us well.

We are likely to see more and more "chaotic mess" solutions in the coming decades. We will need to confront complex problems in ways that are discerning, real-time, responsive, and adaptive. We will need systems capable of doing things that no single designer, however masterful, could envision—things far beyond an individual planner's capacity to comprehend and control, just as the intricate structure of ant colonies is beyond the single ant's 250,000-neuron brain.

Anne Murray Allen, former head of IT and strategy for one of Hewlett-Packard's most profitable divisions, and University of Oregon social network researcher Dennis Sandow teamed up for a series of studies on social network analysis. Reflecting on their research, they wrote, "As the philosophy of the physical sciences dominated the Industrial Age, the philosophy of the biological sciences is beginning to dominate the Knowledge Age. This philosophy views knowledge, people and organizations as living systems . . . [which represents a shift from] (1) focusing on parts to focusing on the whole, (2) focusing on categorization to focusing on integration."

Insofar as organizations—armies, schools, governments, corporations—are essential to solving the biggest problems we face, and the running of those organizations enables or disables their effectiveness, management determines the quality of the world we live in. Management has tapped the power of industry, sent men to the moon, saved the lives of the wounded and the sick, and won and lost wars. And now we need systems that can solve the complex, systemic threats of climate change, brittle development aid flow, and networked terrorism. This makes management one of the fundamental limfacs to the quest for human progress, and as we look to solve bigger and bigger problems, we will need management systems that, like the UT traffic system, can adjust and adapt in real time; that are not constrained by the expired mental models of yesteryear.

As complexity envelops more and more of our world, even the most mundane endeavors are now subject to unpredictability, and we can learn from those at the vanguard. In the 1960s, NASA was the exception, but today it is the rule; only a handful of entities have *not* found themselves surrounded by complexity. Supply chains, once reliable assembly lines, are now spread across the globe and subject to constant, nonlinear disruption—everything from a food shortage in Zambia to a disease outbreak in China to a storm in the middle of the Pacific can impact the delivery of a product packaged in the United States. An American lawn care company came to CrossLead for help because their line-and-block charts had become overwhelmed by the realities of a global economy, a complex supply chain, and the thicketed, overlapping network of relationships with suppliers, marketers, and consumers. Another client—a large technology company—struggled to integrate efforts across continents after a storm in Thailand wiped out production of their flagship product.

Out of necessity, AQI invented a new solution to being effective in this new environment, as did we, and as, sooner or later, will everyone else. There is no such thing as an organizational panacea—the details will always be different for different people, places, and objectives—but we believe that our model provides a good blueprint.

Eventually, we all have to take a leap of faith and dive into the swirl. Our destination is a future whose form we may not find comforting, but which has just as much beauty and potential as the straight lines and right angles of the past century of reductionism: this future will take the form of organic networks, resilience engineering, controlled flooding—a world without stop signs.

Taylor, in the 1880s, gazed into a new era of technology brimming with opportunity and saw that the organization of human behavior would be a limfac. The potential gains in productivity promised by industrialization were being constrained by inconsistent, localized practices.

He threw out the apprenticeship model that had worked so well for centuries and put in its place his doctrine of reductionist, replicable efficiency whose legacy remains threaded through organizations to this day.

In 2003, we were also coming to terms with the reality that technological progress had overwhelmed our management doctrine. We were using the reductionist paradigm that had worked so well since Taylor, but we were faced with a new wave of technologies defined by connectivity—the Internet, the spread of cell phones, and the growth of social media—networks whose power lies in their emergent, nonlinear behaviors, not in the sum of their nodes. This technology produced complex problems—the kind of challenges that, as Warren Weaver observed seventy years ago, refuse to yield to reductionist analysis.

Like Taylor, we found that the same technologies that created these challenges brought solutions. For Taylor, the spread of mechanization offered the opportunity for replicable procedure at scale; for us, the free flow of data unlocked new worlds of teamwork and permutational collaboration. In 2003, our organizational norms regarding information—and, thus, decision-making authority—derived from technological realities of the past: for most of human history, copying and transmitting information was costly. In the past twenty years, the costs of copying, sharing, transmitting, and manipulating data have dropped practically to zero. This enabled us to share in new ways and, consequently, to empower people with new levels of authority.

There was even a nice historical symmetry to the conceptual aesthetics of our organization: our organization, like Taylor's, visually mirrored the technologies of the time. While Taylor developed orderly, machinelike organizational forms to make the most of the orderly machines in his factories, our network resembled the snaking, overlapping, constantly shifting structural makeup of the Web. While Taylor's management structures focused on inputs and outputs, much like a physical assembly line, ours was built on an ecosystem of shared information similar to crowdsourced solutions, just like the architecture of adaptive, evolving Web sites like Wikipedia, which share massive quantities of information among all users and give individuals authority to alter the system.

Just as scientific management fused Smithian thought on efficiency with a new era of technology to create a new kind of organization, we found that our doctrine, by harnessing the ideal of democratic collaboration, had resulted in a fundamentally new type of force—an information-age Task Force.

The Task Force still had ranks and each member was still assigned a particular team and sub-sub-command, but we all understood that we were now part of a network; when we visualized our own force on the whiteboards, it now took the form of webs and nodes, not tiers and silos. The structure that had, years earlier, taunted us from our whiteboards as we failed to prevent the murder of men, women, and children in attacks like the El Amel sewage plant bombing had, like Saddam's bunkers, been repurposed and become our home.

To defeat a network, we had become a network. We had become a team of teams.

RECAP

♦ As our Task Force transformed itself, both our speed and precision improved dramatically. This was not a triumph of fine-tuning it into a hyperefficient machine. *It had become a more transparent, more organic entity.*

♦ Technology had been both a cause of our challenge and a tool for our success. But it was the *culture change in the organization that allowed the Task Force to use it properly.*

♦ At the core of the Task Force's journey to adaptability lay a yin-and-yang symmetry of *shared consciousness,* achieved through strict, centralized forums for communication and extreme transparency, and *empowered execution,* which involved the decentralization of managerial authority. Together, these powered our Task Force; neither would suffice alone.

♦ Our transformation is reflective of the new generation of mental models we must adopt in order to make sense of the twenty-first century. If we do manage to embrace this change, we can unlock tremendous potential for human progress.

ACKNOWLEDGMENTS

Writing a book requires a great deal of organization, discipline, and patience. Writing a book between four authors requires even more coordination, restraint, and editing, although it does provide the added benefit of harnessing different minds and viewpoints to create a unique product. This book is truly a result of a "team of teams" working together to draw on past experiences, analyze and research the stories of others, and visualize what the future could hold.

To help craft the book into a coherent narrative, we relied on the wisdom and advice of professionals, colleagues, and friends. Our co-workers at CrossLead have been essential in both shaping our narrative, developed and continually refined in our past four years of business, and in editing this attempt to capture their shared insights on paper. Brooke Neuman was especially helpful in assisting us by coordinating logistics and managing the publicity surrounding the rollout of the book. The team at Portfolio / Penguin, led by Adrian Zackheim and guided by Bria Sandford, became trusted partners, providing support, patience, and encouragement in a long process.

We could not have produced this book without relying on the research and great works of many, many authors in a wide variety of fields. Drs. Matthew Carty and E. J. Caterson from Brigham and Women's Hospital in Boston, Howard McCurdy of American University, and Preston Cline of the University of Pennsylvania also provided valuable feedback and information that shaped key narratives of the book.

Countless individuals read repeated drafts and provided invaluable feedback in both the early stages of drafting and the late stages of intensive editing. Phil Kaplan provided valuable in-depth research and Michael Eastman gave helpful advice on the book's structure and content. Although we could not begin to thank every single person involved in this project, Mike Hall, Mike Flynn, Coleman Ruiz, Barry Sanders, Steven Spear, Joel Peterson, Tom Friedman, Lea Carpenter, Louis Kim, Dick

Shultz, Lacy Hebert, Melanie Harris, and Jonathan Saw all gave helpful comments and edits on early drafts of the manuscript.

Thanks to Susan Tallman, who read every draft and provided advice throughout the review process.

And of course, major thanks to Jessica Craige, whose fact-checking, patience with *The Chicago Manual of Style*, and thoughtful research and feedback anchored our process.

A personal note from General McChrystal: I met Teddy Collins when he was a student at Yale taking my leadership course. He immediately struck me as an extraordinary, brilliant individual. We maintained our relationship afterward, and when it came time to start considering my next book project, Teddy was the single person who I knew could take the most important role in crafting this book. Teddy became the gravitational pull that brought every idea, every piece of research, every experience, and every personality together, masterfully weaving all of our thoughts into a beautifully written and coherent narrative. I could not be more proud of what we have created together, along with our coauthors.

NOTES

PART I

THE PROTEUS PROBLEM

9 **island of Pharos** . . . Homer, *The Odyssey,* trans. by Robert Fagles (New York: Penguin, 1996), 135.

9 **Eidothea told Menelaus** . . . Homer, *The Odyssey,* 136.

9 **disguised in sealskins** . . . Homer, *The Odyssey,* 138.

9 **"with soaring branchtops"** . . . Homer, *The Odyssey,* 138–39.

CHAPTER 1: SONS OF PROTEUS

16 **Thirty-five children** . . . The events described are based on the actual attack that occurred in El Amel, Baghdad, on September 30, 2004. While it is impossible to know some of the exact operational details of the attack, all of the details supplied are common to how we saw Al Qaeda in Iraq operate throughout the war. Some of the factual elements of the story are reconstructed from Borzou Daragahi, "35 Small Bodies Add Up to Horror: Car Bomb Carnage Shatters Ceremony," *San Francisco Chronicle,* October 1, 2004, http://www .sfgate.com/news/article/35-small-bodies-add-up-to-horror-Car-bomb -2690397.php.

17 **For Al Qaeda in Iraq** . . . Associated Press, "Major Attacks Claimed by Zarqawi," *Guardian,* June 8, 2006, http://www.theguardian.com/world/2006 /jun/09/iraq.mainsection.

21 **exited Suwaqah in 1999** . . . Jean-Claude Brisard, *Zarqawi: The New Face of Al-Qaeda* (Cambridge, UK: Polity Press, 2005), 58–59.

21 **Salafist bent** . . . Hala Jaber, "A Twisted Love," *Sunday Times,* July 31, 2005.

21 **burn off the tattoos** . . . Megan K. Stack, "Zarqawi Took Familiar Route into Terrorism," *Los Angeles Times,* July 2, 2004.

22 **training camp in Herat** . . . Stack, "Zarqawi Took Familiar Route."

22 **Canal Hotel in Baghdad** . . . Kim Ghattas, "Mixed Feelings over UN Iraq Role," BBC News, August 11, 2007, http://news.bbc.co.uk/2/hi/middle_east /6941560.stm.

22 **International Red Cross headquarters** . . . Dexter Filkins and Alex Berenson, "The Struggle for Iraq: Insurgency; Suicide Bombers in Baghdad Kill at Least 34," *New York Times,* October 28, 2003, http://www.nytimes.com

/2003/10/28/world/the-struggle-for-iraq-insurgency-suicide-bombers-in
-baghdad-kill-at-least-34.html.

22 **By December** . . . According to the U.S. State Department, there were 198
"significant" terrorist incidents in Iraq in 2004, compared with the worldwide total of 175 in 2003, 22 of which occurred in Iraq.

22 **more major terrorist attacks** . . . Susan Glasser, "US Figures Show Sharp
Global Rise in Terrorism," *Washington Post,* April 26, 2005, http://www
.washingtonpost.com/wp-dyn/content/article/2005/04/26/AR200504260
1623.html.

22 Statistics on worldwide terrorism have been highly controversial, and the
State Department was forced to retract its annual *Patterns of Global Terrorism* report in 2003, admitting that its initial report tremendously understated
the number of incidents. The issue quickly became politicized, as Democrats
accused the Bush administration of manipulating the numbers in order to
inflate its success in curbing global terrorism. Consequently, the 9/11 Commission recommended creation of a National Counterterrorism Center (NCTC)
in July 2004 to provide an agency for a standardized analysis of global terrorism. In 2005, the State Department's *Patterns of Global Terrorism* report was
renamed *Country Reports on Terrorism,* which did not include a statistical
breakdown of terrorist attacks. However, the NCTC's subsequent reports
included statistics, which we have referenced.

22 **8,300** . . . Mark Mazzetti, "Insurgent Attacks on Iraqis Soared, Report
Says," *New York Times,* April 29, 2006, http://www.nytimes.com/2006/04
/29/world/middleeast/29terror.html?_r=0.

22 **a third of terrorist attacks** . . . Mazzetti, "Insurgent Attacks."

22 **more than a thousand Iraqis dying** . . . Of the twenty thousand deaths world-
wide from terrorist attacks, 65 percent were in Iraq (thirteen thousand deaths).
National Counterterrorism Center, "Report on Terrorist Incidents—2006,"
April 30, 2007, http://www.fbi.gov/stats-services/publications/terror_06.pdf.

23 **20 percent** . . . International Monetary Fund (IMF), *Iraq: Macroeconomic
Assessment* (Washington, D.C.: International Monetary Fund, 2003), 3.
https://www.imf.org/external/np/oth/102103.pdf.

23 **less than 2 percent** . . . The IMF's *Iraq: Macroeconomic Assessment* report
calculated Iraq's GDP per capita in 2003 to be $449. The World Bank calcu-
lated the United States' GDP per capita to be $39,682. (The World Bank did not
have data available for Iraq during this time frame.) World Bank, *World Development Indicators—GDP Per Capita* (Washington, D.C.: World Bank, 2013),
http://data.worldbank.org/indicator/NY.GDP.PCAP.CD?page=2.

23 **"dismal"** . . . United Nations, "Daily Living Conditions in Iraq Dismal, UN
Report Finds," U.N. News Centre, May 12, 2005, http://www.un.org/apps
/news/story.asp?NewsID=14255#.UieEumRxtX9.

23 **electricity shortfalls** . . . Iraqis living in Baghdad had an estimated sixteen to
twenty-four hours of electricity per day before the invasion. By May 2003, it

had fallen to an estimated four to six hours per day. Michael O'Hanlon and Jason Campbell, "Iraq Index: Tracking Variables of Reconstruction & Security in Post-Saddam Iraq," Brookings Institution, October 13, 2009, http://www.brookings.edu/~/media/centers/saban/iraq%20index/index20091013.pdf.

23 **sewage** . . . United Nations, "Daily Living."

23 **Zarqawi's extremism** . . . The most controversial part of Zarqawi's strategy was the unrestrained targeting of Shia Muslims. Lawrence Wright, "The Master Plan," *New Yorker,* September 11, 2006.

24 **swore** *bay'ah,* **allegiance** . . . The message was posted on October 17, 2004. Jeffery Pool, "Zarqawi's Pledge of Allegiance to Al-Qaeda," *Terrorism Monitor,* December 16, 2004.

26 **"everyone in a network is number three"** . . . John Arquilla quoted in Andrew Zoli, *Resilience: Why Things Bounce Back* (New York: Simon & Schuster, 2012), 66.

27 **15 million albums** . . . Zack Greenburg, "Justin Bieber, Venture Capitalist," *Forbes,* May 16, 2012, http://www.forbes.com/sites/zackomalleygreenburg/2012/05/16/justin-bieber-venture-capitalist-the-forbes-cover-story/.

27 **$200 million** . . . "Justin Bieber Net Worth," Celebrity Net Worth, accessed July 28, 2014, http://www.celebritynetworth.com/richest-celebrities/singers/justin-bieber-net-worth/.

28 **five-and-a-half-foot** . . . Adam Nicolson, *Seize the Fire: Heroism, Duty, and the Battle of Trafalgar* (New York: HarperCollins, 2005), 5.

28 **since the Spanish Armada** . . . Roy Adkins, *Nelson's Trafalgar: The Battle That Changed the World* (New York: Penguin, 2006), 5.

28 **thirty-three** . . . Nicolson, *Seize the Fire,* 8.

30 **every commander in the fleet** . . . Adkins, *Nelson's Trafalgar,* 58.

30 **"had patiently instilled"** . . . Adkins, *Nelson's Trafalgar,* 66.

30 **Napoleon had forbidden** . . . Nicolson, *Seize the Fire,* 27.

30 **"this reliance on orders"** . . . Adkins, *Nelson's Trafalgar,* 126.

30 **"weather gage"** . . . Nicolson, *Seize the Fire,* 3.

30 **nineteen of its ships** . . . The exact numbers of the Franco-Spanish fleet after the battle can be debated. Nicolson says in *Seize the Fire* that the British captured nineteen of their ships, while Adkins puts it at twenty-three, adding the four French ships that were captured weeks after the battle ended. All, however, agree that the British did not manage to hold on to their prizes for very long: a violent storm occurred shortly after the battle, destroying all but four (or eight, according to Adkins) of the ships captured by the British.

31 **the very same strategy** . . . Admiral Edward Hawke used it to prevent a French invasion of Britain in the Seven Years' War in 1759, Admiral Richard Howe famously used the tactic against the French on the Glorious First of June in 1794, Admiral Adam Duncan employed it against the Dutch to great success in Camperdown in 1797, and Nelson himself used it at the Battle of the Nile in 1797. As Nicolson describes, these men had already "dared to

recreate the mêlée which 150 years previously the invention of the line of battle had been designed to avoid."

31 "Nelson created the market"... Nicolson, *Seize the Fire*, 26.

CHAPTER 2: CLOCKWORK

34 "bloodless battles" ... This quote is attributed to Flavius Josephus in his work *Bellum Judaicum* (*The Jewish War*). Quoted in Nic Fields, *The Roman Army of the Principate 27 BC–AD 117* (Oxford, UK: Osprey Publishing, 2009), 44.

36 What Taylor unveiled ... Robert Kanigel, *The One Best Way: Frederick Winslow Taylor and the Enigma of Efficiency* (New York: Viking, 1997), 342–43.

36 The norm was nine ... Kanigel, *The One Best Way*, 314

37 People traveled across Europe ... Kanigel, *The One Best Way*, 343–44.

37 The French metallurgist ... Kanigel, *The One Best Way*, 345.

37 A British ... Kanigel, *The One Best Way*, 344.

37 A prominent design ... Kanigel, *The One Best Way*, 405.

37 Taylor had determined ... Kanigel, *The One Best Way*, 326–27.

37 A childhood friend ... Kanigel, *The One Best Way*, 104.

37 At the age ... Kanigel, *The One Best Way*, 107–9.

37 But around that time ... Kanigel, *The One Best Way*, 88–90.

38 He signed up ... Kanigel, *The One Best Way*, 97.

38 He wrote later ... Kanigel, *The One Best Way*, 122.

38 "machinists, as a rule" ... Kanigel, *The One Best Way*, 136.

38 A useful trick ... Kanigel, *The One Best Way*, 100.

38 "It was a tradition" ... Kanigel, *The One Best Way*, 137.

39 Although Taylor claimed ... Kanigel, *The One Best Way*, 117.

39 At his next ... Kanigel, *The One Best Way*, 147.

39 In response ... Kanigel, *The One Best Way*, 166–67.

39 After two years of struggle ... Kanigel, *The One Best Way*, 170.

39 he had an epiphany ... Kanigel, *The One Best Way*, 171.

39 Thus began a ... Kanigel, *The One Best Way*, 175–76.

39 He hired ... Kanigel, *The One Best Way*, 203–4.

39 he followed the reductionist ... Kanigel, *The One Best Way*, 207.

40 *Set tire* ... Kanigel, *The One Best Way*, 206.

40 There was a ... Kanigel, *The One Best Way*, 207.

40 For people who perceived ... Kanigel, *The One Best Way*, 452–53.

40 The cost of ... Kanigel, *The One Best Way*, 206–7.

40 making a cannon projectile ... Kanigel, *The One Best Way*, 229.

41 He measured more ... Kanigel, *The One Best Way*, 222.

41 The physical layout ... Kanigel, *The One Best Way*, 224.

41 rule of thumb ... Kanigel, *The One Best Way*, 171.

41 By 1890, Midvale ... Kanigel, *The One Best Way*, 229.

41 "a workplace" . . . Kanigel, *The One Best Way*, 216.

41 At a paper mill . . . Kanigel, *The One Best Way*, 254, 260.

42 He instituted . . . Kanigel, *The One Best Way*, 260.

42 At a ball bearing . . . Kanigel, *The One Best Way*, 304.

42 At a pig iron plant . . . Frederick Winslow Taylor, *The Principles of Scientific Management* (1911; reprint, New York: Dover Publications, 1998), 21, 35.

42 Under Taylor's . . . Kanigel, *The One Best Way*, 225.

42 managers did . . . Kanigel, *The One Best Way*, 226–27.

42 At the paper mill . . . Kanigel, *The One Best Way*, 253.

43 Taylor could again afford . . . Kanigel, *The One Best Way*, 253.

43 Taylor told . . . Kanigel, *The One Best Way*, 227.

43 he portrayed laborers . . . Taylor, *Principles*, 26.

43 One of the very first . . . Taylor, *Principles*, 28.

43 the laying of bricks . . . Kanigel, *The One Best Way*, 415.

43 Henry Ford's . . . Ford, "Heritage," Ford Motor Company, "The Moving Assembly Line." Accessed July 2, 20014. http://corporate.ford.com/our-com pany/heritage/historic-sites-news-detail/663-highland-park.

44 Historian A. J. P. . . . See A. J. P. Taylor, *War by Timetable* (London: Macdonald, 1969).

44 Historian Samuel Haber . . . Kanigel, *The One Best Way*, 487.

44 the 7,000 ton ship . . . Kanigel, *The One Best Way*, 502.

44 By 1945 . . . "By the Numbers: Wartime Production," National World WarII Museum, http://www.nationalww2museum.org/learn/education/for-students /ww2-history/ww2-by-the-numbers/wartime-production.html (accessed July 3, 2014).

44 Peter Drucker . . . Kanigel, *The One Best Way*, 501–2.

44 "mental revolution" . . . Kanigel, *The One Best Way*, 472.

44 make scrambled eggs . . . Kanigel, *The One Best Way*, 221.

44 an avid tennis . . . Kanigel, *The One Best Way*, 187.

45 *"The same principles"* . . . Kanigel, *The One Best Way*, 12.

45 In 1910 . . . Kanigel, *The One Best Way*, 429, 433.

45 Historian Glenn Porter . . . Kanigel, *The One Best Way*, 412.

45 Robert Kent, wrote . . . Kanigel, *The One Best Way*, 412.

45 Henri Fayol, a mining . . . Henri Fayol, *General and Industrial Management* (1949; reprint, Mansfield Center, CT: Martino Publishing, 2013), 43–107.

45 Luther Gulick . . . Lawrence C. Howard and Jerome McKinney, *Public Administration: Balancing Power and Accountability* (Santa Barbara, CA: ABC-CLIO, 1998), 152.

45 "In my judgement" . . . Kanigel, *The One Best Way*, 479.

46 *"the substitution of"* . . . Kanigel, *The One Best Way*, 473.

46 "by the late 1920s" . . . Kanigel, *The One Best Way*, 490.

46 "No man in the history" . . . Kanigel, *The One Best Way*, 505.

47 Historians attribute . . . Kanigel, *The One Best Way*, 501.

47 "dreamed that in less" . . . Kanigel, *The One Best Way,* 432.

47 Critic Christopher Lasch . . . Kanigel, *The One Best Way,* 501.

48 Peter Drucker . . . Kanigel, *The One Best Way,* 502–3.

48 Jeremy Rifkin believes . . . Kanigel, *The One Best Way,* 8.

CHAPTER 3: FROM COMPLICATED TO COMPLEX

54 Tarek al-Tayeb Mohamed Bouazizi . . . Kareem Fahim, "Slap to a Man's Pride Sets Off Tumult in Tunisia," *New York Times,* January 21, 2011, http://www.nytimes.com/2011/01/22/world/africa/22sidi.html?pagewanted=1&_r=1&src=twrhp.

55 Edward Lorenz . . . James Gleick, *Chaos: Making a New Science,* rev. ed. (New York: Penguin, 2008), 15.

55 initial conditions were exactly . . . Gleick, *Chaos,* 16.

55 "weathers out of a hat" . . . Gleick, *Chaos,* 16.

55 ".506127 and .506" . . . Gleick, *Chaos,* 16.

56 Lorenz presented a paper . . . Lorenz later turned this talk, delivered to the American Association for the Advancement of Science on December 29, 1972, into a book. See Edward Lorenz, *The Essence of Chaos* (Seattle: University of Washington Press, 1995).

56 Footnote: "there was a thing to the air" . . . Excerpt from Ray Bradbury, "A Sound of Thunder," in *R Is for Rocket* (New York: Doubleday, 1952). Found online at http://www.lasalle.edu/~didio/courses/hon462/hon462_assets/sound _of_thunder.htm.

58 197,742 . . . Natalie Wolchover, "How Many Different Ways Can Chess Unfold?," *Popular Science,* December, 15, 2010, http://www.popsci.com/science/article/2010-12/fyi-how-many-different-ways-can-chess-game-unfold.

59 "if a little flap" . . . Lorenz, *Essence of Chaos,* 14.

60 Boeing's primary assembly . . . Dominic Gates, "Boeing 787: Parts from Around World Will Be Swiftly Integrated," *Seattle Times,* September 11, 2005, http://seattletimes.com/html/businesstechnology/2002486348_787global11.html.

61 written entirely by a robot . . . "Robot Writes LA Times Earthquake Breaking News Article," BBC, March 14, 2014, http://www.bbc.com/news/technology-26614051.

61 "co-located" . . . Graham Bowley, "The New Speed of Money, Reshaping Markets," *New York Times,* January 2, 2011, http://www.nytimes.com/2011/01/02/business/02speed.html?pagewanted=all.

61 5.2 milliseconds . . . Matthew Phillips, "Stock Trading Is About to Get 5.2 Milliseconds Faster," *Bloomberg Businessweek,* March 29, 2012, http://www.businessweek.com/articles/2012-03-29/trading-at-the-speed-of-light.

61 "Speed is money" . . . Bowley, "New Speed of Money."

61 646 miles . . . U.S. Department of Defense, "Historian Describes Stonewall Jackson's Rise to Prominence," by John Valcenau, American Forces Press

Service, Washington, D.C., June 17, 2012, http://www.defense.gov/news/newsarticle.aspx?id=116777.

63 **Dow Jones fell 143 points** . . . Heidi Moore and Dan Roberts, "AP Twitter Hack Causes Panic on Wall Street and Sends Dow Jones Plummeting," *Guardian,* April 23, 2013, http://www.theguardian.com/business/2013/apr/23/ap-tweet-hack-wall-street-freefall.

63 **"United Breaks Guitars"** . . . "Singer Gets His Revenge on United Airlines and Soars to Fame," *Guardian,* July 23, 2009, http://www.theguardian.com/news/blog/2009/jul/23/youtube-united-breaks-guitars-video.

63 **$180 million in value** . . . Richard Wilson, "How Saving $1200 Cost United Airlines 10,772,839 Negative Views on YouTube," Sentium Strategic Communications, 2011, http://sentium.com/a-public-relations-disaster-how-saving-1200-cost-united-airlines-10772839-negative-views-on-youtube/.

63 **iTunes** . . . Jesse McLean, "United Loses Luggage of United Breaks Guitars Guy," *Toronto Star,* October, 29, 2009, http://www.thestar.com/entertainment/2009/10/29/united_loses_luggage_of_united_breaks_guitars_guy.html.

63 **two guitars for free** . . . "Singer Gets His Revenge."

63 **global aid system** . . . For a fascinating and much more thorough breakdown of the woes that the development and aid industries have faced due to the complexities of globalization, see Ben Ramalingam, *Aid on the Edge of Chaos: Rethinking International Cooperation in a Complex World* (Oxford: Oxford University Press, 2014).

64 **"emergent, wayward swirl"** . . . Ramalingam, 18.

64 **"organized simplicity"** . . . Warren Weaver, "Science and Complexity," *American Science* 36 (1948): 536–44.

65 **"are more likely to present"** . . . Weaver, "Science," 536.

65 **June 1935** . . . Western Australia Department of Education and University of Western Australia, "Cane Toads: Background Sheet," Spice Science Program, February 2013, http://spice.duit.uwa.edu.au/samples/ast0896/Cane%20toads.pdf.

66 **Ping-Pong balls** . . . Mark Lewis, *Cane Toads: An Unnatural History* (Film Australia, 1988).

66 **poisonous skins** . . . Richard Shine, "The Ecological Impact of Invasive Cane Toads (*Bufo Marinus*) in Australia," *Quarterly Review of Biology* 85, no. 3 (2010): 253–91.

66 **"classic human disaster"** . . . Lewis, *Cane Toads.*

66 **seven million acres** . . . Megan Friedman, "Top 10 Invasive Species," *Time,* February, 2, 2010, http://content.time.com/time/specials/packages/article/0,28804,1958657_1958656_1958305,00.html.

66 **starlings** . . . Friedman, "Top 10 Invasive Species."

67 **"the degree of complexity"** . . . F. A. Hayek, "The Theory of Complex Phenomena," in *Readings in the Philosophy of Social Science,* ed. Michael Martin and Lee C. McIntyre (Cambridge, Mass.: MIT Press, 1994), 56.

67 **"when China gets a cold"** . . . John Urry, *Global Complexity* (Cambridge: Blackwell Publishing, 2003). Quoted in Ben Ramalingam, Harry Jones,

Toussaint Reba, and John Young, *Exploring the Science of Complexity: Ideas and Implications for Development and Humanitarian Efforts*, vol. 285 (London: Overseas Development Institute, 2008), 10.

68 **"The evidence on the folly"** . . . Jonathan Davis, "Folly of Forecasting and Useless Data," *Financial Times,* January 17, 2010, http://www.ft.com/intl/cms/s/0/b8c4adfe-0202-11df-8b56-00144feabdc0.html#axzz36R3YiZLR.

68 **one-in-five-hundred chance** . . . Nate Silver, "The Weatherman Is Not a Moron," *New York Times*, September 7, 2012, http://www.nytimes.com/2012/09/09/magazine/the-weatherman-is-not-a-moron.html?pagewanted=all.

73 **increasingly shorter lifespan** . . . http://www.forbes.com/sites/stevedenning/2011/11/19/peggy-noonan-on-steve-jobs-and-why-big-companies-die/.

73 **Fortune 500 list of 2011** . . . http://www.aei.org/publication/fortune-500-firms-in-1955-vs-2011-87-are-gone/.

73 **"In the last quarter"** . . . Robert M. Grant, "Strategic Planning in a Turbulent Environment: Evidence from the Oil Majors," *Strategic Management Journal* 24, no. 6 (2003): 493.

74 **Gary Hamel writes** . . . Gary Hamel, "Strategy as Revolution," *Harvard Business Review* 74, no.4 (1996): 70.

74 **"Setting oneself"** . . . Harry Mintzberg, "The Strategy Concept II: Another Look at Why Organizations Need Strategies," *California Management Review* 30, no.1 (1987): 26.

CHAPTER 4: DOING THE RIGHT THING

76 **"the capacity of a system"** . . . Brian Walker and David Salt, *Resilience Thinking* (Washington, D.C.: Island Press, 2006), xiii.

77 **Delta Works program** . . . http://www.nytimes.com/2008/09/03/news/03iht-03dutch.15877468.html?_r=0.

77 **"Seven Wonders"** . . . American Society of Civil Engineers, "Netherlands North Sea Protection Works," http://www.asce.org/People-and-Projects/Projects/Seven-Wonders/Netherlands-North-Sea-Protection-Works/.

77 **"came from behind"** . . . Tracy Metz, "Designing for Water: The Sweet & the Salt of It," *Landscape Institute*, Summer 2012, 40.

77 **increased the risks of larger, more devastating floods** . . . Renee Cho, "Making Room for Rivers: A Different Approach to Flood Control," Earth Institute—Water Center Blog, Columbia University, June 7, 2011, http://blogs.ei.columbia.edu/2011/06/07/making-room-for-rivers-a-different-approach-to-flood-control/.

78 **natural dynamics of rivers** . . . T. C. Hein, Antonius Van Stokkom, J. M. Smits, and Rob S. E. W. Leuven, "Flood Defense in the Netherlands," *Water International* 30, no. 1 (2005): 76.

78 **"Room for the River"** . . . Metz, "Designing for Water," 40.

78 **"a radical, even heretical"** . . . Jeff Chu, "Against the Tide," *Fast Company*, October 14, 2013, http://www.fastcompany.com/3018621/against-the-tide.

78 **"If you fight nature"** . . . John McQuaid, "Dutch System of Flood Control an Engineering Marvel," *New Orleans Times-Picayune*, November 13, 2005, http://www.nola.com/frontpage/t-p/index.ssf?/speced/ruinandrecovery/t-p /index.ssf?/speced/ruinandrecovery/articles/dutch13.html.

78 **floods are inevitable** . . . Kuster, "From Control to Management," 72.

78 **"command and control approach not working"** . . . Walker and Salt, 25.

79 **"fragilized"** . . . Nassim Nicholas Taleb, *Antifragile: Things That Gain from Disorder* (New York: Random House, 2012), 5.

79 **"Humans are great optimizers"** . . . Walker and Salt, 38.

79 **"robust-yet-fragile"** . . . Andrew Zolli and Ann Marie Healy, *Resilience: Why Things Bounce Back* (New York: Simon & Schuster, 2012), 27.

79 **Egyptian pyramids** . . . Zolli and Healy, *Resilience*, 13.

80 **damage inflicted by humans** . . . Walker and Salt, 67.

80 **"if we cannot control"** . . . Zolli and Healy, *Resilience*, 5.

81 **"Efficiency is doing"** . . . See Peter F. Drucker, *The Effective Executive: The Definitive Guide to Getting the Right Things Done*, rev. ed. (New York: HarperCollins, 2002).

84 **"It Takes a Network"** . . . J. Arquilla and D. Ronfeldt, *The Advent of Netwar* (Santa Monica, Calif.: RAND Corporation Publishing, 1996), 82.

PART II

FROM MANY, ONE

85 **fifty greatest players** . . . National Basketball Association, "The NBA's 50 Greatest Players," http://www.nba.com/history/50greatest.html.

85 **"It was like"** . . . Quote from Patrick Ewing in *GQ* piece reflecting on the "Dream Team" victory twenty years later, including interviews with the players. Lang Whitaker, "The Dream Team Will Never Die: An Oral History of the Dream Team," *GQ Magazine*, July 2012, http://www.gq.com/sports/pro files/201207/dream-team-20th-anniversary-1992-olympics-usa-basketball.

85 **"Dream Team III"** . . . William Rohden, "Competitors Without a Competition," *New York Times*, July 23, 1996, http://www.nytimes.com/1996/07/23 /sports/sports-of-the-times-competitors-without-a-competition.html?page wanted=all&src=pm.

85 **2004 team's stars** . . . US Men's National Team, "Games of the XXVIIIth Olympiad—2004," USA Basketball, http://archive.usab.com/mens/national /moly_2004.html.

85 **"humiliated by minnows"** . . . "Dream Team Beaten by Puerto Rico," CNN, August 18, 2004, http://www.cnn.com/2004/SPORT/08/15/olympics.basketball/.

86 **Argentina won gold** . . . US Men's National Team, "Games of the XXVIIIth Olympiad."

CHAPTER 5: FROM COMMAND TO TEAM

87 **twenty-seven thousand flight hours** . . . National Transportation Safety Board, *Aircraft Accident Report: United Airlines, Inc., McDonnell-Douglas, DC-8-61, N8082U*; Portland, Oregon, December 28, 1978, NTSB Number AAR-79-07 (Washington, D.C., 1979), 32. http://libraryonline.erau.edu /online-full-text/ntsb/aircraft-accident-reports/AAR79-07.pdf.

87 **46,700 pounds of fuel** . . . National Transportation Safety Board, *AAR* 1978, 2.

87 **13,209 lbs per hour** . . . National Transportation Safety Board, *AAR* 1978, 10.

88 **"Heading for runway 28"** . . . National Transportation Safety Board, *AAR* 1978, 2.

88 **"thump"** . . . National Transportation Safety Board, *AAR* 1978, 3.

88 **"Less than three weeks to retirement"** . . . National Transportation Safety Board, *AAR* 1978, 37–38.

88 **"last guy to leave"** . . . National Transportation Safety Board, *AAR* 1978, 37.

89 **5:48** . . . National Transportation Safety Board, *AAR* 1978, 3.

89 **"a million rubberneckers"** . . . National Transportation Safety Board, *AAR* 1978, 45.

89 **"Why don't you put"** . . . National Transportation Safety Board, *AAR* 1978, 46.

89 **"I don't want to hurry 'em"** . . . National Transportation Safety Board, *AAR* 1978, 47.

89 **"They're pretty calm"** . . . National Transportation Safety Board, *AAR* 1978, 48.

89 **At 6:02** . . . . . . National Transportation Safety Board, *AAR* 1978, 6.

89 **"Okay, we're going to go in"** . . . National Transportation Safety Board, *AAR* 1978, 7.

89 **"I think you just lost"** . . . National Transportation Safety Board, *AAR* 1978, 53.

90 **"There's, ah, kind of an interstate highway"** . . . National Transportation Safety Board, *AAR* 1978, 59.

90 **Two minutes later** . . . National Transportation Safety Board, *AAR* 1978, 8.

90 **"Okay, declare a mayday"** . . . National Transportation Safety Board, *AAR* 1978, 9.

90 **1,500 feet** . . . National Transportation Safety Board, *AAR* 1978, 9.

90 **above twenty thousand feet** . . . National Transportation Safety Board, *Aircraft Accident Report: Loss of Thrust in Both Engines, US Airways Flight 1549 Airbus Industrie A320-214, N106US*; Weehawken, New Jersey, January 15, 2009, NTSB Number AAR-10-03 (Washington, D.C., 2010), 87.

92 **the USS** *Bainbridge* ... "More Pirates Searching for Lifeboat, Official Says," CNN, http://www.cnn.com/2009/WORLD/africa/04/10/somalia.u.s .ship (accessed July 8, 2014).

92 **lethal force could be** ... Robert McFadden, "Navy Rescues Captain, Killing 3 Pirate Captors," *New York Times*, http://www.nytimes.com/2009/04 /13/world/africa/13pirates.html?pagewanted=all (accessed June 30, 2014).

92 **seventy-five feet away, the three** ... Elisabeth Bumiller, "To Rescue Captain, U.S. Snipers Held Steady Despite Many Moving Parts," *New York Times*, http:// www.nytimes.com/2009/04/14/world/africa/14sniper.html (accessed July 8, 2014).

93 **"The operation was nothing"** ... "Three Perfect Strikes: Inside the Rescue of Captain Phillips," Fox News, http://www.foxnews.com/story/2009/04/14 /three-perfect-strikes-inside-rescue-captain-phillips/ (accessed July 8, 2014).

93 **"has got the whole country brushing up"** ... Rachel Maddow, "April 13, 2009," *The Rachel Maddow Show*, MSNBC, April 13, 2009, http://www.nbc news.com/id/30210708/ns/msnbc-rachel_maddow_show/#.UzCDrRZNLlc.

93 **through his own scope** ... Jim Spencer, "A Quiet Man Uniquely Qualified to Stalk and Kill," *Chicago Tribune*, http://articles.chicagotribune.com /1986-09-07/features/8603060789_1_winchester-viet-cong-north -vietnamese-army/2 (accessed July 8, 2014).

93 **eight thousand feet** ... Ian Drury, "The Super Sniper; Hero Picks Off Two Taliban from a Mile and a Half Away," *Daily Mail*, May 3, 2010, http:// www.dailymail.co.uk/news/article-1270414/British-sniper-sets-new -sharpshooting-record-1-54-mile-double-Taliban-kill.html (accessed July 8, 2014).

94 **"Hell Week"** ... "Navy SEALs," U.S. Navy, http://www.navy.com/careers /special-operations/seals.html (accessed July 8, 2014).

95 **around 90 will drop** ... Interview with Coleman Ruiz, former Navy SEAL.

96 **1.47 million people** ... "2013 State of the Sport—Part III: U.S. Race Trends," RunningUSA.com, http://www.runningusa.org/state-of-sport-2013-part-III ?returnTo=annual-reports (accessed July 7, 2014).

96 **a seven-minute pace** ... Nancy Hart, "Typical 10K Times of a Runner or Jogger," Livestrong.com, http://www.livestrong.com/article/536048-typical -10k-times-of-a-runner-or-jogger/ (accessed July 8, 2014).

96 **seventy-six minutes** ... "How Much Time Does It Take to Finish an Ironman Triathlon? Average Ironman Finish Times," RunTri.com, http://www .runtri.com/2011/06/how-long-does-it-take-to-finish-ironman.html (accessed July 8, 2014).

96 **fifty-six hours** ... Lizette Alvarez, "Sharks Absent, Swimmer, 64, Strokes from Cuba to Florida," *New York Times*, September 2, 2013, http://www .nytimes.com/2013/09/03/sports/nyad-completes-cuba-to-florida-swim .html?_r=1& (accessed July 8, 2014).

97 **Diving activities include** ... Interview with Coleman Ruiz, former Navy SEAL.

98 **"Great teams consist of"** . . . Amy C. Edmondson, *Teaming: How Organizations Learn, Innovate, and Compete in the Knowledge Economy* (San Francisco: Jossey-Bass, 2012), 11.

102 **"that limb is nonviable"** . . . Interview with Dr. Matthew Carty and Dr. E. J. Caterson.

102 **70 percent increase** . . . "Energy Expenditure of Amputees," The War Amps, http://www.waramps.ca/nac/health/energy.html (accessed July 8, 2014).

103 **news reports played up the drama** . . . Robert Johnson, "Detailed Account of Bin Laden Raid Reveals How It Nearly Ended in Disaster," *Business Insider*, May 17, 2011, http://www.businessinsider.com/detailed-account-abbottabad-2011-5 (accessed July 8, 2014).

104 **"town dump"** . . . Steven Johnson, *Emergence: The Connected Lives of Ants, Brains, Cities, and Software* (New York: Scribner, 2001), 30–32.

104 **produce new ants** . . . Johnson, *Emergence*, 31.

104 **250,000 brain cells** . . . Maryland Department of Natural Resources, Project Wild, "All About Ants," http://dnr.maryland.gov/wildlife/education/projectwild/pdfs/allaboutants.pdf.

104 **pheromone trails** . . . Johnson, *Emergence*, 52.

104 **simple, low-level interactions** . . . Johnson, *Emergence*, 15.

105 **"connectedness and organization"** . . . Johnson, *Emergence*, 117.

105 **"could have landed safely"** . . . National Transportation Safety Board, *AAR* 1978, 24.

106 **"The probable cause of the accident"** . . . National Transportation Safety Board, *AAR* 1978, 29.

106 **"This accident exemplifies"** . . . National Transportation Safety Board, *AAR* 1978, 26.

107 **NASA** . . . The NASA study analyzed accidents in the period between 1968 and 1976.

107 **70 percent of air crashes** . . . J. Bryan Sexton and Robert L. Helmreich, "Analyzing Cockpit Communications: The Links Between Language, Performance, Error, and Workload," *Journal of Human Performance in Extreme Environments* 5, no. 1 (2000): 63. (Study referenced is Murphy, Miles (1980), *Review of Aircraft Accidents*. In G. E. Cooper, M. D. White, and J. K. Lauber, eds., *Resource Management on the Flightdeck: Proceedings of a NASA/Industry Workshop* (NASA CP-2120) (Moffett Field, Calif.: NASA-Ames Research Center, 1980).

107 **At 5:48** . . . National Transportation Safety Board, *AAR* 1978, 39.

107 **"fifteen minutes"** . . . National Transportation Safety Board, *AAR* 1978, 40.

108 **"We got about three** . . . National Transportation Safety Board, *AAR* 1978, 40.

108 **continue to try to mitigate** . . . Robert L. Helmreich, "On Error Management: Lessons from Aviation," *British Medical Journal*, 320, no. 7237 (2000): 782.

109 **CRM-trained** . . . http://www.apa.org/research/action/crew.aspx.

109 **In 1981, United Airlines** . . . Robert L. Helmreich, Ashleigh C. Merritt, and John A. Wilhelm, "The Evolution of Crew Resource Management Training in

Commercial Aviation," *International Journal of Aviation Psychology* 9, no. 1 (1999): 20.

109 **juniors to speak more assertively** . . . Helmreich et al., "Evolution of Crew Resource Management Training," 20.

109 **"charm school"** . . . Helmreich et al., "Evolution of Crew Resource Management Training," 21.

109 **In 1989, another United** . . . National Transportation Safety Board, *Aircraft Accident Report: United Airlines Flight 232 McDonnell Douglas DC-10-10 Sioux Gateway Airport*; Sioux City, Iowa, July 17, 1989, NTSB Number AAR-90-06 (Washington, D.C., 1991), 75.

109 **no safety procedure** . . . http://clear-prop.org/aviation/haynes.html.

109 **185 of the 296 people** . . . American Psychological Association, *Making Air Travel Safer Through Crew Resource Management,* February 2014, http://www.apa.org/research/action/crew.aspx.

110 **thirty-one communications per minute** . . . American Psychological Association, *Making Air Travel Safer.*

110 **"If we had not let"** . . . http://clear-prop.org/aviation/haynes.html.

110 **"greatly exceeded"** . . . National Transportation Safety Board, *AAR* 1989, 76.

110 **more than 90 percent** . . . Barbara G. Kanki, Robert L. Helmreich, and José M. Anca, "Why CRM? Empirical and Theoretical Bases of Human Factors Training," in *Crew Resource Management*, 2nd ed. (Amsterdam: Academic Press/Elsevier, 2010), 35. See original study: R. L. Helmreich and J. A. Wilhelm, "Outcomes of Crew Resource Management Training," *International Journal of Aviation Psychology* 1 (1991): 287–300.

110 **2012 and 2013 had the fewest deaths and fatalities** . . . 2012 had fewer crashes, but 2013 had the fewest casualties, with 265 fatalities (compared with the past ten-year average of 720 fatalities). From "Airliner Accident Fatalities at Record Low," Aviation Safety Network, January 1, 2014, http://news.aviation-safety.net/2014/01/01/aviation-safety-network-airliner-accident-fatalities-at-record-low/.

110 **1 percent of today's air travel** . . . In 1947, 12.3 million passengers flew 6.2 billion passenger miles. In 2012, 642 million passengers flew 568 billion passenger miles. From Bart Jansen, "Safety Expert Urges Against Complacency with Few Crashes," *USA Today*, August 3, 2013, http://www.usatoday.com/story/travel/news/2013/08/08/flight-safety-airline-crash-ntsb/2632307/.

110 **time between serious airline incidents** . . . "Longer Spans Without Serious Airline Accidents," *New York Times*, February 11, 2013, http://www.nytimes.com/interactive/2013/02/11/business/Longer-Spans-Without-Serious-Airline-Accidents.html?ref=business&_r=0.

110 **one per million aircraft departures** . . . Boeing Co., 2012 Statistical Summary of Commercial Jet Plan Accidents 1959–2012, August, http://www.boeing.com/news/techissues/pdf/statsum.pdf.

110 **mortality risk per flight for passengers since the 1960s** . . . See Arnold Barnett, "Is It Really Safe to Fly?," Table 1, in *Tutorials in Operations Research: State-of-the-Art Decision-Making Tools in the Information-Intensive Age,*

ed. Zhi Chen (Hanover, Md.: INFORMS, 2008), 20. Unfortunately, flying in the developing world is less safe, but still safer than it once was. Barnett noted that, for the same 2000–2007 period, a passenger flying within the developing world faced a one in two million chance of mortality.

110 Footnote: "the most obvious validation . . . Helmreich, Merritt, and Wilhelm, "The Evolution of Crew Resource Management Training in Commercial Aviation."

111 98 percent . . . American Psychological Association, *Making Air Travel Safer.*

111 No procedure for low-altitude . . . National Transportation Safety Board, *AAR* 2009, 88.

111 "Because of time constraints" . . . National Transportation Safety Board, *AAR* 2009, 91.

111 "The captain credited" . . . National Transportation Safety Board, *AAR* 2009, 91.

111 A 1966 report . . . See National Academy of Sciences and National Research Council, *Accidental Death and Disability: The Neglected Disease of Modern Society* (Washington, D.C.: National Academies Press, 1966).

112 "We have trained, hired, and rewarded physicians" . . . Mary Mosquera, "One Surgeon's Take on Need for Culture Change in Medicine," *Healthcare IT News*, http://www.healthcareitnews.com/news/one-surgeons-take-needculture -change-medicine?single-page=true (accessed July 8, 2014).

112 military surgeons discovered . . . Preston Cline, "A Mission Centric Professional Development Model for U.S. Army Special Operations Command" (working paper, Center for Leadership and Change Management, Wharton School, University of Pennsylvania, Philadelphia, 2014): 8.

112 "cross-functional trauma teams" . . . Yun Seokhwa, Faraj Samer, and Henry P. Sims Jr., "Contingent Leadership and Effectiveness of Trauma Resuscitation Teams," *Journal of Applied Psychology* 90, no. 6 (2005): 1288.

112 122 to 56 minutes . . . P. A. Driscoll and C. A. Vincent, "Organizing an Efficient Trauma Team," *Injury* 23, no. 2 (1992): 107–10.

112 every single one survived . . . Interview with Dr. Matthew Carty and Dr. E. J. Caterson; Deborah Kotz, "Injury Toll from Marathon Bombings Rises," *Boston Globe*, April 23, 2013, http://www.bostonglobe.com/metro/massachusetts /2013/04/22/just-bombing-victims-still-critically-ill-but-count-injured-rises /7mUGAu5tJgKsxc634NCAJJ/story.html (accessed July 8, 2014).

113 "A combination of increased" . . . Interview with Preston Cline.

CHAPTER 6: TEAM OF TEAMS

124 "No decision was made . . . Interview with Dr. Carty and Dr. Caterson.

124 "a nurse or technician" . . . Alison Diana, "Marathon Bombing Lessons: Boston Hospital Revamps Information Systems," *Information Week*, April 26, 2014.

124 44,000 to 98,000 . . . See Linda T. Kohn, Janet M. Corrigan, and Molla S. Donaldson, eds., *To Err Is Human: Building a Safer Health System*, vol. 627 (Washington, D.C.: National Academies Press, 2000).

124 **motor vehicle accidents** ... Centers for Disease Control and Prevention (National Center for Health Statistics), Births and Deaths: Preliminary Data for 1998, National Vital Statistics Reports 47, no. 25 (1999): 6. In *To Err Is Human*.

124 **210,000 to 400,000** ... John T. James, "A New, Evidence-Based Estimate of Patient Harms Associated with Hospital Care," *Journal of Patient Safety* 9, no. 3 (2013): 122.

124 **third-leading cause** ... Centers for Disease Control and Prevention (National Center for Health Statistics), "Deaths: Preliminary Data for 2011," National Vital Statistics Reports 61, no. 6 (2012): 4, http://www.cdc.gov/nchs/data/nvsr /nvsr61/nvsr61_06.pdf

124 **twenty Boeing 747** ... Charles R. Denham et al., "An NTSB for Health Care—Learning from Innovation: Debate and Innovate or Capitulate," *Journal of Patient Safety* 8 (March 2012): 8.

125 **MIT economist Paul Osterman** ... Found in J. Richard Hackman, *Leading Teams: Setting the Stage for Great Performance*, referencing Paul Osterman, "How Common Is Workplace Transformation and Who Adopts It?," *Industrial and Labor Relations Review* 47 (1994): 233.

125 **survey by the Work in America Institute** ... Found in Hackman, *Leading Teams*, referencing a news release Work in America Institute, July 15, 1998.

127 **between 100 and 230** ... See: Robin Dunbar, "Neocortex Size as a Constraint on Group Size in Primates," *Journal of Human Evolution* 22, no. 6 (1992): 469–93.

127 **"[It's a] fallacy"** ... Diane Coutu interviewing J. Richard Hackman, "Why Teams Don't Work," *Harvard Business Review*, May 1, 2009, http://hbr.org /2009/05/why-teams-dont-work.

128 **"has no better chance"** ... Richard J. Hackman, *Leading Teams: Setting the Stage for Great Performances* (Boston, Mass.: Harvard Business School Press, 2002), 116.

130 **eighty-seven per day** ... Dexter Filkins, "General Says Less Coercion of Captives Yields Better Data," *New York Times*, September 7, 2004, http://www .nytimes.com/2004/09/07/international/middleeast/07detain.html?fta=y&_r=0.

130 **death toll had passed one thousand** ... "Fierce Fighting in Fallujah as US Death Toll Tops 1,000," NBC News, September 9, 2004, http://www.nbcnews.com/id /5911852/ns/world_news-mideast_n_africa/t/fierce-fighting-fallujah-us-toll-tops/.

130 **2 percent** ... Michael Knights and Eamon McCarthy, "Provincial Politics in Iraq: Fragmentation or New Awakening?," Washington Institute for Near East Policy, April 2008, 6.

PART III

SHARING

133 The details in the 9/11 vignette were taken from *The 9/11 Commission Report* (New York: W. W. Norton, 2004). National Commission on Terrorist Attacks upon the United States (Philip Zelikow, Executive Director; Bonnie

D. Jenkins, Counsel; Ernest R. May, Senior Advisor), *The 9/11 Commission Report*, 271.

133 *"inordinate number of individuals"* . . . 9/11 Commission Report, 272.

133 *did not read the memo* . . . 9/11 Commission Report, 272.

133 *"were not put together"* . . . 9/11 Commission Report, 277.

CHAPTER 7: SEEING THE SYSTEM

139 *"One man draws out the wire"* . . . Adam Smith, *The Wealth of Nations, Books 1-3* (New York: Penguin, 1986), 109–10.

143 *"240,000 miles away"* . . . "Address at Rice University on the Nation's Space Effort," John F. Kennedy Presidential Library & Museum, July 21, 2014, http://www.jfklibrary.org/Asset-Viewer/MkATdOcdU06X5uNHbmqm1Q.aspx.

144 600 million . . . "Apollo 11 Moon Landing: Ten Facts About Armstrong, Aldrin and Collins' Mission," *Telegraph,* July 18, 2009, http://www.telegraph.co.uk/science/space/5852237/Apollo-11-Moon-landing-ten-facts-about-Armstrong-Aldrin-and-Collins-mission.html.

144 bleached white . . . Clara Moskowitz, "American Flags Planted on the Moon Are Still Standing Decades Later," *Business Insider,* July 30, 2012, http://www.businessinsider.com/american-flags-planted-on-the-moon-still-stand-2012-7.

145 "The Apollo project" . . . R. C. Seamans and F. I. Ordway, "The Apollo Tradition: An Object Lesson for the Management of Large-Scale Technological Endeavors," *Interdisciplinary Science Reviews* 2, no. 4 (1977): 270–303.

145 The escape rocket . . . Johnson, *Secret of Apollo*, 128.

145 An almost identical issue . . . Johnson, *Secret of Apollo*, 128.

146 "systems issues" identified by NASA . . . Johnson, *Secret of Apollo*, 9.

146 electromagnetic interference . . . Johnson, *Secret of Apollo*, 10–11.

146 And then there was gravity . . . Johnson, *Secret of Apollo*, 12.

146 "Most of us" . . . Howard E. McCurdy, "Inside NASA: High Technology and Organizational Change in the US Space Program," *New Series in NASA History* (Baltimore: Johns Hopkins University Press, 1993), 75.

146 "How do you get liquid" . . . McCurdy, "Inside NASA," 75.

146 Fuel cell technology . . . McCurdy, "Inside NASA," 75.

147 Apollo program would eventually employ . . . Johnson, *Secret of Apollo*, 5.

147 old management model . . . Johnson, *Secret of Apollo*, 5.

147 "The switch from research" . . . Johnson, *Secret of Apollo*, 81.

147 George Mueller . . . Johnson, *Secret of Apollo*, 142.

147 "nervous system" . . . Johnson, *Secret of Apollo*, 151.

147 "wreaked havoc at NASA" . . . Johnson, *Secret of Apollo*, 134.

147 "almost iron-like discipline" . . . Johnson, *Secret of Apollo*, 124.

148 central control room . . . Johnson, *Secret of Apollo*, 138.

148 "teleservices network" . . . Johnson, *Secret of Apollo*, 148.

148 "I think we had 250" . . . McCurdy, "Inside NASA," 66.

148 "You cannot simply" ... McCurdy, "Inside NASA," 48.
148 take apart and rebuild ... Johnson, *Secret of Apollo*, 124.
149 "The reason that it" ... McCurdy, "Inside NASA," 68.
149 tightly run development organization ... Johnson, *Secret of Apollo*, 142.
149 only by sharing information ... Johnson, *Secret of Apollo*, 113.
149 "The real mechanism" ... McCurdy, "Inside NASA," 48.
150 the United Kingdom had ... Johnson, *Secret of Apollo*, 159–60.
150 ELDO teams worked independently ... Johnson, *Secret of Apollo*, 161.
150 There was no single location ... Johnson, *Secret of Apollo*, 166.
150 Contractors reported only ... Johnson, *Secret of Apollo*, 165.
150 "half-hearted and mutually suspicious" ... Johnson, *Secret of Apollo*, 163.
150 connecting rings ... Johnson, *Secret of Apollo*, 169.
150 second stage sequencer ... Johnson, *Secret of Apollo*, 173.
150 ELDO's final launch attempt ... Johnson, *Secret of Apollo*, 175.
151 *"methods of organization above all"* ... Jean-Jacques Servan-Schreiber, *The American Challenge*, trans. Robert Steel (New York: Avon Books, 1969), 168. Quoted in Johnson, *Secret of Apollo*, 157.
151 "technological gap" ... Johnson, *Secret of Apollo*, 157.
151 Congress held hearings ... Johnson, *Secret of Apollo*, 5.
151 aerospace research and development ... Johnson, *Secret of Apollo*, 3.
152 "maintaining ... organizational culture" McCurdy, "Inside NASA," 98–99.
152 "Post Office and the IRS gone to space" ... McCurdy, "Inside NASA," 132.
152 "formal, elaborate, and expensive" ... McCurdy, *Faster, Better, Cheaper*, 10.

CHAPTER 8: BRAINS OUT OF THE FOOTLOCKER

157 "counting houses" ... Nikil Saval, *Cubed: A Secret History of the Workplace* (New York: Random House, 2014),17–18.
157 "exporter, wholesaler, importer" ... Alfred D. Chandler Jr., *The Visible Hand* (Cambridge, Mass.: Harvard University Press, 1993), 15. In Saval, *Cubed*, 20.
157 750,000 ... Saval, *Cubed*, 36–40.
158 New technologies enabled ... Saval, *Cubed*, 36.
158 building blocks of beehives ... Saval, *Cubed*, 109.
158 Dictaphones and pneumatic tubes ... Saval, *Cubed*, 40.
158 Executives moved ... Saval, *Cubed*, 144.
158 the term "ladder" ... Saval, *Cubed*, 39.
158 efficient flow of paperwork ... Saval, *Cubed*, 5, 67.
158 *"The girl at the end"* ... Saval, *Cubed*, 151.
159 turning their desks away ... Saval, *Cubed*, 61.
159 Bell Labs ... Saval, *Cubed*, 148.
159 "nonterritorial" offices ... Saval, *Cubed*, 257.
159 "serendipitous encounters" ... Saval, *Cubed*, 146.
159 "Don't fence me in again" ... Saval, *Cubed*, 258.

160 "I've always believed" . . . Michael Bloomberg and Matthew Winkler, *Bloomberg by Bloomberg* (New York: John Wiley & Sons, 2001), 163.

160 reserved parking spots . . . Bloomberg and Winkler, 165.

160 "Anyone could come up" . . . Bloomberg and Winkler, 21.

160 "If you lock yourself" . . . Michael Barbaro, "The Bullpen Bloomberg Built: Candidates Debate Its Future," *New York Times*, March 22, 2013, http://www.nytimes.com/2013/03/23/nyregion/bloombergs-bullpen-candidates-debate-its-future.html.

160 "The great urban contraption" . . . Bill Keller, "The Bloomberg Legacy," *New York Times*, July 14, 2013, http://www.nytimes.com/2013/07/15/opinion/keller-the-bloomberg-legacy.html?_r=0.

162 "Action Office II" . . . Saval, *Cubed*, 206.

162 "the completely enclosed 'boxes'" . . . Saval, *Cubed*, 214.

163 squeeze more people . . . Saval, *Cubed*, 217.

163 "the inevitable expression" . . . Saval, *Cubed*, 216.

163 93 percent . . . Saval, *Cubed*, 2.

163 "The dark side of this" . . . Saval, *Cubed*, 220.

170 "This disclosure is not just" . . . "Remarks to the Press on Release of Purportedly Confidential Documents by Wikileaks," U.S. State Department, November 29, 2010, http://www.state.gov/secretary/20092013clinton/rm/2010/11/152078.htm.

170 "all this leaked information" . . . James P. Pinkerton, "America Needs Willpower—and the Right Leaders," Fox News, July 29, 2010, http://www.foxnews.com/opinion/2010/07/29/james-pinkerton-world-trade-centre-arizona-alqaeda-wikileaks-ground-zero-mosque.

170 854,000 people . . . Dana Priest and William Arkin, *Top Secret America: The Rise of the New American Security State* (New York: Little, Brown, 2011), 158.

CHAPTER 9: BEATING THE PRISONER'S DILEMMA

183 "just four lines of code" . . . Robert Axelrod, Introduction to *The Evolution of Cooperation*, rev. ed. (New York: Basic Books, 2006), vii.

183 "the punishment lasted only" . . . Metta Spencer, "Rapoport at Ninety," *Peace Magazine* 17, no. 4 (2001): 23.

183 "system 1" . . . Daniel Kahneman, *Thinking, Fast and Slow* (New York: Farrar, Straus & Giroux, 2011), 19–21.

188 On April 1, 2014 . . . *General Motors Ignition Switch Recall: Hearing Before the Committee on Energy & Commerce, Oversights & Investigations Subcommittee, United States House of Representatives* (2009), 113th Cong., 2014, http://energycommerce.house.gov/hearing/%E2%80%9C-gm-ignition-switch-recall-why-did-it-take-so-long%E2%80%9D.

188 GM had issued a recall . . . Maggie McGrath, "General Motors Recalls Another 7 Million Vehicles, Some Dating Back to 1997," *Forbes*, June 30, 2014, http://

www.forbes.com/sites/maggiemcgrath/2014/06/30/general-motors-recalls
-another-7-million-vehicles-some-dating-back-to-1997/.

188 **victims were teenagers** . . . Tom Krisher, "GM Recall: Many Victims Were
Young Drivers," Associated Press, March 31, 2014, http://bigstory.ap.org
/article/gm-recall-many-victims-were-young-drivers.

188 **"As soon as the Chevy Cobalt"** . . . *General Motors Ignition Switch Recall.*

189 **"the piece . . . cost pennies"** . . . *General Motors Ignition Switch Recall.*

189 **spree of corporate acquisitions** . . . In total, Durant bought twenty-five com-
panies between 1908 and 1910 and another fourteen between 1916 and 1920.
From William Holstein, *Why GM Matters: Inside the Race to Transform an
American Icon* (London: Bloomsbury Publishing, 2010), 4.

189 **"any effective over-all"** . . . Alfred D. Chandler, *Strategy and Structure:
Chapters in the History of American Enterprise* (Beard Books, 2003), 125.

189 **Footnote: 153 deaths** . . . Ben Klayman, "Deaths Linked to GM Ignition-
Switch Defect Rise to 23," Reuters, September 29, 2014, http://www.reuters
.com/article/2014/09/29/us-gm-recall-compensation-idUSKCN0
HO1F220140929.

190 **"Organizational Study"** . . . William Pelfrey, *Billy, Alfred, and General
Motors: The Story of Two Unique Men, a Legendary Company, and a Remarkable Time in American History* (New York: AMACOM Books, 2006), 11.

190 **"none of it sounds"** . . . Pelfrey, *Billy, Alfred, and General Motors,* 249.

190 **Durant ignored the plan** . . . Pelfrey, *Billy, Alfred, and General Motors,* 11.

190 **"the largest turn around"** . . . Pelfrey, *Billy, Alfred, and General Motors,* 265.

190 **"Alfred Sloan institutionalized"** . . . Pelfrey, *Billy, Alfred, and General
Motors,* 272.

190 **even through the Great Depression** . . . Pelfrey, *Billy, Alfred, and General
Motors,* 237.

190 **net profit of $248.3 million** . . . Pelfrey, *Billy, Alfred, and General Motors,* 265.

190 **first company to earn a billion dollars** . . . Taylor, *Sixty to Zero,* 15.

190 **"grew from less than 10 percent"** . . . Pelfrey, *Billy, Alfred, and General
Motors,* 268. Alex Taylor, *Sixty to Zero: An Inside Look at the Collapse of
General Motors and the Detroit Auto Industry* (New Haven, Conn.: Yale Uni-
versity Press, 2010), 14.

190 **"was eventually copied"** . . . Pelfrey, *Billy, Alfred, and General Motors,* 11.

191 **"GM couldn't keep up"** . . . Alex Taylor, *Sixty to Zero: An Inside Look at
the Collapse of General Motors and the Detroit Auto Industry* (New Haven,
Conn.: Yale University Press, 2010), 2.

191 **"speed and agility were much more crucial"** . . . Taylor, *Sixty to Zero,* 37.

191 **separate divisions and a competitive culture** . . . Taylor, *Sixty to Zero,* 45.

191 **result of a task force** . . . Taylor, *Sixty to Zero,* 39.

191 **airbags and ignition systems** . . . Rana Foroohar, "We've All Got GM Problems," *Time,* June 12, 2014, http://time.com/2863214/weve-all-got-gm-problems/.

192 **placed on the back burner** . . . Anton Valukas, "Report to Board of Directors of General Motors Company Regarding Ignition Switch Recalls," Jenner

& Block LLP, May 29, 2014, 54. Full report available at http://www.nytimes.com/interactive/2014/06/05/business/06gm-report-doc.html?_r=0.

192 **"GM *did not have a process in place*"** . . . Valukas, "Report to Board of Directors of General Motors Company Regarding Ignition Switch Recalls," 95.

192 **the information was not passed on** . . . Valukas, "Report to Board of Directors of General Motors Company Regarding Ignition Switch Recalls," 44, 50.

192 **took years for engineers and investigators** . . . Valukas, "Report to Board of Directors of General Motors Company Regarding Ignition Switch Recalls," 256–57.

192 **"passed through an astonishing number"** . . . Valukas, "Report to Board of Directors of General Motors Company Regarding Ignition Switch Recalls," 255.

192 **"permeates the fabric"** . . . Valukas, "Report to Board of Directors of General Motors Company Regarding Ignition Switch Recalls," 250.

193 **"GM nod"** . . . Valukas, "Report to Board of Directors of General Motors Company Regarding Ignition Switch Recalls," 255.

193 **GM's CEO and general counsel did not learn** . . . Valukas, "Report to Board of Directors of General Motors Company Regarding Ignition Switch recalls," 227.

193 **"Two dollars"** . . . Todd Spangler, "Mom of GM Crash Victim: 'My Heart Is So Broken,'" *USA Today,* April 1, 2014, http://www.usatoday.com/story/money/cars/2014/04/01/families-gm-deaths/7152985/.

193 **"failure to take basic steps"** . . . Valukas, "Report to Board of Directors of General Motors Company Regarding Ignition Switch Recalls," 143.

193 **"We can continue"** . . . Bryce Hoffman, *American Icon: Alan Mulally and the Fight to Save Ford Motor Company* (New York: Crown Publishing Group, 2013), 38.

194 **most financially successful passenger planes** . . . Hoffman, *American Icon,* 62.

194 **"working together"** . . . Hoffman, *American Icon,* 57.

194 **computer system to maintain live-updated** . . . *21st Century Jet: The Building of the 777,* directed by Karl Sabbagh, PBS Home Video, 1996. Available on YouTube.

194 **"design build teams"** . . . *21st Century Jet: The Building of the 777.*

194 **"One Ford"** . . . Hoffman, *American Icon,* 145.

194 **"business plan review"** . . . Hoffman, *American Icon,* 102.

194 **BlackBerry use** . . . Hoffman, *American Icon,* 106–7.

194 **"shine a light into the darkest corners"** . . . Hoffman, *American Icon,* 102.

194 **"tried unsuccessfully to draw"** . . . Hoffman, *American Icon,* 103.

194 **"inundated with esmails"** . . . Hoffman, *American Icon,* 103.

194 **Japanese automakers** . . . Hoffman, *American Icon,* 131.

195 **"A designer who knew nothing"** . . . Hoffman, *American Icon,* 132.

195 **"shared purpose"** . . . Hoffman, *American Icon,* 201.

195 **keeping these suppliers alive** . . . Hoffman, *American Icon,* 222.

195 **"Mulally had done"** . . . Hoffman, *American Icon,* 235.

195 **Detroit celebrated Mulally's magic** . . . Hoffman, *American Icon,* 380.

195 **"the greatest turnaround artist of all time"** . . . Hoffman, *American Icon,* 380.

195 "the biggest threat to Ford" . . . Hoffman, *American Icon*, 395.

195 "Working together always works" . . . Hoffman, *American Icon*, 393.

196 Sandy Pentland, an MIT . . . Alex Pentland, *Social Physics: How Good Ideas Spread—the Lessons from a New Science* (New York: Penguin Press, 2014), 88.

196 "The best ideas" . . . Pentland, *Social Physics*, 61.

196 spread of the flu . . . Pentland, *Social Physics*, 33–34.

196 "engagement" and "exploration" . . . Pentland, *Social Physics*, 19–20.

196 "when the flow of ideas" . . . Pentland, *Social Physics*, 60.

196 more than 6 percent . . . Pentland, *Social Physics*, 38.

196 Footnote: Pentland, *Social Physics*, 37.

196 tone of voice . . . Pentland, *Social Physics*, 88.

196 1,900 hours of data . . . Pentland, *Social Physics*, 95–96.

196 engagement was the central predictor . . . Pentland, *Social Physics*, 89.

196 880 emails . . . Pentland, *Social Physics*, 99.

197 higher levels of creative output . . . Pentland, *Social Physics*, 100.

197 87.5 percent . . . Pentland, *Social Physics*, 102.

197 high and low-performing groups . . . Pentland, *Social Physics*, 106.

197 Bank of America call center . . . Pentland, *Social Physics*, 93.

197 average call handle time . . . Pentland, *Social Physics*, 94.

197 $15 million in productivity . . . Pentland, *Social Physics*, 95.

PART IV

LETTING GO

199 No captain . . . Nicolson, *Seize the Fire*, 25.

CHAPTER 10: HANDS OFF

203 largest naval force . . . John H. Schroeder, *Matthew Calbraith Perry: Antebellum Sailor and Diplomat* (Annapolis, Md.: Naval Institute Press, 2001), 171.

203 isolation of *sakoku* . . . Geoffrey Gunn, *First Globalization: The Eurasian Exchange, 1500 to 1800* (Lanham, Md.: Rowman & Littlefield, 2003), 151.

203 enlisted in the Navy at age fourteen . . . Schroeder, *Matthew Calbraith Perry*, 11.

204 assisted colonists . . . Schroeder, *Matthew Calbraith Perry*, 25.

204 goodwill to the Ottoman Empire . . . Schroeder, *Matthew Calbraith Perry*, 47.

204 promotion to captain . . . Schroeder, *Matthew Calbraith Perry*, 76.

204 he had campaigned for . . . Schroeder, *Matthew Calbraith Perry*, xiv.

204 in 1851 . . . Schroeder, *Matthew Calbraith Perry*, 168.

204 trade between Asia and the United States . . . Schroeder, *Matthew Calbraith Perry*, 257.

204 "It is my duty" . . . Perry quoted in Samuel Eliot Morison, *"Old Bruin": Commodore Matthew C. Perry 1794–1858* (Boston: Little, Brown, 1967), 279.

204 "write his own ticket" . . . Morison, *Old Bruin,* 282.

204 U.S. priorities in Japan . . . Schroeder, *Matthew Calbraith Perry,* 76.

205 "The Secretary of the Navy will" . . . Morison, *"Old Bruin,"* 283.

205 white flag . . . Schroeder, *Matthew Calbraith Perry,* 257, note 44, and Yosa-burō Takekoshi, *The Economic Aspects of the History of the Civilization of Japan,* volume 3 (London: Taylor & Francis, 2004), 285–86.

205 "Perry, halfway around the globe" . . . Carl Builder, *Masks of War: American Military Styles in Strategy and Analysis* (Santa Monica, Calif.: RAND Corporation, 1989), 18–19.

205 plant gardens . . . William F. Strobridge, *Regulars in the Redwoods: The U.S. Army in Northern California 1852–1861* (Glendale, Calif.: Arthur H. Clark, 1994), 31.

206 hold junior officers accountable . . . Strobridge, *Regulars in the Redwoods,* chapter 1.

206 "HEADQUARTERS ARMIES OF THE U.S." . . . Ulysses S. Grant, *Personal Memoirs of U. S. Grant, Complete* (New York: Charles L. Webster and Co., 1885). Retrieved from Project Gutenberg at http://www.gutenberg.org /files/4367/4367-h/4367-h.htm; chapter LI.

207 "A ship at sea" . . . Joseph Conrad quoted in James Stavridis and William P. Mack, *Command at Sea,* 5th ed. (Annapolis, Md.: U.S. Naval Institute, 1999), 4.

208 workers feed Fayol's cycle . . . Gary Hamel, "Strategy as Revolution," *Harvard Business Review,* 74, no. 4 (1996): 20.

208 Footnote: Similarly, . . . Builder, *Masks of War,* 18–21.

210 eighty-five hotels in thirty countries . . . "Fact Sheet," The Ritz-Carlton Hotel Company, http://corporate.ritzcarlton.com/en/Press/FactSheet.htm.

210 regularly tops Zagat lists . . . Zagat named the Ritz-Carlton's Dallas location as the nation's best large hotel in 2009. "Zagat Names the Ritz-Carlton Dallas Number One Large Hotel," *Luxury Travel Magazine,* November 19, 2008, http://www.luxurytravelmagazine.com/news-articles/zagats-names-the -ritz-carlton-dallas-number-one-large-hotel-12612.php.

210 fifty thousand executives . . . Joseph Michelli, *The New Gold Standard: 5 Leadership Principles for Creating a Legendary Customer Experience Courtesy of the Ritz-Carlton Hotel Company* (New York: McGraw Hill, 2008), 9.

210 Employess can spend up to $2,000 . . . Robert Reiss, "How Ritz Carlton Stay at the Top," *Forbes,* October 30, 2009, http://www.forbes.com/2009/10/ 30/simon-cooper-ritz-leadership-ceonetwork-hotels.html.

210 "Instant guest pacification" . . . Sandra J. Sucher and Stacy McManus, "The Ritz-Carlton Hotel Company," Harvard Business School Case 601-163, March 2001 (revised September 2005).

210 "almost mythic levels" . . . Jason S. Wrench, *Workplace Communication for the 21st Century: Tools and Strategies That Impact the Bottom Line,* Volume 1 (Santa Barbara, Calif.: ABC-CLIO, 2013), 216.

211 "WELCOME TO NORDSTROM" . . . See Robert Spector and Patrick D. McCarthy, *The Nordstrom Way to Customer Service Excellence: The*

Handbook for Becoming the "Nordstrom" of Your Industry (New York: John Wiley & Sons, 2012).

211 **"empowerment improved employee satisfaction"** . . . Jay A. Conger and Rabindra N. Kanungo, "The Empowerment Process: Integrating Theory and Practice," *Academy of Management Review* 13, no. 3 (July 1988): 474.

211 **"intrinsic task motivation"** . . . Kenneth W. Thomas and Betty A. Velthouse, "Cognitive Elements of Empowerment: An 'Interpretive' Model of Intrinsic Task Motivation," *Academy of Management Review* 15, no. 4 (October 1990): 666.

211 **nursing in China** . . . S. Ning, H. Zhong, W. Libo, and L. Qiujie, "The Impact of Nurse Empowerment on Job Satisfaction," *Journal of Advanced Nursing* 65, issue 12 (December 2009), http://www.ncbi.nlm.nih.gov /pubmed/19941547.

211 **five-star hotels in Turkey** . . . Elbeyi Pelit, Yüksel Öztürk, and Yalçın Arslantürk, "The Effects of Employee Empowerment on Employee Job Satisfaction: A Study on Hotels in Turkey," *International Journal of Contemporary Hospitality Management* 23, no. 6 (2011), http://www.emeraldinsight .com/journals.htm?articleid=1944210.

211 **"primarily upon two important elements"** . . . Kanigel, *One Best Way,* 377.

212 **only 20 percent of workers** . . . Josh Bernoff and Ted Schadler, "Empowered," *Harvard Business Review* (July 2010): 5, http://hbr.org/2010/07/empowered/ar/1.

212 **"the number of 'exceptions'"** . . . Rosabeth Moss Kanter, *Change Masters: Innovation & Entrepreneurship in the American Corporation* (New York: Touchstone, 1984), 18.

212 **"In a world where one angry tweet"** . . . Bernoff and Schadler, "Empowered," introduction.

212 **Citing United Airlines' sluggish** . . . Bernoff and Schadler, "Empowered," 2.

212 **frustration with Maytag** . . . Bernoff and Schadler, "Empowered," 2.

212 **assaulted Nestlé's Facebook page** . . . Bernoff and Schadler, "Empowered," 2.

212 **Comcast found itself** . . . Mark Berman, "A Long Day's Journey into Cancelling Comcast Service," *Washington Post,* July 15, 2014, http://www.wash ingtonpost.com/news/post-nation/wp/2014/07/15/a-long-days-journey-into -canceling-comcast-service/.

212 **"anyone with a smartphone"** . . . Bernoff and Schadler, "Empowered," 2.

213 **When an iPhone bought from Best Buy** . . . Bernoff and Schadler, "Empowered," 3.

213 **"just as susceptible to online customer"** . . . Bernoff and Schadler, "Empowered," 3.

216 **battle reached its climax** . . . Adam Nicolson, *Trafalgar and the Making of an English Hero* (New York: HarperCollins, 2005), 256.

217 **"To any other Nation"** . . . Unlike Nelson, Villeneuve survived the battle. He was taken a prisoner of war, but favorably treated (he even attended Nelson's funeral) and was released in a prisoner exchange. Upon returning to France, Villeneuve allegedly committed suicide, although there is much speculation

that Napoleon had him murdered. Quoted in Nicolson, from N. H. Nicolas, *The Dispatches and Letters of Vice Admiral Lord Viscount Nelson*, vol. 7 (London, 1846), 314.

CHAPTER 11: LEADING LIKE A GARDENER

220 **"Torpedo impact, 20 seconds"** . . . See *The Hunt for Red October,* directed by John McTieran (Hollywood, Calif.: Paramount Pictures, 1990).

223 **"In 2011 Americans took"** . . . Daniel J. Levitin, *The Organized Mind: Thinking Straight in the Age of Information Overload* (New York: Penguin, 2014), 6.

223 **multitasking dramatically degrades** . . . Levitin, *Organized Mind*, 16.

PART V
LOOKING AHEAD

233 **"The first duty imposed"** . . . Alexis de Tocqueville, *Democracy in America*, trans. George Lawrence (New York: Harper & Row, 1966), 12.

CHAPTER 12: SYMMETRIES

239 **Finally, after seventeen days** . . . The events of the ensuing operation are based upon my recollection as well as multiple interviews with participants at all levels of the Task Force.

241 **But he died twenty-four minutes later** . . . Time line emerges from Multi-National Force–Iraq June 12 and June 15 press briefings. Multi-National Force–Iraq (Major General William B. Caldwell IV), "Iraq Operational Update" (briefing), June 12, 2006, and June 15, 2006.

243 **"almost complete equality of conditions"** . . . Alexis de Tocqueville, *Democracy in America*, trans. Henry Reeve, ed. John Canfield Spencer (New York: Gerard Adlard, 1839), 11.

243 **"in no country of the world"** . . . Alexis de Tocqueville, *Democracy in America*, ed. Phillips Bradley (New York: Vintage Books, 1945), 198.

244 **"in the United States"** . . . Alexis de Tocqueville, *Selections from Democracy in America* (New York: Sterling Publishing, 2005), 202.

244 **"The first duty imposed"** . . . Alexis de Tocqueville, *Democracy in America*, trans. George Lawrence (New York: Harper & Row, 1966), 12.

244 **"charged with the task"** . . . Brian Danoff, *Educating Democracy: Alexis de Tocqueville and Leadership in America* (New York: SUNY Press, 2010), 7.

244 **"a proper kind of education"** . . . J. H. Blits, "Tocqueville on Democratic Education: The Problem of Public Passivity," *Educational Theory* 47, no. 1 (1997): 15.

246 **University of Texas at Austin computer simulation** . . . The Autonomous Intersection Management project is conducted by Professor Peter Stone at the

Artificial Intelligence Laboratory in the University of Texas at Austin's Department of Computer Science.

246 **Instead, ears going in all four . . .** "Computer Scientist Developing Intersections of the Future with Fully Autonomous Vehicles," *University of Texas News*, February 20, 2012, http://www.utexas.edu/news/2012/02/20/autonomous_intersection/.

246 **25 percent of accidents . . .** "No Lights, No Signs, No Accidents: Future Intersections for Driverless Cars," Reuters Video, March 22, 2012, http://www.reuters.com/video/2012/03/22/no-lights-no-signs-no-accidents-future-i?videoId=232193655.

246 **95 percent are attributable . . .** "No Lights," Reuters Video.

247 **"stereotypes are a real timesaver" . . .** "Stereotypes Are a Real Timesaver," *The Onion,* August 14, 2002, http://www.theonion.com/articles/stereotypes-are-a-real-timesaver,10696/.

248 **"Our theories determine what we measure" . . .** Peter Senge, *The Fifth Discipline: The Art & Practice of the Learning Organization* (New York: Random House, 2006), 164.

248 **teamed up for a series of studies . . .** Senge, *Fifth Discipline,* 270.

248 **"As the philosophy of the physical sciences" . . .** See Anne Murray Allen and Dennis Sandow, "The Nature of Social Collaboration," *Reflections, the SoL Journal* 6, no. 2, cited in Senge, *Fifth Discipline,* 271.

INDEX

Page numbers in *italics* refer to illustrations. Page numbers beginning with 255 refer to endnotes.

ABOUT THE COAUTHORS

TANTUM COLLINS

Tantum "Teddy" Collins completed his undergraduate studies at Yale University, where he earned a BA in global affairs and took General McChrystal's course on leadership. While at Yale, he focused on regional studies of China and the Middle East, and institutional design.

He is currently pursuing an MPhil in international relations and politics as a Marshall Scholar at the University of Cambridge, with a concentration in global institutional design.

DAVID SILVERMAN

David Silverman is the cofounder and chief executive officer of Cross-Lead, a leadership and management system he cofounded with General Stan McChrystal to enable organizations to adapt and win in complex environments.

A graduate of the United States Naval Academy, David served in the U.S. Navy as a SEAL officer for twelve years. He is an experienced and combat-decorated veteran with six operational deployments worldwide, including Iraq, Afghanistan, and Southeast Asia.

David and his wife, Hollis, live in Washington, D.C., with their two children.

CHRIS FUSSELL

Chris Fussell is a partner at CrossLead, where he oversees development, client relations, and marketing efforts.

Prior to joining CrossLead, Chris spent over fifteen years as an officer in the Navy SEAL Teams. His time with SEAL Teams Two and Eight, and with the Naval Special Warfare Development Group, put him in multiple combat zones around the world.

During his career, Chris served as aide-de-camp to then–Lieutenant General Stan McChrystal during General McChrystal's final year commanding the Joint Special Operations Command, then went on to earn his master's degree in unconventional warfare from the Naval Postgraduate School in Monterey, California.

Chris is also a senior fellow for naval security at New America, a Washington, D.C.–based nonpartisan think tank dedicated to understanding the next generation of challenges facing the United States.

Chris and his wife, Holly, live on Capitol Hill in Washington, D.C., with their two young children.

He just wanted a decent book to read ...

Not too much to ask, is it? It was in 1935 when Allen Lane, Managing Director of Bodley Head Publishers, stood on a platform at Exeter railway station looking for something good to read on his journey back to London. His choice was limited to popular magazines and poor-quality paperbacks – the same choice faced every day by the vast majority of readers, few of whom could afford hardbacks. Lane's disappointment and subsequent anger at the range of books generally available led him to found a company – and change the world.

'We believed in the existence in this country of a vast reading public for intelligent books at a low price, and staked everything on it'
Sir Allen Lane, 1902–1970, founder of Penguin Books

The quality paperback had arrived – and not just in bookshops. Lane was adamant that his Penguins should appear in chain stores and tobacconists, and should cost no more than a packet of cigarettes.

Reading habits (and cigarette prices) have changed since 1935, but Penguin still believes in publishing the best books for everybody to enjoy. We still believe that good design costs no more than bad design, and we still believe that quality books published passionately and responsibly make the world a better place.

So wherever you see the little bird – whether it's on a piece of prize-winning literary fiction or a celebrity autobiography, political tour de force or historical masterpiece, a serial-killer thriller, reference book, world classic or a piece of pure escapism – you can bet that it represents the very best that the genre has to offer.

Whatever you like to read – trust Penguin.